D0742798

Westminster Public Library
3705 W. 112th Avenue
Westminster, CO 80031
www.westminsterlibrary.org

DID THE CHILDREN CRY?

DID THE CHILDREN CRY?

Hitler's War against Jewish and Polish Children, 1939-1945

Richard C. Lukas

HIPPOCRENE BOOKS

New York

WESTMINSTER PUBLIC LIBRARY
3031 WEST 76th AVE.
WESTMINSTER, CO 80030

Copyright © 1994 by Richard C. Lukas
All rights reserved.

For information, address:
HIPPOCRENE BOOKS, INC.
171 Madison Avenue
New York, NY 10016

Library of Congress Cataloging-in-Publication Data
   Lukas, Richard C., 1937-
      Did the children cry? : Hitler's war against Jewish and Polish children,
   1939-1945 / Richard C. Lukas.
         p. cm.
      Includes bibliographical references and index.
      ISBN 0-7818-0242-3
      1. World War, 1939-1945—Children—Poland. 2. Holocaust, Jewish
   (1939-1945)—Poland. 3. Jewish children—Poland—History—20th century.
   4. Children—Poland—History—20th century. 5. World War, 1939-1945—
   Atrocities. I. Title.
   D810.C4L82   1994
   940.53′161—dc20
                                                        94-4509
                                                        CIP

Printed in the United States of America.

Children are the real princes of feelings,
the poets and thinkers.
-Janusz Korczak

Acknowledgments

I AM GRATEFUL to several individuals and institutions for assistance I received. To Dr. Wojciech Kostecki, who helped me secure documentary materials in Polish archives, I am especially obliged. Several colleagues, friends and supporters, especially John Gmerek, Joseph Gore, R. Tyndorf, Alex Pittman, Arthur Molitierno, and Sister Mary Beatrix, deserve recognition for help they gave to me during my research.

Without the financial assistance of the Kosciuszko Foundation and its New York Metropolitan Chapter, the Polish American Teachers Association, and the Anti-Defamation Committee of California, I would have been unable to complete this project.

This book is dedicated to my wife, Marita, my partner in life.

Contents

Introduction

HISTORIANS AND PHILOSOPHERS have written a great deal about the Holocaust, though far less about the genocide perpetrated by the Germans against the Poles, other Slavs and the Gypsies, with a view to try to understand this horrible chapter in the history of western civilization. This nightmare is so divorced from our values and thought processes, I doubt that anyone will ever really understand it. To write a history of this period presents almost an insurmountable challenge, reminiscent of that which confronted a character in one of Jorge Borges's stories who tried but failed to write a poem that described the universe.

What makes this chapter in history stand out is not the fact that millions of people were slaughtered. Millions of human beings had been killed in earlier times—one-third of the German people lost their lives in the Thirty Years War, Joseph Stalin murdered 11 million people in the forced collectivization campaign, and on the grim litany of human losses goes. But the mass murder of 5 to 6 million Jews in the Holocaust was extraordinary because this was the first time a state seriously intended to murder completely an entire group of people. At the same time the Nazis murdered 9 million Christians, also victims of the fanatical racist nationalism that intended to reduce Poles and other Slavs in numbers so substantial they would never be able to hinder Nazi imperialism in eastern Europe.

One of the most extraordinary aspects of Nazi genocide was the cold deliberate intention to kill children in numbers so great that there is no historical precedent for it. Killing Jewish children was intended to prevent Jews from perpetuating themselves, which explains why the Nazis were as ruthless in slaughtering Jewish children as they were in killing Jewish adults. Starving, killing and Germanizing Polish children was intended to reduce substantially the reproductive capacity of a people relegated by the Nazis to the class of sub-humans. All this was part of the grotesque Nazi racial plan, facilitated by modern technology, to eliminate Jews and to reduce Poles and other Slavs to such small numbers that the Germans would dominate the heartland of Europe.

This book deals with the life and times of Jewish and gentile children of Poland, where the Nazis had established the most efficient killing center in history. While it does not relativize the unique place Jewish children had in the scale of suffering, this account does not downplay either the tragedy experienced by Polish children.

Among the Jewish and gentile victims in Poland were infants who could not talk or walk yet, primary school youngsters who had just begun to discover the wonders of life, and teenagers who dreamed dreams of going to a university and marrying their high-school sweethearts. You will meet many of them in a personal way in this book—Liliana, Franciszek, Sonia, Marysia, Wojciech, and many others. Most perished. Some survived. All of them were an important part of a significant chapter in the history of genocide of children, a chapter that is a mixture of inhumanity and altruism, villainy and courage.

Chapter I

Invasion

"GOD IS ANGRY," 8-year-old Waclaw Major said as he and his younger friend, Pietrek, looked up to the sky and saw noisy German airplanes dropping bombs on the inhabitants of Lodz on September 1, 1939. Terrified by the "black crosses" in the sky, as Waclaw described them, he and Pietrek scurried under a mound of potatoes where friendly Polish peasants had directed the youngsters. The noise and confusion seemed to go on forever, even though the two boys hid for only twenty minutes, the duration of the Luftwaffe attack. Someone yelled, "Are you alive?" Engulfed by earth and debris, Waclaw and Pietrek were reluctant to open their mouths. "You will live. You will live," came a reassuring voice.[1]

A few days earlier Liliana, a young Jewish girl, was on a train with her grandparents bound for the Polish resort of Naleczow. Her parents, anticipating that the grim warnings of war with Germany would soon become all too real, decided that Warsaw was not the best place for their daughter. Yet they opted to remain in the capital, Liliana's father ready to serve in the Polish army reserve.[2]

Twelve-year-old Franciszek Kopec was with his father in a wagon drawn by the family's gray horse. They were on their way to the city of Tomasz Mazowiecki, where they regularly exchanged rye for flour. It was a beautiful day for a ride. Suddenly, Franciszek and his father heard the sound of gun fire. German planes flew low, striking the city's factory and railroad station. Franciszek and his father hid under the wagon where the man turned to the boy and solemnly declared, "Son, this is the war!"[3]

Young Jerzy Wolski was in school on that fateful September day when word came that the Germans had invaded Poland. Boys and girls fled in panic. When he made it to the street, Jerzy read official notices of the government mobilizing the country and calling upon Polish citizens to contribute their firearms to the national defense effort. On his way home Jerzy saw Polish soldiers, dressed in new uniforms and boots, carrying gas masks. People scurried about, buying out bread from the town's bakeries. Soldiers placed machine-guns on the roof of the post office but these proved of little value when the Germans succeeded the next day in hitting the Lublin Airplane Factory and killing and wounding many people.[4]

This is how World War II began for the children of Poland.

Liliana remembered the patriotic bravado of young Poles on the train to Naleczow, singing Poland's national anthem, *Jeszcze Polska nie zginela (Poland Is Not Yet Lost)*, and shouting, "Kill Hitler! Hang him by his—!"[5] Franciszek remembered how Poles in his village triumphantly exclaimed, "No one will do anything to us, no one will take anything." And another favorite, "We won't give [them] even a button!"[6] Such proclamations of patriotism and confidence in Poland's victory against the Germans were common during the hot sticky days of late August and early September, 1939. No doubt this confidence was bolstered on September 3 when Poland's allies, England and France, declared war on Berlin.

No one would ever challenge the patriotism of Poles during those dark days. Even children—Jewish and gentile—were caught up in the national resolve to fight the enemy. They were everywhere, doing whatever they could to help. Many joined the armed forces. Others, too young to become soldiers, helped in non-combatant roles as the Boy Scouts and Girls Scouts did. Sixteen-year-old Zbigniew Bokiewicz was a Scout who served as a telephone operator for an antiaircraft unit in Warsaw. Marian Dabrowski, orphaned before the war, lived in the Henryk Dietz Orphanage in Bydgoszcz when the Germans invaded the country. He and the other boys in the orphanage, proudly wearing their Scout uniforms, performed intelligence and observation work for the Polish army in the area.[7] Scouts defended the provincial government building in Katowice and died at their posts.[8]

Franciszek Kopec's fifteen-year-old brother was a Scout. So intent on fighting Germans was he that not even the tearful pleas of his mother deterred him from leaving the sleepy village of Lubochnia for Warsaw. Reconciling herself to the inevitable, the boy's mother filled his knapsack with bread and salt pork for the journey.[9]

Students of the Regiment of the Academic Legion, originally established in 1920 during the Russo-Polish War, joined adults in defending key cities—Warsaw, Gdynia, Vilna, and Lwow. After Poland's defeat, many of these young Poles crossed illegally into Romania and Hungary from where they eventually joined the Polish army then being formed in France. Many of them were under eighteen years of age.

A German solder, Werner Kluck, recalled seeing a young boy, perhaps 13 years old and wearing a Polish officer's uniform, during the German attack on Warsaw on September 9. The boy held a bottle with an incendiary liquid while he ran toward an enemy tank. A German machine-gun hit him. "The boy spreads his arms to the sides but he still takes a few steps forward," wrote Kluck. "He falls onto the ground close to the tank; the liquid that has spilled from the bottle explodes on the armour in a bright flame."[10]

Dawid Sierakowiak, a young Jewish boy, was so moved by the appeal of Lodz's mayor, Jan Kwapinski, for volunteers to dig anti-aircraft ditches that he signed up immediately at the police station after he received his parents' permission. Two days later, Dawid recorded in his diary, "My bones ache like everyone else's from yesterday's work. Fifty thousand people were out digging."[11]

If they weren't digging trenches or building barricades, children were carrying messages, collecting supplies for hospitals or looking for wounded. A twelve-year-old boy and a nine-year-old girl found a man under a German tank and brought him to the hospital for treatment.[12] Several years after the war, a Polish priest, a survivor of Dachau, said that the courage and patriotism of Polish youth—Jewish and gentile—should be commemorated by a permanent monument.[13]

13

As the fierce power of the Wehrmacht unleashed itself on the Poles, the Germans quickly revealed that this would not be a conventional war against the Polish government and its armed forces. Rather, the Germans intended to destroy the Polish nation. The Germans attacked hospitals, homes and schools with the same ferocity that they bombed factories and military installations. Civilians, including women and children, were considered worthy targets even as they joined the hegira of refugees trying to flee from cities and towns. When the refugees got to outlying villages, they discovered that the villages, too, had come under attack. "Along the Warsaw-Kutno road during the entire month of September," one Polish report stated, "mounds of decomposing cadavers were to be seen, consisting for the most part of women and children. The same thing was repeated on the other roadways."[14] German aviators seemed to search deliberately for women and children and then pursued these unfortunate victims with machine-guns. The American ambassador to Poland, Anthony J. Drexel Biddle, Jr., personally saw the slaughter of Polish civilians. He was the first western observer to describe what he witnessed as German genocide against the Polish nation.[15]

Franciszek Kopec helped his family load a wagon with their personal possessions as they fled from Lubochnia. Franciszek's job was to ensure that the family's cow kept pace with the wagon. The family found to its dismay that everyone in Poland seemed to be running somewhere. A few days on the road brought the Kopec family to a column of trucks, loaded with laughing soldiers who spoke a language Franciszek did not understand. There the flight of the Kopecs ended. Returning to their village, they found their farm partially destroyed. Many of their friends and neighbors had been shot. "A new life began," recalled Kopec, "which spawned defiance and hatred."[16]

The Wolskis did the same thing as the Kopec family. Jerzy Wolski, a schoolboy, accompanied his family on a brief trek from Lublin to a village ten kilometers away. Forced to return home a little more than a week later, they found the Germans in Lublin. Jerzy was struck by the youth of the German soldiers who gawked at and took pictures of the Poles whom they had made refugees in their own land.[17]

As the bombs of the Luftwaffe rained down on the people of Warsaw, Halina Birenbaum and her family tried to protect themselves from the air raids by hiding in the hallway of their apartment. "As we crouched together, listening to the ominous rumblings, we prayed to God for help," Halina said. "But the uproar had evidently deafened God Himself. Houses collapsed in ruins, burying people underneath; fires broke out. Death had its hands full." Halina believed the Germans deliberately bombed the Jewish districts of the Polish capital with special force on Yom Kippur, the holiest of Jewish holy days.[18]

Liliana's visit to Naleczow was cut short because government officials and their staffs flocked there to continue the semblance of a government. Civilians, like Liliana and her grandparents, had to leave. They opted for Lublin. "It was panic, with screams, families separated, mothers running around looking for their children," Liliana later recalled. "People wanted to move faster but couldn't. Some were angry and just pushed others around." Liliana, like thousands of other Jewish and Polish refugees, was terrified. She could not believe that she and her grandparents were heading in the direction of explosions and burning villages. "As we neared Lublin it became worse, with more burning villages, more retreating soldiers, and more German planes trying to kill them."[19]

Outmatched by the bloated military power of Germany, the Polish armed forces fought bravely but hopelessly. One Polish veteran remembered seeing so many German planes, "You couldn't even see the sky. I just couldn't believe how they had built so many planes. We kept retreating as they bombed; we lost our horses; we didn't have any ammunition, so we attacked with bayonets. We retreated back to Warsaw, with no food or water."[20]

The bravado and confidence before September 1 soon gave way to the grim reality that Poland would be defeated. Germany's 65 military formations, numbering 1,850,000 men, 10,000 guns and mortars, 2,800 tanks and over 2,000 airplanes, overwhelmed the Poles who depended upon the English and French to launch an offensive which never came. As the Germans invaded from the west, the Soviets marched into the country on September 17 from the east.[21]

The Poles had beaten back a German effort to take Warsaw

on September 9. The Polish capital did not fall for almost another three weeks, thanks to the stubborn defense organized by General Walerian Czuma and Warsaw's popular mayor, Stefan Starzynski. However, by October 5, 1939, Poland's last military units capitulated. Meanwhile, in conformity with the Soviet-German Non-Aggression Pact, the Germans and the Soviets each seized a share of the Polish nation. The German slice followed a boundary closely resembling the prewar Curzon Line that netted the Reich 189,000 square kilometers inhabited by 21.8 million Polish citizens. The Soviets acquired 200,000 square kilometers inhabited by 13.2 million people.[22]

The ordeal for the children of Poland had begun.

The grim pronouncements of Hitler and his cronies prior to and during the early stages of the war did not yet make clear distinctions between Polish Christians and Polish Jews. That would come later when Jews were singled out for ghettoization and mass extermination.

Because of their belief that there was a biological foundation for the diversity of the human race, the Nazis differentiated between superior and inferior people. Germans were superior while Jews, Gypsies, Poles and other Slavs were inferior. Thus the Nazi theory of empire was based on the denial of humanity to Jews and Poles. Hitler made this clear when he told his commanders before the Polish campaign, "I have sent to the East only my 'Death's Head Units' with the order to kill without pity or mercy all men, women, and children of Polish race or language. Only in such a way will we win the vital space we need...."[23] Even if his invasion of Poland provoked a war with the West, Hitler told his commanders that "the destruction of Poland shall be a primary objective." He declared, "Be merciless! Be brutal! The war is to be a war of annihilation."[24]

Concerned about the implications for Germany of the high Polish birth rate—40 percent of Polish citizens were under 18 years of age, one of the largest percentages of any country in Europe[25]—Hitler was obsessed with *Lebensraum* (living space) in Poland for his superior German race. A few weeks after Poland's surrender, Hitler minced no words when he told Field Marshal Wilhelm Keitel that Germany's relationship to Poland involved "a hard racial struggle which will not allow any legal restrictions.... Shrewdness and severity must be the maxims in this racial struggle in order to spare us from going into battle on account of this country again."[26] That is why Hitler's lieutenants grimly repeated with monotonous regularity the theme of blood and destruction. A few months after Polish surrender, Himmler declared, "All Poles will disappear from the world....It is essential that the great German people should consider it as its major task to destroy all Poles."[27]

Polish children—Jewish and gentile—immediately felt the brunt of the German policy of terrorism. During the Wehrmacht's administration of Poland, which went on until the end of October, 1939, the German armed forces joined the SS and police in what some historians have described as "a merciless and systematic campaign of biological destruction." During this period alone, the Germans burned 531 towns and villages and executed over 16,000 people, many of whom were children.[28]

Among the first victims of indiscriminate murder were a number of Boy Scouts in Bydgoszcz. Most of them were twelve to sixteen years of age. The Germans lined them up against a wall and shot them to death. A priest who rushed to administer the last rites to them was shot five times.[29]

In a small town near Gdynia, someone smashed a window of the local police station. The Germans immediately arrested 50 school boys and ordered them to denounce the culprit. When the boys refused to do so, the Germans ordered their parents to flog them in front of the church. When the parents refused, the SS attacked and beat them with rifle butts. Ten boys were shot.[30] The pretext for killing three Boy Scouts, 16 and 17 years old, in the village of Zielonka was the appearance of a handmade poster with the words of writer Maria Konopnicka, "No German will spit in our faces or make Germans of our children."[31]

One of the most notorious German massacres during the early months of the occupation occurred at Wawer, a summer resort near Warsaw. Poles killed two German soldiers in a restaurant. Within a few hours, German soldiers arrived and in reprisal shot every tenth inhabitant of Wawer and of the adjoining thermal station of Amin. Thirty-four of the victims were under 18 years of age. The owner of the restaurant was hanged and buried. And then the Germans exhumed the body and hanged it again.[32]

The gruesome episode in Wawer was consistent with the wishes of Hans Frank, administrator of the General Government, who declared, "My relationship with the Poles is like the relationship between ant and plant louse.... I would not even hesitate to take the most draconic action." The Germans routinely killed 100 Poles for the death of one German, but there were instances where 200-400 Poles lost their lives in reprisal for the death of a German. In Lublin, the Germans wiped out the entire village of Jozefow—men, women, and children—for the death of a German family. Germans killed children not only in reprisal actions but also in response to children making anti-German statements or displaying what the Germans called a "hostile mentality."[33]

Perhaps no other calamity early in the German occupation of Poland suggests the commonality of suffering of Jewish and Polish children more than the mass deportations of families from western Poland, which the Germans annexed and renamed Reichsgau Danzig-Westpreussen and Reichsgau Wartheland, in 1939 and 1940. The remainder of Poland, renamed the General Government, became a dumping ground for displaced Jews and Poles from the Wartheland.

With little or no notice, Germans ordered families to clear out of their homes. Regardless of the weather, women and children were often separated from men who frequently were deported to some unknown destination and never seen again. The Germans terrified the women and children by blows from gun butts. In the transition camp at Lodz, where thousands of women and children were detained, epidemics decimated especially the children who were forced to live in such horrible conditions that many drowned in the lavatories there. "Coughing and the heart-rending sobs of dying children were the usual music of those camps," one official report stated. "How many child-victims these camps accounted for it is impossible to say and we shall never learn the whole truth."[34]

After being detained for days and even weeks in these camps and already exhausted from the lack of food, water and clothing, children had to walk with their parents several miles to the loading point and wait in the bitter cold until dawn when the

Germans loaded them up in cattle cars for the trip to the General Government. More often than not, they had to travel in unheated cars when the Polish winter temperatures fell to 30 degrees below zero.

So many people froze to death that the Germans stopped the trains along railroad sidings to dispose of frozen corpses, a large number of which were children.[35] In a transport that arrived in Krakow in January, 1940, 26 bodies were found in one wagon. At the station in Debica, 30 bodies of children were discovered.[36] Thirty children froze to death in one car at the railroad station at Sandomierz. In December, 1939, a train loaded with Jewish children, women and aged adults stood for four days while the people sat in cold cars without food or water.[37] When trains stopped and the Polish Red Cross tried to hand a pot of hot tea or water to mothers with children, they were usually met with the rifle butts or bayonets of the German police.[38]

Zygmunt Gizella was one of these deportees who was in a thirty-seven wagon rail transport that left Poznan for Lublin in 1939. Packed into a cattle car with 39 others, he recalled how at first everyone tried to maintain their dignity and refused to relieve themselves in front of others. But when people became ill, modesty gave way, Gizella said. "It was necessary to overcome all shame and take care of one's needs like an animal."[39]

Out of approximately 600,000 people deported from the Wartheland to the General Government, half were children.[40]

In the midst of these German-inspired horrors, Poles tried to maintain a sense of humor. After Governor Frank assumed his duties as head of the General Government, he issued a proclamation in which he explained the operation of his administration and outlined a German version of utopia for the unfortunate residents of the area. As soon as Frank's speech was posted in Warsaw, someone glued a slip of paper to it that read, "As Commander Pilsudski would say: 'Kiss my ass.'"[41]

Before the massive expulsions of Jews and Poles from western Poland, Sonia, a young Jewish girl, recalled the brief period when she not only lived near German families in Polish Silesia but also played with their children. Sonia's family kept a low profile as the town began to swarm with Germans in various uniforms—soldiers in gray, the SS in black and the local police in green. "The town, after all, had to be restructured to fit into the German mold in a hurry," Sonia said. "Still, it took the Germans a little while to feel their way about and become well organized."

Sonia played with Anna Weiner, a German official's daughter, who invited her home one day for lunch. But the budding friendship between the two children was not allowed to blossom. Soon the Germans required all Jews, including children, to wear a yellow star sewn on the front and back of everything they wore so everyone could tell from any direction that it was a Jew they saw. "After that little Anna stopped knocking at my door," Sonia recalled.[42]

Although murder had become a routine part of life in German-occupied Poland, where thousands of Jews and Poles had perished in executions, raids, and deportations by 1940, Hitler's threats to totally exterminate Jews and Poles could not be implemented immediately. It was only late in 1940 that the Germans began to corral Jews into congested unsanitary ghettos, where thousands of people, especially children, died of disease and hunger before the so-called Final Solution got underway in 1942.

As much as the Nazis hated Poles, there were too many of them to kill outright, as they did later the Jews. Besides, the Germans soon recognized they needed Polish labor to win the war. As the Nazis drafted more Germans into the armed forces and deported more Jews to the death camps after January, 1942, Polish labor filled growing German labor shortages. Thus there was always tension between the racist ideology to exterminate Poles and the pragmatic necessity to exploit them. Governor Frank pointed up the problem when he grimly said, "You must not kill the cow you want to milk. However, the Reich wants to milk the cow and... kill it."[43]

In contrast to their policy against the Jews, the Germans used more varied and often indirect means in conducting genocide against the Poles. They sought to destroy the Polish intelligentsia by killing them outright or sending them to concentration camps where most of them later died. They tried to eradicate Polish culture by destroying the educational system and reducing the influence of the Roman Catholic Church, a major force in Polish nationalism. They hampered normal biological propa-

gation by separating young Polish men and women and deporting them to work camps and factories, forcing Poles to
delay marriages, forbidding Poles of the annexed lands to
marry those who resided in the General Government, legaliz-
ing abortions, encouraging homosexuality, removing aid to
mothers with children and reducing the availability of food and
medical care. Genocide against Poles also involved de-Poloniz-
ing Polish land and Germanizing Polish children who met
German racial criteria.[44]

Above all, they tried to work and starve Poles to death in and
out of concentration camps. As one young Polish survivor of
Auschwitz said, "The real reason for the work was not the job,
but the beating and killing."[45] In this way millions of Poles
would eventually perish while the remnant that survived the
war would presumably either be deported beyond the pale of
German settlement or annihilated as the Jews had been. Martin
Bormann, the secretary of the Nazi Party, suggested the kind of
future that awaited the Poles when he grimly stated, "The Slavs
are to work for us. Insofar as we don't need them, they may
die."[46]

"It was impossible to settle the Slavic problem in the East
during the war in a manner as effective as that applied in the
Jewish case," one historian astutely observed. "The number
and economic importance of the Slavs were too great to be
disposed of in the circumstances of a prolonged war. But partial
measures for their reduction were well under way."[47]

Chapter Notes

1. Waclaw Major, "Znienawidzilem Psy," in *Byli Wowczas Dziecmi*, ed. by Marian Turski (Warsaw: Ksiazka i Wiedza, 1975), pp. 156-57.

2. Liliana Zuker-Bujanowska, *Liliana's Journal: Warsaw. 1939-1945* (New York: Dial, 1980), pp. 6-8.

3. Franciszek Kopec, "Numer 109063," in Turski, *Byli Wowczas Dziecmi*, p. 552.

4. Jerzy Wolski, "Dziennik z Lublina," in Turski, *Byli Wowczas Dziecmi*, pp. 163-65.

5. Zuker-Bujanowska, *Liliana's Journal*, p. 6.

6. Kopec, "Numer 109063," p. 552.

7. Richard C. Lukas, ed., *Out of the Inferno: Poles Remember the Holocaust* (Lexington: The University Press of Kentucky, 1989), pp. 23, 51.

8. *Polish Fortnightly Review*, November 15, 1942.

9. Kopec, "Numer 109063," p. 553.

10. *Polish Fortnightly Review*, November 15, 1942; Roman Hrabar, Sofia Tokarz and Jacek Wilczur, *The Fate of Polish Children During the Last War* (Warsaw: Interpress, 1981) p. 54.

11. Portions of Dawid Sierakowiak's diary, along with other revealing diaries and memoirs, can be found in Alan Adelson and Robert Lapides, comps. and eds., *Lodz Ghetto: Inside a Community under Siege* (New York: Viking, 1989), p. 7.

12. Dorothy Macardle, *Children of Europe: A Study of the Children of Liberated Countries: Their War-Time Experiences. Their Relations, and Their Needs. With a Note on Germany* (Boston: The Beacon Press, 1951), p. 67.

13. Interview with the Reverend Jan Januszewski, August 1, 1982.

14. Republic of Poland, The Polish Territory Occupied by the Germans, March 1940, in PRM 10/3, Polish Institute and General Sikorski Historical Museum. Hereinafter cited as PI/GSHM.

15. Anthony J. Drexel Biddle, Jr., "The Biddle Report," pp. 17ff, in Franklin D. Roosevelt Library, Hyde Park, New York; Msg., Gun-

ther to Secretary of State, September 16, 1939, in U.S., Department of State, *Foreign Relations of the United States: Diplomatic Papers. 1939* (Washington: United States Government Printing Office, 1956), II, 554-57.

16. Kopec, "Numer 109063," p. 554.

17. Wolski, "Dziennik z Lublina," pp. 169-72.

18. Halina Birenbaum, *Hope Is the Last to Die: A Personal Documentation of Nazi Terror*, Trans. by David Welsh (New York: Twayne, 1971), p. 2.

19. Zuker-Bujanowska, *Liliana's Journal*, p. 9.

20. Quoted in Barbara Stern Burstin, *After the Holocaust: The Migration of Polish Jews and Christians to Pittsburgh* (Pittsburgh: University of Pittsburgh Press, 1989), p. 9.

21. Richard C. Lukas, *The Forgotten Holocaust: The Poles Under German Occupation, 1939-1944* (New York: Hippocrene Books, 1990), p. 2.

22. *Ibid.*, pp. 2-3.

23. Statement by Hitler to Commanders, August 22, 1939, in U.S., Office of United States Chief of Counsel for Prosecution of Axis Criminality, *Nazi Conspiracy and Aggression* (10 vols.; Washington: USGPO, 1946), VII, 753.

24. *Ibid.*, III, 665.

25. Macardle, *Children of Europe*, p. 67.

26. Protocol of Conversation between Hitler and Keitel, October 25, 1939, in U.S. Counsel, *Nazi Conspiracy and Aggression*, II, 631-32.

27. Karol Pospieszalski, *Polska pod Niemieckim Prawem* (Poznan: Wydawnictwo Instytutu Zachodniego, 1946), p. 189.

28. Lukas, *Forgotten Holocaust*, p. 3.

29. Quoted in Polish Ministry of Information, *Black Book of Poland* (New York: G.P. Putnam's Sons, 1942), p. 134.

30. Republic of Poland, The Polish Territory Occupied by the Germans.

31. Wladyslaw Bartoszewski, *Warsaw Death Ring. 1939-1945* (Warsaw: Interpress, 1968), p. 28.

32. Republic of Poland, The Polish Territory Occupied by the Germans.

33. Lukas, *Forgotten Holocaust*, pp. 34-35.

34. Memo, undated, in WR/22/18; PAG-4/2.0.62: Box 15, United Na-

tions Relief and Rehabilitation Administration Records, United Nations Archives. Hereinafter cited as UNRRA/UNA.

35. *Ibid.*

36. Czeslaw Pilichowski, *Zbrodnie Hitlerowskie na Dzieciach i Mlodziezy Polskiej* (Warszawa: Rada Ochrony Pomnikow Walki i Meczenstwa, 1972), p. 10.

37. Republic of Poland, The Polish Territory Occupied by the Germans.

38. Memo, undated, UNRRA/UNA.

39. Protokol, Zygmunt Gizella, in NTN/27, Archiwum Glownej Komisji Badania Zbrodni Hitlerowskich w Polsce. Hereinafter cited as AGKBZHP.

40. Pilichowski, *Zbrodnie Hitlerowskie*, p. 10.

41. Jan Tomasz Gross, *Polish Society under German Occupation:The General Gouvernement, 1939-1944* (Princeton, N.J.: Princeton University Press, 1979), p. 48.

42. Sonia Games, *Escape into Darkness: The True Story of a Young Woman's Extraordinary Survival during World War II* (New York: Shapolsky, 1991), pp. 40-41.

43. Central Commission for Investigation of German Crimes in Poland, *German Crimes in Poland* (2 vols.,; New York: Howard Fertig, 1982), II, 18-21.

44. Most of this is discussed in Lukas, *Forgotten Holocaust*.

45. Zbigniew Drecki, *Freedom and Justice Spring from the Ashes of Auschwitz* (Exeter, England: BPCC Wheatons Ltd., n.d.), p. 30.

46. Statement by Bormann, in U.S. Counsel, *Nazi Conspiracy and Aggression*, II, 904.

47. Ihor Kamenetsky, *Secret Nazi Plans for Eastern Europe: A Study of Lebensraum Policies* (New York: Bookman Associates, 1961), p. 175.

Chapter II

Deportations

"FROM THAT TIME ON the Jews were not Poles anymore; just Jews," Liliana Zuker-Bujanowska recalled when in October, 1940, the Germans forced her and her family to live in the Warsaw Ghetto.[1] Liliana was one of 100,000 Jewish children under the age of 15 who were confined there.[2]

No one could have predicted that when the Germans established some 300 ghettos in Poland, they intended not only to isolate all the Jews of Poland from the surrounding Polish community but also eventually to deport those who survived the horrible conditions in them to the death camps. The most vulnerable element—the sick, aged and children—had the least chance to survive the hunger and disease of these Nazi corrals and they perished by the hundreds of thousands even before the deportations to the gas chambers got underway in 1942.

Despite the constant "actions" of the Germans which established an ongoing pattern of murder and the decimation of the population by hunger and disease, children displayed an amazing ability to adapt to the surrealistic world of the ghetto. Thousands of them were involved in the underworld of smuggling food without which many families would have starved to death. They also attended schools and participated in cultural events which brought some semblance of normality to their lives and offered a kind of spiritual resistance against the Nazi onslaught.

Warsaw was the largest center of European Jewry. After the

Nazis established the ghetto, Jewish Warsaw became "a city unto itself, with characteristics quite different from those of Aryan Warsaw," one diarist wrote. "Anyone passing from the Jewish district to the Aryan district gets the impression of having entered a new city with a different appearance and a different way of life and have nothing to do with its Jewish neighbor."[3]

Soon the Warsaw Ghetto became a cramped, ugly city, a graveyard where, according to Chaim Kaplan, "only here the skeletons of the dead walk about in the streets." Compared to Lodz, the Warsaw Ghetto was a "mess," according to Emmanuel Ringelblum. In early 1942, a former Polish inmate of Auschwitz, who went to the Warsaw Ghetto to visit Jewish friends and to warn them of what the Germans had in store for them, said, "The Ghetto was, like Auschwitz, cut off from the world, simply awaiting extermination, according to Hilter's verdict of total destruction. I shall never be able to forget the sights I saw then."[4]

The ghetto drew Jews not only from the gentile sections of the city but also from surrounding villages and towns. Most of the immigrants had neither money nor relatives and were forced to live wherever they could. Apartments were packed with too many people and soon became breeding grounds for infectious diseases.

An eleven-year-old Polish boy, Lech Wisniewski, was an eyewitness to the establishment of a Jewish ghetto in his town in the summer of 1940. The conditions were so horrible there, Lech recalled, that he had never seen anything so bad. The poverty, disease and hunger were indescribable. The moans of sick elderly Jews melded with the cries of the children. It was eerie how some Jews prayed loudly while others, equally loudly, cursed their plight.[5]

With an average daily food allotment in Warsaw of 184 calories for Jews (Poles received 669 and Germans 2,613),[6] which translated into a few bowls of watery soup and a small amount of bread, people became so weak they fell on the sidewalk where they died of hunger. One teenage survivor recalled:

> Walking on the streets was like a nightmare. On every block there were corpses, sometimes covered with paper, other times half

naked—someone had already stolen pieces of their clothing. At first I could not look at them. I would get off the sidewalk in order to pass them as far away as I could. As days passed everyone grew used to the sight, but I couldn't. It seemed that those frozen bodies always had their eyes open and nobody would come close enough to shut them. Most of the time, the family did not know what had happened to them, and many had no family. There was no such place as a morgue. Most of these corpses were taken by the garbage men—the streets had to be kept clean.[7]

It was common for people to rob others for food. *Hapers* were children and adults who grabbed food from other people and ate it on the spot. One young man was so famished that he took a loaf of bread from a teenage girl, bit off a piece and threw it back to her. By the time she became aware of what had happened, a swarm of hungry children consumed what was left of the bread. The girl returned home, crying and empty-handed.[8]

The revealing chronicle of the Lodz Ghetto graphically described the garbage pits where there was an incredibly bad stench. Yet young Jewish boys dug in these pestilential pits hoping to scrounge something out of the refuse. Since everyone tried to salvage what they could, anything they dumped into the pits was not fit to eat. As the chronicle explained, "And there it was covered with fetid rubbish, excrement, and sweepings; no one would ever have imagined that people would grub in this abyss of misery, undaunted by the obnoxious stench, the ghastly pestilence. And yet every tiny remnant is extracted with the fringes, carefully checked, and collected in a little sack or bowl."[9]

A teenage girl recorded the pervasive hunger in Lodz. She noted on February 21, 1942, "I stay at home..., I, too, get only 20 dkg. of bread for the entire day.... Hunger is terrible; people drop like poisoned flies. Today I got 1 kg. of parsley. Father, brother and I ate it raw. What fate, what irony! Will it ever end? I despise this life, we live like animals. How wretched human life is, a constant struggle." She asked forlornly on March 1, "Will there be more of this terrible hunger? Will they go on deporting us? Will death devastate us again?" A few days later, she wrote: "There is no food for supper. I tried all day to get something. Finally in the evening I bought ½ kg. of flour for 20RM. One needs thousands, millions to buy food. No way to live like this." Despairingly, she records on March 9, 1942, "Hunger is unbelievable, people fall off their feet.... We have no food for supper. I am owed 1.25 kg. of noodles, 50 dkg. of oil, 75 dkg. of honey, but I didn't get these. What misfortune has befallen our house. My head hurts, I cannot see right, our house is empty, not even a crumb of bread or a bit of coffee."[10]

The constant hunger and death that enveloped the young girl hardened her: "You can drop dead and nobody will help you, a human being means nothing, dozens are of no importance. People are nasty, everyone for himself.... Nothing moves me any more, not even the worst suffering. People have taught me this...."[11]

Jews were no different than gentiles. Some acted selfishly toward others. A Polish woman who visited the Warsaw Ghetto where she looked after some Jews remarked, "I noticed that wealthier Jews did not help poorer ones.... There were plenty of bread and rolls on display, while outside, under the shop window, Jews died of hunger."[12] Rabbi Shimon Huberband witnessed Jews who ignored the plight of hungry, naked children in the Warsaw Ghetto. In December, 1941, he saw a sixteen-year-old boy lying on the ground in freezing weather. Three small children lay beside him. They were all nearly naked. Scores of people passed them and only a few gave them alms. Huberband remarked, "My attention was drawn to a young man who was walking arm in arm with two girls. All three of them were elegantly dressed, in fine furs and fine boots.... The three young people stopped next to the unfortunate Jewish children, and I was certain that they were about to open their purses and the bags of goodies which they held in their hands, to give something to the children. But the young people just stood there for awhile. Occasionally, one of the girls pulled at the young man. They burst out in laughter and left."[13]

People with money acquired food. Vendors sold different delicacies on the streets. In the heart of the Warsaw Ghetto, Cafe Hirschfeld's clientele were the monied and the debauched. People could buy anything they wanted there—duck, chicken, goose, pickled fish. And young girls came to sell their bodies for a meal. "Sixteen-year-old girls come here with their lovers, the few scoundrels who work for the Gestapo," Mary Berg wrote. "These girls do not think of what will happen to them later—they are too young for that. They come here to eat well. The next day such girls may be found shot to death together with their lovers. The organized youth of the ghetto deals ruthlessly with traitors."[14]

Halina Birenbaum, who lived in the Warsaw Ghetto, could not bear to see the endless numbers of beggars and starving people who day and night cried out, *"A shtykele broit, a shtykele broit !" ("A piece of bread, a piece of bread!")* Moved by what she witnessed, Halina stole bread and potatoes from her own family's nearly empty larder and gave it to people on the street. She could not help all of them.[15]

Hunger and disease took so many lives in the Warsaw Ghetto that they could not keep up with hauling the bodies away to the cemetery. Birenbaum watched "the carts moving through the ghetto carrying boxes into which they piled ten or more dead bodies at a time, so that the lids would not shut...."[16]

By January, 1941, 900 people died every day in the Warsaw Ghetto. By the summer, the figure rose to 5,000. During the years of the existence of the Warsaw Ghetto, approximately 100,000 people died, a large proportion of whom were children. In Lodz in 1941, there was a minimum three day waiting period to bury a dead person. At times there was such a backlog in transporting bodies to the cemetery, a large hauling wagon, which had the capacity to handle several dozen bodies, had to be used. Before the war, 12 gravediggers worked at the cemetery. In 1941, there were 200. "You can't die either these days," complained a woman who tried to arrange the burial of her mother.[17]

The lack of order and social restraints led to selfishness, callousness, and even criminal behavior by some youths on both sides of the ghetto walls. Because of hunger and poverty, people engaged in behavior they never would have considered before the war. Women from good backgrounds became prostitutes. Both Jewish and gentile youths engaged in promiscuous sex. "Open marriages" were common among urban Polish teens involved in the underground conspiracy. Perhaps the constant danger to which they were exposed brought boys and girls closer together. Moral norms, especially in the cities, were in dissolution.[18]

The physical and moral injury experienced by Jewish youth

in the ghetto was graphically expressed in a youth movement newspaper: "The worsening economic and housing situation has caused a huge decline in the authority of parents. The father, who does not earn a living for his family, the pressured couple, always arguing—these are the elements which bring the child to lack of respect for his father and mother. It is clear that such a boy is prey to the trap of the slogan 'grab and eat,' and that the absence of care and authority brings about a rejection of all conventions, excessive card-playing, smoking, wild dancing and sexual abandon."[19]

On the other side of the ghetto walls, the Germans systematically pauperized the Polish people by economic exploitation. In June, 1941, a Warsaw worker earned 120-300 zlotys monthly; yet, it cost 1,568 zlotys to feed a family of four.[20] Next to the Jews, the Poles had the lowest rations of any people in German-occupied Europe. In Warsaw, in the middle of 1942, Polish children actually received rations amounting to 375 calories instead of the 640 that the Germans allowed.[21] Compared to the Germans, Polish youth 14-20 years old received 33 percent less food while Polish children 10-14 got 65 percent less food. Children under 10 years of age got 60 percent less food than their German counterparts.[22]

Hunger led to greater susceptibility to sickness and death. Medical examinations of children in Warsaw's primary schools in 1942-43 showed 42.5 percent of the children were threatened with tuberculosis. In Krosno, 80 percent of Polish children were anemic. Dr. Wilhelm Hagen, the German medical officer in Warsaw, stated in 1941 that tuberculosis in the General Government had increased by 50 percent.[23] The level of rickets among Polish children increased 70 to 90 percent during the war.[24]

When Polish officials complained about the dreadful food situation to Governor Frank in December, 1941, he promised not to export more foodstuffs to the Reich. Yet, eight months later he approved a six-fold increase of grain to Germany from the General Government for 1942-43. He admitted that the new exactions would be taken at the expense of the Poles and Jews. "It must be done cold-bloodedly and without pity," he said.[25] Obviously, as Goering bluntly declared, "If anyone goes hungry, it certainly would not be the Germans."[26] This was consistent with the Nazi view, expressed by Reichsminister Robert

Ley that since the Poles were racially inferior, they "needed less food."[27] Pursuing genocide by malnutrition was precisely what Field Marshal Gerd von Rundstedt, a Wehrmacht officer, had in mind when he said, "We, Germans, must overcome our neighbors twice. Consequently, we shall be forced to destroy one-third of the population in the neighbouring territories. We can do this through systematic malnutrition which ultimately produces better results, particularly among the young."[28]

> Past rubble, fence, barbed wire
> Past soldiers guarding the Wall,
> Starving but still defiant,
> I softly steal past them all.
> Clutching a bag of sacking,
> With only rags to wear,
> With limbs numbed by winter,
> And hearts numbed by despair.[29]

These touching lines of the poem by Henryka Lazowertowna honor the child smugglers of the ghetto. If people in and out of the ghetto had to depend upon official allotments of food, more Jews and Poles would have died of hunger and disease. Thanks to extensive smuggling operations in Poland, in which Jewish and Polish children played an important role, the lives of many people were either prolonged or even saved. Smuggling was so extensive that Adam Czerniakow, head of the Warsaw Judenrat before his suicide in July, 1942, estimated that 80 percent of the food that found its way into the ghetto came through smugglers.[30] The statistics for other ghettos were similar—Krakow, 75 percent; Lodz, 50 percent; Czestochowa, 80 percent.[31]

Hundreds of Jewish and Polish child smugglers operated in virtually every city. Their cooperation on both sides of the ghetto wall, Emmanuel Ringelblum, a noted Jewish historian who lived in the Warsaw Ghetto, observed, "is one of the finest of all stories in the history of the relations between Poles and Jews during the Second World War."[32] United against a common enemy, these youngsters risked their lives in an activity that carried the death penalty. Jewish and Polish children could be found anywhere smuggling was going on.

They managed to squeeze through cracks and holes in ghetto walls. Sometimes they daringly climbed over them. Or they simply snuck out through the entrances under the noses of preoccupied guards. When they returned, the lucky ones boasted of pockets filled with food.

Abraham Lewin, a teacher at a private Zionist school for girls in Warsaw, personally observed the extensive smuggling operations where he lived:

> I live by the wall that divides the ghetto from Przejazd Street. A gap has appeared in the wall through which someone could quite easily crawl, or which is wide enough for a sack with 100 kg. of potatoes or corn or other foodstuffs. The smuggling goes on without a break from dawn at half past five until nine in the evening.[33]

As for Jewish youngsters crossing over to the Aryan side for a few potatoes, Lewin said, "These they hid in their little coats, with hems swollen so that the children look like balloons. While hosts of them can be seen climbing over the walls, crawling through the gaps or so-called 'targets' and passing through the official entrances where gendarmes and Polish police stand guard."[34] Chaim Kaplan commented on one of the distinctive characteristics of Jewish child smugglers—namely, the "humps on their backs," which was "an artificial manufactured hump whose inside is filled with potatoes and onions."[35]

Often Poles out of pity gave food to the children. Ewa Bukowska, a Pole, remembered when she was in Otwock, which had a large Jewish ghetto, she saw ragged Jewish children six or seven years old who were small enough to slip through the barbed wire of the ghetto and beg for food from the Poles. "They always approached very carefully and my aunt gave them what she had," Bukowska said. "Then they would disappear as quickly and quietly as they had come."[36]

In Krakow, some Jewish child smugglers boldly left the ghetto on a streetcar. One boy, displaying great skill at his work, exchanged fountain pens for food on the Polish side of the city. He was never caught by the Germans.[37]

One enterprising smuggler was a 14 year-old Pole called Zawadzki, who supplied saccharine, vaccines and medicines to the Jews of the Lodz Ghetto. Caught by the Germans, he told them he wanted to go to the bathroom, where the stalls were set up so that only a person's feet were visible. Zawadzki left his shoes in the stall to deceive the guards while he slipped to safety through a window.[38]

Sonia Games, who lived in the Czestochowa Ghetto, embarked on a career of smuggling to help feed her family. One day she took advantage of preoccupied guards who were checking the identification papers of a group of people and sneaked out of the ghetto. She bought food on the black market from Polish farmers and even took a trolley to the suburbs before returning to the ghetto before curfew.[39]

Frequently sympathetic policemen—German and Polish—pretended not to see the young smugglers and allowed them to move in and out of the ghettos. Often police received bribes for looking the other way, especially when it involved professional smugglers. Sometimes greed disrupted the arrangements between the police and smugglers and resulted in the death of the smugglers.[40]

Often young smugglers were not as fortunate as Zawadzki and Games. When child smugglers were caught, they were beaten and lost their food they had so painstakingly collected. Even worse, sadistic guards shot and killed them. As Mary Berg wrote, "Most of the German guards fire in cold blood at the running children, and the Jewish policemen must then pick up the bleeding victims, fallen like wounded birds, and throw them on passing rickshas."

On a walking tour of the city, Hans Frank, accompanied by several officials, explained to the Italian attache in Warsaw how smuggling operated in the ghetto. He referred to the children who engaged in it as "rats." "We play a game of hide and seek with them," he said. "It's a game much like cricket." While Frank spoke, a German soldier, who walked ahead of the group, placed his rifle into a hole in the ghetto wall and fired at a child smuggler. When Frank inquired why he had fired, the soldier replied, "I shot a 'rat.'" On the other side of the hole was a young boy, frightened but still alive. Frank took the gun from the soldier saying, "You missed the mark," and fired at the child.[41]

Ghetto diarists celebrated the courage and determination of the smugglers. Abraham Lewin said they "reached the stature of heroes in my eyes, and the day will come when the whole people will surely sing of them in celebration of their great heroism."[42] Another poetically described the smuggler as "the grey soldier on the walls of the besieged city." Leon Berensohn urged that a monument to the "unknown smuggler" be erected after the war.[43]

Smuggling operations were so pandemic that in one prison for Jews on Gesia Street in May, 1941, most of the nearly 1,300 prisoners were smugglers. Many of them were children. During the last half of 1941, Heinz Auerswald, who supervised the Warsaw Ghetto, ordered the execution of all smugglers, including women and children.[44] But smuggling continued. "Three things were unconquerable," wrote Ringelblum, "The German Army, the British Isles, and Jewish smuggling."[45]

Amidst the pain and tragedy in the lives of smugglers, there was a comical side too. One smuggler managed to hide a dead pig, dressed up as a peasant woman, into a train compartment. When the police discovered the pig, even they exploded in laughter.[46]

But the Polish market women of Warsaw deserved special tribute because they managed to provide meat and bread to the residents of Warsaw. Often they were aided by young Polish girls and boys, who intentionally distracted policemen with childish antics to enable the women to get their goods to their destination. "They moved like pillars carrying and transporting by rail or carts tons of foodstuffs in little bags sewn into their underskirts and blouses," Stefan Korbonski, the last chief of the Polish underground, wrote. "Never before have I seen such oversized busts as in Poland at this time." He remembered seeing one of these kindly amazons hit a gendarme on the head with a basket of eggs because he tried to take it away from her; the gendarme ran away when he saw other hefty women coming to their friend's aid. "No one else would have dared to treat a gendarme in such fashion," Korbonski said.[47]

Despite Nazi pronouncements before and during the war about destroying the Poles, the shortage of labor in Germany militated—at least in the short term—against the kind of wholesale slaughter the Jews experienced. This did not mean, however, the Germans abandoned their genocidal goals against the Poles. Working Poles to the point where thousands died at hard labor accomplished the objectives of economic exploitation and genocide.

Even before the Second World War, Polish labor had been important to the Germans. In 1914, there were 300,000 Poles employed in Germany, mostly on farms. Nevertheless, prior to the rise of Hitler to power, the Germans expressed their prejudice against them by the term *Polnische Wirtschaft*, which suggested stupidity and incompetence.[48]

Due to the increased tempo of the German war effort, which took men from farms and factories and put them in uniform, and the reluctance to force the existing labor force to work longer hours and to employ more women, foreign labor was essential to fill the growing labor shortages in the Reich. Since the labor supply in the annexed lands was inadequate, the 15 million Poles living in the General Government were an obvious source to exploit.

Early in 1940, Berlin asked Governor Frank to send one million workers, both male and female, from the General Government to work in agriculture and industry.[49] In view of the harshness of the conditions for Polish laborers already in Germany, Poles were understandably reluctant to volunteer. The Germans resorted to *lapanki* or dragnets which kidnapped men, women and children. Anyone who appeared healthy could be deported at any time.[50]

Even with forced conscription, the flow of Polish workers to Germany did not keep pace with demand. In January, 1941, there were 798,000 Poles working in the Reich, considerably short of the number the Nazi authorities wanted. But a year later this figure increased to slightly over 1 million. By August, 1943, the number of Polish laborers, mostly from the General Government, swelled to over 1.6 million. In addition, the Germans used approximately 300,000 Polish prisoners of war who, along with regular Polish laborers, lived and worked in appalling conditions.[51]

Exploitation of Polish children was a major part of Nazi Germany's labor policy. Children as young as 12 in the annexed lands and 14 years of age in the General Government were obligated to work. But in practice the Germans conscripted younger children, especially as the war dragged on and German fortunes declined.[52] By 1944, heavy casualties had to be met by drawing more Germans from the labor pool which was increasingly filled by children, some as young as 8 years old.[53]

The result was the Germans deported 10-15 percent of Polish children to forced labor in the Reich, contributing to what has been described as "the most horrible and the largest slave program in history."[54]

The major industrial giants of Germany profited from conscripted child labor. For every child laborer it received, I.G. Farben paid the SS 1½ Reichsmarks, considerably less than it paid for adults. Twenty-five percent of the workers employed by Siemens-Halske were conscriptees, including women and children. Krupp employed a large number of children; by 1944, they even employed 6-year-olds. Krupp had so many children working for it that they even organized a special camp for them.[55]

So intent were the Germans to fill their labor needs, they seized children from schools without their parents even being aware of it and sent them to Germany. At a trade school in Gorlice, where the pupils ranged in age from 12 to 16, the Germans surrounded the school building and detained the children until trucks arrived to take them to the railroad station for deportation to the Reich.[56]

The circumstances surrounding these deportations were reminiscent of the expulsions of men, women and children, Jews and Poles, from the annexed lands to the General Government earlier in the war. A 16 year-old Polish girl recalled her deportation to Germany: "After three days of a ghastly journey, half-choked, we were put down at the railway station.... Next we were driven to the *Arbeitsamt* (Labor Office) where buyers waited for us. Each of these buyers inspected us like cattle. Young strong girls were fought for."[57]

Most Polish children sent to Germany usually worked as agricultural laborers, though many also worked in factories. Martin Bormann wanted Polish children over 12 years old to work in German munitions plants. Generally, more Polish boys than girls could be found in industrial plants. Up to 1943, over 50 percent of Polish women, including a high percentage of girls, worked as forced laborers on farms. In the lands annexed to the Reich, there were 390,000 Polish children employed by 1944, comprising 25 percent of the labor force of the Wartheland.[58]

Children who remained in the General Government also

worked in a large number of German establishments, including labor camps. Thousands of youngsters worked for the *Baudienst* (Construction Service). As early as 1941, 120,000 Poles of the Baudienst worked in demolitions, road building, and laying railroad tracks. One former laborer said, "We [were] treated like beasts. Our inspector swore at us constantly and what is engraved most in my memory is the term *Polnische Schweine* (Polish Swine). Our Vorwerker's cruelty was sophisticated, a brute, drunkard, he ill-treated us." Liban was a Baudienst camp in Krakow where the Germans sent young Poles for any number of reasons. Working in the quarries and stone pits of Liban, many prisoners were chained during work.[59]

Lech Wisniewski's father insisted his son learn German well enough to shield him from deportation to Germany. It paid off, though it wasn't easy for the 13-year-old boy who was employed with a German firm in the General Government. On a trip to Kutno in connection with his job, German officials on the train asked for his identification papers. Missing one document, Lech was taken off the train and beaten so badly he lost two of his teeth. When the Germans established that the boy was on a legitimate business trip, they released him. Railroad stations like Kutno were convenient places for Poles to leave messages on walls to alert their families about what had happened to them. Lech remembered one that read, "They caught us without passes near Lowicz. Jurek was killed probably yesterday during the interrogation when he lost consciousness. Tell his mother. Janka S."[60]

Germans treated child workers as adults, forcing them to work 12 hours a day, which increased to 14 after 1943 when German military needs were greater than they had been when Germany held the military initiative. Ill-fed and poorly clothed, they were often subjected to draconic discipline, usually in the form of beatings, which sometimes seriously injured or killed them. One boy finished his work three minutes before the end of his shift; he was beaten so badly he died from his wounds. In some cases, the Germans sent the children to concentration camps for alleged infractions.[61]

Children deported to Germany lived in camps or barracks near the factories in which they worked. Conditions in these places were so bad that the workers frequently became ill and only the hardiest survived. Later in the war, according to one account, "German inspectors visiting the camps used to point to any people who seemed weak or ill and to children who looked fragile, saying, 'Kaput!' or merely giving a sign, and all these were put to death."[62]

Poles deported to work on German farms had to put up with long hours, abuse and even beatings but they were able to slake their hunger by stealing food on the farm to supplement their meager meals, an advantage those working in factories did not have. Sixteen-year-old Marian Dabrowski, kidnapped with several of his friends from an orphanage, ended up in a German labor exchange where the children were purchased by the son of a local farmer. The man took them to the family farm where the children's quarters consisted of a small cubbyhole off the stable. Their supper was a bowl of watery soup and a slice of bread.

Working in 20 below zero weather without gloves or adequate shoes, the boys had to use pickaxes and hammers to break up the frozen soil to dig out beet roots. "Soon our hands were frost bitten," Marian related. "We used to pull down our sweater sleeves over our hands, but this was hopeless." Condescending toward the Polish boys, the overseer punished Marian usually by denying him food or, like most local farmers in that area, by threatening to send him to Stutthof concentration camp where, until 1942, 90 percent of the inmates were Poles. "The longer the war lasted, the more likely this seemed," Marian later wrote. "All of us had heard of people who had been sent there and nothing more was ever heard of them." Thanks to a 15-year-old Polish girl, who worked in the farmer's kitchen, Marian got extra food. "I also augmented my diet by stealing cream from the milk churns. I used my only cup for this purpose."

Despite the hardships, Marian adjusted, as most young Poles in Germany seemed to do:

> The older ones had more problems. I was once sent to another farm to translate for a Polish woman, about forty years of age, who was said to have gone insane. The day I saw her, she was still coherent, though clearly upset. She kept repeating, 'What have they done to us?' When I went to see her a week or so later, she no longer recognized me. She was taken away and I never heard of her again.

It later transpired that she came from the Bydgoszcz area. Her own farm had been taken by the Germans and her husband had been sent to a concentration camp.[63]

For the Nazis hundreds of thousands of Poles working in Germany raised the question of racial contamination. Polish workers deported to the Reich had to wear a violet letter "P" on their clothing to distinguish them from the Germans, who were admonished with monotonous regularity not to treat them too humanely or to have any social relations with them. Poles could not go to churches or movies, use public transportation or have sexual intercourse with women. "No remorse whatever should restrict such action," one directive declared.

Many Germans refused to accept the Nazi racial code concerning the Poles. Catholic priests in Erlangen collected money, books and food to be sent to worker families in Poland. The gauleiter's office in Wurzburg felt the attitude of the German people toward the Poles left much to be desired: They were too kind to them!

Many Germans received stiff prison sentences for showing kindness to Poles. Karl Lossin paid for a railway ticket for a Pole and attended a movie with him; for that a German court sentenced him to nine months' imprisonment. A forty-nine-year-old German at Halberstadt earned a month in prison for offering a box of cigarettes to a Pole. When a middle-aged German enabled a Pole to correspond with his family, he was sent to prison for four months. One Nazi exhortation read: "Germans! The Poles can never be your comrades. Poles are beneath all Germans whether in the farm or in the factory ... never forget that you belong to the Master Race."[64]

Poles could not have sexual intercourse even with Poles, but if a Polish man had intercourse with a German woman, it called for the death penalty. In 1941, Himmler directed the execution of 190 Polish agricultural workers who allegedly had sexual intercourse with German women. The Germans selected the youngest prisoners at Buchenwald and forced them to administer the hangings.[65]

Notwithstanding Nazi doctrines of racial purity, Germans initiated sex with Polish and Jewish women—often violently. A German farmer and his son sexually assaulted a 16-year-old girl, a domestic servant, and neither suffered any penalty, even though German guidelines provided for a short prison term. German farm workers often had liaisons with their Polish female counterparts. Young Jewish women were sexually violated by German soldiers. There was even a report of someone representing himself as a member of the Gestapo who wanted the cooperation of Jewish leaders in the Warsaw Ghetto in supplying girls for two brothels—one for officers and one for enlisted men.[66]

When Polish and other eastern European women became pregnant in Germany, at first they were allowed to return home for the delivery of the child. That changed in February, 1943, due to the strain on the German labor supply, when pregnant Polish women were either aborted or, if they delivered to term, the babies were raised in German nurseries.

In Wolfsburg, hundreds of babies were delivered at the maternity hospital of KDF Stadwerk. After delivery, the Germans placed the babies in the company's nursery. Conditions were appallingly primitive. Children lived in wooden barracks, infested with lice and bugs. There were no provisions to isolate sick children from healthy ones. Food was inadequate and of poor quality. In a little over one year, 25 percent of the children in the company's nursery died. When the Germans moved the nursery to Ruehen, the mortality of infants soared. During the last ten months of the war, 350-400 Polish and Russian infants died in the nursery barracks. Death certificates for the deceased children read simply, "Too Weak to Live," or "Feebleness." One of the supervisors at the nursery allegedly told a German worker there, "We will take care that not so many Russian and Polish children grow up."

The same appalling conditions existed at Brunswick where dead children were allowed to remain for days in the bathroom before their bodies were placed in margarine containers for burial or burning. The mortality rate at Brunswick was as staggering as at Ruehen. At the nursery in Spital, even an SS officer was so appalled at the small daily allowance of milk for the infants, he reported to Himmler, "On these rations the babies will die of starvation in several months."[67]

With confinement of Jews in ghettos, Jewish children worked either in factories and shops in or near the ghetto in which they lived or in scores of labor camps which dotted the landscape of the General Government. All Jewish children from the age of 14 joined adult men and women in compulsory labor. Children, like adults, had to register with the *Judenrat* (Jewish Council) which supervised the execution of German labor laws. By the end of 1940, 700,000 Jews were on forced labor in German-occupied Poland.[68]

The prevailing view in the major ghettos of Poland was that if Jews worked long and hard enough, the Germans would allow them live. Thus the ghettos became beehives of activity, veritable labor camps which, as in the case of the Lodz Ghetto, produced everything from boots to telecommunication devices for the Germans.[69]

Nowhere was the "work to survive" mentality more pronounced than in Lodz where its controversial leader, Chaim Rumkowski, sacrificed thousands of children, aged and sick Jews late in 1942 to meet the German demand for over 20,000 victims for their death camps. "They requested 24,000 victims," he told his audience. "I succeeded in reducing the number to 20,000, but only on the condition that these would be children below the age of ten. Children ten and older are safe...." Thus more productive Jews would be spared to work for the German war machine. "Give into my hands the victims," he said, "*so that we can avoid having further victims,* and *a population of a hundred thousand Jews can be preserved* (author's italics). So they promised me: if we deliver our victims ourselves, there will be peace...."[70] Of course, the Nazi demands for more Jewish lives continued with Rumkowski eventually becoming a victim himself. Yet Lodz continued under forced labor until its liquidation in August, 1944.

Rumkowski's views were naive at best and criminal at worst because they deluded Jews in the belief that cooperation, not resistance, was the best course to follow. "It is hard to see how Rumkowski's desperate gamble was less catastrophic than if cooperation with the Germans had been refused or resisted," two students of the subject astutely observed. "The naked truth is that Rumkowski's plan, unless the war ended quickly and the Nazis were removed, was bound to result in the death of the sick and of children below working age."[71]

Some ghettos were spared, at least for the time being, the tragedy of Lodz. In Kovno, for example, it was not until the end of March, 1943, that the German demand for an increase in the number of workers forced the *Judenrat* to co-opt teenagers 16 and 17 years old into the labor force. Kovno, the eighth largest ghetto in the area occupied by the Germans after June, 1941, had a labor force of 10,000 people but there were an additional 8,000, mostly young children, women, and sick Jews, who depended upon those who worked. Interestingly, the *Judenrat* courageously did not register 2,000 of the 8,000, most of whom were orphaned children from the German slaughter of Jews that followed the invasion of the Soviet Union in 1941. Had the Germans known about the orphans, they undoubtedly would have deported and killed them.[72]

Life for the child laborer was grim. As one diarist recorded at the time, "Most of them can hardly eke out a living. Many are orphans or the children of deported parents. Because their meager wages are too small, they must sell a part of their ration... and their working hours make their lives even more miserable." He was also critical of those who oversaw child laborers in the workshops: "Unfortunately, the attitude toward them in the workshop is far from proper. The workshop management shows a total lack of concern for the conditions and needs of the children."[73]

Shortly before the complete liquidation of the Lodz Ghetto, one young Jewish diarist wrote in desperation:

> Curse those who are able to cause such agony—as I suffer now—for their fellow creatures. I write and I don't know if tomorrow I shall be able to read this, because our disgustingly untiring oppressors 'want' a thousand unhappy Ghettonians to be sent for 'work.'... How much longer will this senseless cruelty be continued? What am I guilty or accused of? My little poor sister of 12! It is already more than 4 years since you've been toiling in the most unimaginable manner,... Will all this horror, trouble, agony, tears and beastly fears have been in vain? Ah, if it is to turn out that way, why didn't we die 5 years ago?[74]

In many ghettos there were arrangements to train children in various trades. None was as well organized as Lodz. There, the ghetto chronicle recorded on July 23, 1942, the vast scale of operations in tailoring alone: "Putting such an institution into operation has provided a rational solution to the problem of completing the education of children and young people in tailoring, which is a basic trade in the ghetto. At present, the tailoring workshops employ around 2,000 children as apprentices. All the tailoring divisions, as well as the related manufacturers (the hosiery factory, the saddlery workshop, and so forth), are sending their most gifted children to attend the courses."[75]

Jewish children also worked in a number of labor camps in the General Government. As early as 1940, there were 29 labor camps in the Lublin district alone. Conditions in these camps were extremely bad—inadequate food, few, if any, sanitary facilities, and, of course, the ever present beatings.[76] Poniatowa was one of the more infamous camps in this district where approximately 18,000 Jews worked before the Germans liquidated the camp in 1944.[77]

In order to appreciate how appalling conditions were for Jews in these camps, there is the vivid example when the Germans sent 6,000 men from the Warsaw Ghetto to nearby locations; two weeks later, 1,000 of them were no longer capable of working again.[78] One of these camps was located in Kampinos where, in the spring of 1941, many Jewish youths died. Kampinos was important to the Germans because it was connected with the area's water industry. The laborers had to work in knee-deep water on a starvation diet.[79]

Twelve-year-old Sammy Rosenbaum lived in the town of Rabka, not far from the ski resort of Zakopane in the Carpathian Mountains. Forced to work in a stone quarry in Zakryty, Sammy learned that his father, mother, and sister had been shot by the SS. He was saying *Kaddish*, the Jewish prayer for the dead, when the head of the German police school in the area, SS Untersturmfuhrer Wilhelm Rosenbaum, who had the same name as Sammy's family and hated the Jews for it, summoned him. The SS leader and his "students" waited for him in a clearing in the woods where the frail young boy was shot to death. Simon Wiesenthal, the famous Nazi hunter, learned about Sammy and his family years after the war, presumably from a Polish woman who had known the youngster. "Every year, one day in June, I light two candles for him and say *Kaddish*," Wiesenthal said.[80]

On his way to a secret tutorial session with his teacher, a young gentile boy made a grim discovery concerning what happened to Jews who ran away from a nearby labor camp and were caught by the Germans. As he walked through the town's Jewish cemetery, the boy noticed several odd rectangular depressions in the ground. Intensely curious, he went inside an abandoned sentry post where he rummaged through boxes of documents which graphically recorded the gruesome circumstances surrounding the deaths of Jewish workers. One of the documents matter-of-factly recorded how the Jews had to agree to work for three days cleaning the town's streets in order to pay for the ammunition that was later used to kill them![81]

One of the most amazing aspects of the lives of Polish and Jewish children during the German occupation of Poland was their role in helping to maintain the entire fabric of their community's cultural life—schools, theater, music, the press. Much of this had to be done clandestinely because the Germans prohibited most forms of intellectual and cultural expression. Attending a secret class, participating in Purim festivities or helping to distribute an underground newspaper were some of the many ways Jewish and Polish children asserted their individuality and contributed to the resistance against the Germans. These manifestations of resistance were no less damaging to the Nazis than sabotage or reprisal operations because they defied Nazi racist doctrines and regulations which sought to destroy the Jews and to obliterate the country of Poland.

The Nazi prescription for the education of a Polish child reflected the subservient role the Germans wanted the Poles who survived their genocidal policies to play in the postwar world. Himmler wanted Polish children to be able to sign their own name, be obedient to the Germans and count at most to 500.[82] Thus only primary schools, which did not operate throughout the year, would be tolerated in the General Government. In the annexed lands the Germans abolished Polish primary schools entirely.

A major achievement of the Poles during the occupation was the establishment of an underground network of schools. By 1942-43, almost 5,300 teachers taught over 86,000 elementary school children and over 5,600 teachers instructed over 48,000 secondary school children in the General Government. In the annexed lands, the difficulties in establishing secret schools were greater than in the General Government. Nevertheless, over 1,400 Polish teachers taught almost 19,000 elementary school children and 200 teachers taught almost 1,700 secondary school students.[83] This was quite an impressive achievement considering the decimation of teachers, 15 percent of whom were killed during the war[84] and thousands more incarcerated in prisons.

Children met secretly in small groups in attics, cellars, and apartments with their teachers. These "flying schools" were everywhere. Zbigniew Bokiewicz was a 16-year-old student at the prestigious Stefan Batory gymnasium before the war. Shortly after Poland's surrender in October, 1939, he recalled the day the Germans arrived and seized the building. Teachers and students, anticipating the worst, removed and hid school records and paintings of the school's patron, King Stefan Batory, and a copy of Jan Matejko's famous painting of the Battle of Grunwald. "A week later," he said, "our studies resumed as a technical school.... After about a year, the Germans realized what was going on and closed that school too. My education then continued in secret. Groups of six or seven students met in private apartments and the teachers went to the various apartments to give their lessons."[85]

A Catholic nun remembered the misfortunes of her order and the 400 boys and girls in a boarding school outside of Katowice, the area annexed by the Germans to the Reich. The SS and the NSV (Nazi Welfare Organization) took over the school and divided the children into groups based on intelligence. They placed 150 of the most intelligent children in the care of the NSV, forbidding the nuns to have anything to do with them. The Germans told the nuns they could remain at the school provided they agreed to educate the children "in the German spirit" and under supervision of the NSV. They arrested the mother superior and the remaining nuns, 80 of them, left the institution on foot, seeking a home elsewhere. The 150 most intelligent children remained at the school for several months. The Germans later sent them away. No one knew where.[86]

Despite the closing of 28 schools of university status and the arrest of hundreds of professors by the Germans, university-level classes began late in 1940 at the secret University of Warsaw. About the same time, professors and students deported from the University of Poznan established a secret university of their own in Warsaw. This unique institution, which had 250 teachers and more than 2,000 students, even offered extension work in Czestochowa and Kielce. Due to the loss of almost 200 professors from the Jagiellonian University early in the occupation, university studies in Krakow were delayed.[87]

Students attended secret classes, took examinations and received diplomas, usually drawn up in code and signed by professors using pseudonyms. Sometimes a student received a calling card that could be exchanged for a diploma after the war. One card read: "Thank you for your charming visit on September 19, 1942. I was most satisfied. You told me such *interesting* things. Bravo." Even though the ghetto had university classes of its own, some Jewish students attended sessions on the Christian side of the wall.[88] Attending underground schools had its price: hundreds of Polish students were sent to concentration camps. On May 24-25, 1944, a transport of 867 young Poles, many of them students in underground schools, arrived at Stutthof concentration camp.

Ironically, illegal schools operated in many camps—Sachsenhausen, Ravensbruck, Buchenwald, Majdanek—to name some of the major ones. There was even a "Walking University" at Mauthausen-Gusen, where prisoners walked in threes and after they heard a lecture, they repeated it to another set of three prisoners. Students at different levels of their education heard lectures in different places—toilets, bathhouses, storerooms and barracks. Sometimes a specially designated prisoner walked around the area where the lessons took place and warned teachers and students when a guard appeared. "Learning took one's thoughts away from the gloomy reality of the camp," one participant in the underground educational system said. "It somehow connected the prisoners with a normal world. The whole camp knew about the lectures, nevertheless, they were never betrayed. Nowhere was the hunger for knowledge so strong and never was the truth so forcefully revealed, that man cannot live by bread alone." Children's plays and choirs also performed in several camps.[89]

The Germans set up elementary schools for Jewish children in the General Government, but ghetto leaders established their own underground elementary and secondary schools as the Poles had done. Despite the enormous obstacles which were even greater for Jews than Poles, the Warsaw Ghetto by 1942 boasted of 20 primary and secondary schools which served 7,000 children. Polish educators, organized in the *Tajna Organizacja Nauczycielstwa* (Secret Organization of Teachers) cooperated with Jewish teachers and students by providing them with money, books, and food and they even hid several Jewish students from the Germans.[90]

Most of the clandestine high schools followed the pattern on the other side of the ghetto wall—namely, unemployed teachers gathering small groups of students and giving them lessons. In Warsaw, however, there was also a Hebrew high school which drew students from Zionist elementary schools, and functioned more like a normal school by meeting in a designated place rather than in private homes. Dr. Nathan Eck, the principal, recalled: "Two months prior to the end of the school year we held registration for the following year and scores of students re-enrolled. After vacation, we were able to reopen with three complete classes—freshmen, sophomores and juniors. In other words, only one class was lacking to make it a complete high school. We completed our studies at the end of June, 1942, three weeks before the Jews of the Ghetto were massacred!"[91]

Prior to the outbreak of the war, approximately 3,500 Hasidic youth studied in the *shtiblekh* and hundreds of others in yeshivas in Warsaw. Since many rabbis and their students fled eastward during the German invasion of Poland, studies at these centers ended. Despite the fact that it was impossible for Jews to assemble in synagogues and houses of study during most of the occupation, Hasidic youth in the Warsaw ghetto informally met for Torah study. The majority of them exchanged their traditional Jewish garb for European dress.[92]

The pattern was similar in other ghettos. Shortly after the establishment of the Vilna Ghetto, Moshe Ulitzky spearheaded the organization of a unified educational system there. The disinterest of Jacob Gens, the ghetto chairman, allowed Ulitzky and his collaborators a free hand in creating a school system which by September, 1941, enrolled 2,700 children, ages 6 to 14. Like Jews in other ghettos, Vilna residents had various political and ideological loyalties which influenced the school curriculum. As Dr. Meir Dworzecki, eye-witness and historian of the Vilna Ghetto, noted, "They succeeded in fixing an equality between Hebrew and Yiddish and a suitable synthesis of the ideological orientations: Zionist, Socialist and Communist." For Orthodox parents who wanted their children to have an Orthodox Hebrew education, special schools, including a yeshiva, were established.[93]

Surviving accounts of school children suggest they were eager to attend school. Often children in Vilna came to school early. During recess, they danced and sang, "We are young, we will overcome." Perhaps the few hours with friends and a loving teacher helped them to deal with the pervasive tragedy that enveloped them and their families. This was clearly reflected in the subjects of compositions they wrote: "How I Saved Myself from Camp Ponar (Vilna Death Camp)," "They Led My Parents to Death," "I Hid in an Underground Bunker."

The Vilna Ghetto also boasted of a music school, specializing in piano, violin and choir, which enrolled approximately 100 students. They gave frequent concerts, enriching the cultural life of the residents of the ghetto.[94]

One of the most inspirational aspects of the lives of children in Poland during the war was their ability to cope with the terror and tragedy that characterized life in wartime Poland. For Jewish children the horror increased substantially in 1942 when the Germans singled out the Jews, including children, for systematic deportations to the death camps.

Surviving accounts reveal that many children, especially those confined in ghettos and hiding from German deportation actions, read a great deal. Halina Birenbaum was a typical teenager who loved to read: "I would sit over my books until late at night, by a smelly carbide lamp, or a candle, or a little gas flame that often provided the only light in our room." No doubt reading took Halina and countless other children away from the terrible world of the Nazis to other happier worlds. "I believed I would wake up one morning to find no more Germans left in Warsaw," Halina wrote, "that they would vanish, disappear forever like figures in a nightmare."[95] Yehuda Nir, hiding his Jewish identity, spent much of his time reading the obituaries of German soldiers in the leading German newspaper, the *Volkischer Beobachter*. It pleased him that young, German boys died, he said, "So I wasn't the only orphan boy."[96]

Judging by the number of libraries in Poland's ghettos, reading was a favorite activity of children and adults. The Vilna Ghetto library celebrated the second year of its existence by awarding a 14-year-old girl first prize for reading the most books. She continued to borrow and read books until the Germans liquidated the ghetto.[97]

Young children played games that reflected the tragedy around them. Ghetto children played a game of "Jews caught by Germans" by feigning beating and killing. Janusz Korczak, the well-known physician and child psychologist, noted in his diary that he saw three boys playing "Horses and Drivers." Their reins became tangled and as they tried to disengage them, they stumbled over a young boy who was dying or perhaps already dead. Used to seeing dead and dying people every day, one of the boys said, "Let's move on, he's getting in the way!" Zofia Szymanska, a pioneer in child psychiatry in Poland, observed the same indifference. While observing a group of children playing at a child center, Szymanska saw a boy fall dead to the floor, a victim of hunger. The others, inured to what was a daily occurrence, ignored the boy and continued to play.[98]

There was another child's game that went something like this: A child took a handful of sand, saying "I had so many children." He then threw the sand in the air. While most of it fell to the ground, he said matter-of-factly, "Those are all dead." He looked at the few remaining grains of sand on his hand, saying "And these are still alive."[99]

Gentile children during the Warsaw Uprising of 1944 used to divide into opposing sides and play "Insurgents." They went into "battle," complete with wooden pistols and rifles. They even made grenades out of ashes and paper, and hurled them at each other. To the great disappointment of one group of children, they had to relinquish the only real weapon, a bayonet they found in the rubble, to a member of the *Armia Krajowa* (Home Army). One boy complained how unfair the enemy team was when they "attacked" his group during supper when there were few defenders.[100]

There was an imaginative variety of toys that amused youngsters too. In Lodz, the ghetto toys of the summer of 1943 were two slabs of wood; one held between the forefinger and the middle finger and the other between the middle finger and ring finger. Pressing the fingers together produced a noise resembling the clicking of castanets. As the Lodz Chronicle recorded: "The instrument imposes no limit on the individual's musical ability. There are children who are content to use the primitive clicking of the slabs to produce something like the sounds of a Morse code transmitter. Other children imitate the beating of a drum, improvising marches out of banging sounds as they parade with their playmates like soldiers." The streets of Lodz witnessed barefoot boys earnestly performing their music. "Here the musical instinct of Eastern European Jews is cultivated to the full," the Chronicle continued. "An area that has given the world so many musicians, chiefly violinists—just think of Hubermann, Heifetz, Elman, Milstein, Menuhin—now presents a new line of artists."[101]

Children also collected empty cigarette boxes and removed the colorful tops which they methodically stacked in decks and played with them as playing cards. Arranging the cards by color and name, they played imaginative games they invented themselves.[102]

In a children's home where Polish and Jewish children were cared for by nuns, one of the games the children played was tied to the survival of the Jewish youngsters. Playing at the grim reality of German roundups (lapanki), a child yelled, "The Germans are coming! Jews hide yourselves!" (Niemcy ida! Zydzi, Chowajcie sie!) The Jewish children quickly hid under tables and chairs until the danger had passed.[103]

On the other side of the ghetto walls, it was common for young boys to walk the streets, often singing self-authored songs for which passersby would give them a coin. Earlier in the war they sang, "March, March, Sikorski from London to Poland," a reference to the head of the Polish government-in-exile and commander of Polish forces abroad. Another favorite was, "Now You Beloved Warsaw are Burned," the last stanza of which looked forward to happier days: "Don't worry brothers, God's grace is with us, we will rebuild Poland from sea to sea."[104]

There was a large number of Jewish organizations which tried to help as many of the ghetto children as possible. Obvious priority had to be given to orphaned and abandoned children. The leading organization involved in a variety of welfare activities in behalf of children was CENTOS (*Centralna Zwiazku Towarzystw nad Sierotami*), headed by Adolf Berman. CENTOS had dormitories, public kitchens, child centers, clinics, orphanages and boarding schools. In Warsaw alone, CENTOS ran approximately 100 establishments offering relief to about 40,000-45,000 children. According to one welfare official, without CENTOS, Jewish children would have starved to death within a few months of the creation of the Warsaw Ghetto.[105]

CENTOS and other groups associated with it recognized that physical care of children was important, but emphasis also had to be placed on the psychological integrity of the youngsters. "The upholding of the morale of the child was a prime consideration from the very beginning," Genia Silkes, a former Warsaw Ghetto teacher wrote. "Efforts were directed by the initiators of the relief action to distract the children, to allay their fears and to minimize hazards that were lurking in every corner of the home, yard, the street."[106]

That was why welfare and relief officials emphasized education and other cultural activities for the children. In order to raise money to fund various cultural activities for the youngsters, CENTOS sponsored a "Month of the Child" (*Miesiac Dziecka*) and succeeded in raising 1 million zlotys in 1941. CENTOS planned a similar event the following year. It was scheduled for August, 1942, and was to be commemorated by the opening of a new home for 800 orphaned and abandoned children. Ten days before the event, the Germans began the liquidation of the Warsaw Ghetto.[107]

Similar activities on behalf of children took place in other ghettos. Unable to save adults, ghetto officials in Vilna concentrated on the children, establishing child centers and clinics. To ensure that children had milk to drink, they resorted to extensive smuggling. "There was a time," one survivor recalled, "when every school child received a glass of milk." Like Warsaw and other ghettos, great emphasis was placed on educational, cultural, and vocational activities for youngsters. "The children knew well their destiny," a leading Jewish educator in Vilna wrote. "They knew what was coming and they were helpless. They were imagining a magic circle around them, keeping out the horrors of the ghetto life. A measure of such solace they found inside the schools and institutes. Here they could spin a dream life."[108]

Some children apparently managed to cope with the horror around them. If the revealing wartime diary of Eva, an adolescent girl who lived in the Krakow Ghetto, is representative of other youngsters her age, it is clear that some children tried to minimize not only the terrible events around them, but also the terror they felt in response to them. Eva gave surprisingly little attention to the events of the Holocaust in her diary. Rather, she seemed preoccupied with relationships with her family and awakenings of sexual interest.

Her diary is studded with mundane matters. On October 16, 1940, "Yesterday was Mommy's birthday...." One month later, she notes simply, "I'll write more details another time, because today I'm too busy." On December 5, 1940, she speaks of the possibility of leaving Krakow: "Now I realize how much I love this city and this, my second, fatherland." Or, when she alluded to the tragedy around her, as in an entry on December 19, 1940, it is starkly brief: "Wladek died. We are barely staying alive. It's freezing out."[109]

This psychic numbing was her way, no doubt true of others her age, of coping with the traumatic experiences that affected her and her loved ones. Yet, one psychologist noted, "In Eva's case one is impressed by the basically normal course of adolescent development observed in her diary. Surrounded by death, despair, cold, hunger, and relentless persecution, Eva emerges from her memoirs in many ways like the ninth grader next door."[110]

Not all Jewish children adapted so well to the horrors the Germans imposed upon them. In the same ghetto where Eva lived, one teacher spoke of the severe emotional conflicts experienced by children under her care. These youngsters expressed their conflicts through aggression. Often they exhibited aggressive behavior toward their own parents whom they considered traitors, unable to understand the helplessness of their elders. When parents came to visit their children after working all day, Renee Padar observed, "They had nothing to offer them; to bring them closer. Gradually the child-parent connection was severed. It also became apparent that some parents were obsessed with saving their own lives. Many children felt that. There were cases when children went into hiding when their parents came." Teachers tried to distract the children with some handiwork or story-telling but these activities did not interest them. Instead, the children would cry and scream. Many times older children would try to escape through the windows, somehow believing they would free themselves of the constant pain they had to endure. "When we held them back," Padar said, "they would attack us, accusing us that we were preventing them from reaching their goal."[111]

Jews and Poles produced a rich variety of performances of plays, reading, music and puppetry. Children performed in many of these performances or, in many cases, performed in their own productions. Hundreds of these events were performed under the noses of the Germans; yet, amazingly in the five years of the Nazi occupation, the Gestapo failed to break up a single theatrical performance, despite the fact that these productions occurred hundreds of times.[112]

Among the favorite events celebrated by ghetto children was Purim, which commemorated the deliverance of the Jews in the Persian Empire from a diabolical plan by Haman, the king's minister, to commit genocide. Queen Esther thwarted Haman's plan by revealing to King Ahasuerus that she herself was Jewish. Purim is also known as the Feast of Lots because of the lots Haman cast to determine the day of the annihilation of the Jews.

To ghetto Jews during the war, the story of Purim offered obvious parallels with Hitler and the Nazi terror. Purim offered hope that Haman's fate would also befall Hitler and that the Jews would survive as they had done in Ahasuerus' day. Little wonder, then, that Purim was the most popular festival among Jews, especially children, who eagerly anticipated the event. Purim festivals, rich in artistry and literary quality, often featured gifted artists like Marisha Eisenstat, known as the "Singing Nightingale."

Acting in Purim plays, children assumed various disguises and imitated the Germans cursing and beating Jews. Improvising their own scripts, the play ended with a Jewish boy leading Hitler to the gallows, the fate that had befallen Haman.[113]

When the children's performance in Kovno ended, one observer noted, "Mothers and guardians of the children wiped single tears from their eyes. But these are tears of joy at the sight of their sons and daughters who, at this moment, give free expression to their youthful experience."[114]

Following the Purim custom of giving gifts, especially to children, mothers scrounged to offer their youngsters some delicacy. Those who could afford it bought smuggled items from Christians. As one observer recalled, "The best Purim present for a child in the public kitchen was a piece of potato floating in his soup—that would make his holiday."[115]

The Germans knew their attempts to destroy the cultural life of Poles and Jews failed miserably. Nowhere did this manifest itself more profoundly than in the dynamic underground press which helped not only to unify people from all walks of life but also to forge bonds between Poles and Jews who before the war lived side by side but, except for a small number of assimilated Jews, had little to do with one another.

Poland exceeded all other countries in the number of titles regularly published under German occupation. There were 1,257 confirmed titles of the Polish underground press, though one historian estimates that there were probably as many as 1,400. They were published in various forms—mimeographed, printed, typed, written by hand. Although most of them were organs of various political groups, many publications—newspapers and journals—met the interests of special groups, including children. For example, there were 30 publications for Scouts and a children's journal, *Biedronka* (*Ladybird*). Several student organizations published their own newspapers.[116]

In Warsaw alone, there were 56 titles of the Jewish press that appeared before the deportations to the death camps in the summer of 1942. They were published in three languages—Polish, Yiddish and Hebrew. Jewish youth groups, Zionist and Bundist, published a number of newspapers that addressed political and cultural matters. The only printed newspaper in the Warsaw Ghetto, *Ha Medina*, was published by the Zionist youth group Betar. The *Bund* and its youth section, at odds with the Zionists, mimeographed its newspapers on large thick paper, making it cumbersome to hide or to pass to others secretly.[117]

Newsboys played a critical role in distributing underground

newspapers which never seemed to quench the public's thirst for news. People were so eager for news they even stole copies of newspapers from others.[118] "Every item of more important news, or even rumour," one leading Polish underground official recalled, "was the talk of Warsaw after a few hours."[119]

But it was as dangerous to produce and distribute as it was to read an underground publication. In one Warsaw district, the Gestapo surrounded a villa where an illegal printing press operated. When the Germans got no response to their knocking on the doors, they blasted the villa with machine-gun fire and grenades. The owner of the villa, his wife and two adolescent sons were arrested and shot. For good measure, the Gestapo arrested and shot all the residents of nearby homes. Altogether, 83 people died.

Somewhat earlier, the Germans apprehended two girls—one 14, the other 16 years of age—on a Warsaw street. They found illegal publications on them. Taken to prison, the girls were later shot. They did not betray any secrets and the publication continued to be distributed illegally in Warsaw.[120]

Little wonder, then, that hawkers and customers had to be cautious about transactions involving underground newspapers. One eyewitness observed how sophisticated the system was:

> Newsboys on the streets of Warsaw and Krakow sold the German local papers, *Krakauer Zeitung, Warschauer Zeitung,* or the *Ostdeutscher Beobachter* in Poznan, or Adolph Hitler's own *Voelkischer Beobachter* in every small and large Polish city. No Pole bought these papers, unless the boy smilingly said to him:
>
> "Today you have extraordinary news about German victories... Buy it," and handed him a copy.
>
> The passerby knew the copy was worth buying, for it was stuffed. Between the pages full of German dispatches describing incredible successes of the swastika-bearing flag, he found a hidden copy of his underground paper.
>
> A butcher would say to a woman customer, while wrapping her steak: "Put it on ice immediately when you reach home, will you?" And she would know that the paper was wrapped inside.[121]

Chapter Notes

1. Zuker-Bujanowska, *Liliana's Journal*, p. 28.
2. Hrabar, *The Fate of Polish Children*, pp. 154-55.
3. Chaim A. Kaplan, *Scroll of Agony: The Warsaw Diary of Chaim A. Kaplan* (New York: Collier, 1973), pp. 219-20.
4. *Ibid.*, Emmanuel Ringelblum, *Kronika Getta Warszawskiego*, ed. by Artur Eisenbach (Warsaw: Czytelnik, 1983), p. 244; Drecki, *Freedom and Justice*, p. 40.
5. Lech Wisniewski, "Likwidacja Getta," in Turski, *Byli Wowczas Dziecmi*, p. 395.
6. Eugeniusz Duraczynski, *Wojna i Okupacja: Wrzesien 1939-Kwiecien 1943* (Warsaw: Wiedza Powszechna, 1974), p. 69.
7. Zuker-Bujanowska, *Liliana's Journal*, p. 29.
8. *Ibid.*
9. Lucjan Dobroszycki, ed., *The Chronicle of the Lodz Ghetto, 1941-1944* (New Haven: Yale University Press, 1984), p. 479.
10. Quoted in Adelson and Lapides, *Lodz Ghetto*, pp. 236-39.
11. *Ibid.*, pp. 239-40.
12. Lukas, *Out of the Inferno*, p. 135.
13. Shimon Huberband, *Kiddush Hashem: Jewish Religious and Cultural Life in Poland during the Holocaust* (Hoboken, N.J.: KTAV Publishing House and Yeshiva University Press, 1987), pp. 240-41.
14. Mary Berg, *Warsaw Ghetto: A Diary*, ed. by S.L. Shneiderman (New York: L.B. Fischer, 1945), pp. 88-89.
15. Birenbaum, *Hope Is the Last to Die*, p. 8.
16. *Ibid.*
17. Hrabar, *Fate of Polish Children*, p. 159; Dobroszycki, *Chronicle of the Lodz Ghetto*, p. 9.
18. Concerning the morality of Polish youth see PRM 45c/23 in PI/GSHM. For a summary of the moral decline of Jewish youth, see Yisrael Gutman, *Fighters Among the Ruins: The Story of Jewish Heroism during World War II* (Washington, D.C.: B'nai B'rith, 1988), p. 83.

19. Quoted in *Ibid.*, pp. 83-84.

20. Joanna K. M. Hanson, *The Civilian Population and the Warsaw Uprising of 1944* (Cambridge: Cambridge University Press, 1982), pp. 22-23.

21. Hrabar, *Fate of Polish Children*, pp. 168-69.

22. Pilichowski, *Zbrodnie Hitlerowskie*, p. 37.

23. Hrabar, *Fate of Polish Children*, pp. 33-34.

24. Hanson, *Civilian Population*, p. 69.

25. Gross, *Polish Society*, pp. 102-03; U.S. Counsel, *Nazi Conspiracy and Aggression*, II, 637-38.

26. *Polish Fortnightly Review*, November 1, 1942.

27. Republic of Poland, *German Occupation of Poland* (New York: Greystone Press, 1942), p. 2.

28. Quoted in United Nations Information Organization, *Today's Children Tomorrow's Hope: The Story of Children in the Occupied Lands* (London: United Nations, 1945), p. 40.

29. Quoted in Hrabar, *Fate of Polish Children*, p. 159.

30. Abraham Lewin, *A Cup of Tears: A Diary of the Warsaw Ghetto*, ed. by Antony Polonsky (London: Basil Blackwell, 1988), p. 21.

31. Interview with Stefan Korbonski, June 7, 1982. Korbonski, the highly respected head of the Polish Underground's Directorate of Civil Resistance and the last chief of the Polish Underground, had many contacts with Jewish leaders before and during the war and was very well informed about what went on in Poland's ghettos. It was his messages from Poland that first alerted the world about the massive German deportations of Jews from the Warsaw Ghetto to the death camps in the summer of 1942. For the first time, these messages were quoted in Lukas, *Forgotten Holocaust*, pp. 156-57.

32. Lewin, *Cup of Tears*, p. 266. It was not uncommon for a Pole to give a Jewish child food and shelter after having done business with him. Joseph Ziemian, *The Cigarette Sellers of Three Crosses Square*, trans. by Janina David (London: Vallentine, Mitchell, 1970), p. 72.

33. Lewin, *Cup of Tears*, p. 77.

34. *Ibid.*, p. 89.

35. Kaplan, *Scroll of Agony*, pp. 327-28.

36. Lukas, *Out of the Inferno*, p. 36.

37. Zenona Strozyk, "W Krakowie i Gdzie Indziej," in Turski, *Byli Wowczas Dziecmi*, p. 231.

38. Dobroszycki, *Chronicle of the Lodz Ghetto*, p. 70.

39. Games, *Escape into Darkness*, p. 89.

40. Ringelblum, *Kronika Getta Warszawskiego*, p. 368; Interview with Korbonski.

41. Berg, *Warsaw Ghetto*, pp. 72-73; Azriel Eisenberg, *The Lost Generation: Children in the Holocaust* (New York: The Pilgrim Press, 1982), pp. 53-54.

42. Lewin, *Cup of Tears*, p. 132.

43. *Ibid.*, p. 23.

44. *Ibid.*, pp. 18, 23.

45. Ringelblum, *Kronika Getta Warszawskiego*, p. 369. Jewish children also smuggled arms and ammunition to the Jewish resistance from Polish sources. Rosenblum, "Jewish Children," p. 28.

46. Stefan Korbonski, *Fighting Warsaw: The Story of the Polish Underground State, 1939-1945*, trans. by F.B. Czarnomski (N.C.: Minerva Press, 1968), p. 219.

47. *Ibid.*, pp. 219-20; Interview with Korbonski.

48. Robert Gellately, *The Gestapo and German Society: Enforcing Racial Policy, 1933-1945* (Oxford: Clarendon Press, 1990), pp. 216-17.

49. *Ibid.*, p. 220.

50. Lukas, *Forgotten Holocaust*, p. 32.

51. Czeslaw Madajczyk, *Polityka III Rzeszy w Okupowanej Polsce* (2 vols.; Warsaw: Panstwowe Wydawnictwo Naukowe, 1970), I, 251; U.S. Counsel, *Nazi Conspiracy and Aggression*, II, 800.

52. Hrabar, *Fate of Polish Children*, p. 38.

53. Aleksander Wierzejewski, "Praca Przymusowa Dzieci i Mlodziezy Polskiej w Wielkopolsce," in *Dzieci i Mlodziez w Latach Drugiej Wojny Swiatowej*, ed. by Czeslaw Pilichowski (Warsaw: Panstwowe Wydawnictwo Naukowe, 1982), pp. 271-72.

54. Pilichowski, *Zbrodnie Hitlerowskie*, p. 38.

55. Robert Jay Lifton, *The Nazi Doctors: Medical Killing and the Psychology of Genocide* (New York: Basic Books, 1986), p. 187; Czeslaw Kempisty, *Spraw Norymbergi Ciag Dalszy* (Warsaw: Panstwowe Wydawnictwo Naukowe, 1975), p. 45: Hrabar, *Fate of Polish Children*, p. 41.

56. Memo, undated, WR 22/18; in PAG-4/2.0.62: Box 15, UN-RRA/UNA.

57. Quoted in Hrabar, *Fate of Polish Children*, p. 40.

58. Wierzejewski, "Praca Przymusowa," pp. 270-71.

59. Hrabar, *Fate of Polish Children*, pp. 42-43; Reports on the Situation in Occupied Poland, No. 6/42, in RG 226, Records of the Office of Strategic Services, National Archives. Hereinafter cited as OSS/NA.

60. Wisniewski, "Likwidacja Getta," pp. 397-98.

61. Wierzejewski, "Praca Przymusowa," pp. 272-74; Czeslaw Luczak, "Eksploatacja Sily Roboczej Polskich Dzieci Przez III Rzesze," in Pilichowski, *Dzieci i Mlodziesz*, pp. 267-69.

62. Macardle, *Children of Europe*, p. 68.

63. Lukas, *Out of the Inferno*, pp. 51-55.

64. U.S. Counsel, *Nazi Conspiracy and Aggression*, I, 905-06; Polish Ministry of Information, *Black Book of Poland*, pp. 124-25, 427-28; The Appeal can be found in Appendix 107 of Republic of Poland, *German Occupation of Poland*, pp. 187-89; Gellately, *The Gestapo and German Society*, p. 226.

65. Bohdan Wytwycky, *The Other Holocaust: Many Circles of Hell* (Washington, D.C.: Novak Report, 1980), pp. 77-78.

66. Gellately, *Gestapo and German Society*, pp. 233-34; Republic of Poland, *The Polish Territory Occupied by the Germans*.

67. Proceedings of Military Court for Trial of War Criminals, May 16, 1946, in WO 203/263-389, Public Record Office, Kew, Richmond. Hereinafter cited as PRO; Wnuk, *Dzieci Polskie Oskarzaja*, pp. 81-82.

68. Israel Gutman (ed.), *Encyclopedia of the Holocaust* (4 vols.; New York: Macmillan, 1990), II, 500-501.

69. Dobroszycki, *Chronicle of the Lodz Ghetto*, pp. lix-lx.

70. Speech by Chaim Rumkowski, September 4, 1942, quoted in Adelson and Lapides, *Lodz Ghetto*, p. 330.

71. *Ibid.*, p. 513.

72. Avraham Tory, *Surviving the Holocaust: The Kovno Ghetto Diary* (Cambridge: Harvard University Press, 1990), pp. viii, xvii, 261.

73. Quoted in Adelson and Lapides, *Lodz Ghetto*, pp. 373-74.

74. *Ibid.*, p. 423.

75. Dobroszycki, *Chronicle of the Lodz Ghetto*, p. 228.

76. Gutman, *Encyclopedia of the Holocaust*, p. 500.

77. Hrabar, *Fate of Polish Children*, p. 39.

78. Gutman, *Encyclopedia of the Holocaust*, p. 501.

79. Huberband, *Kiddush Hashem*, pp. 71ff.

80. Simon Wiesenthal, *The Murderers Among Us: The Simon Wiesenthal Memoirs* (New York: McGraw Hill, 1967), pp. 263-68.

81. Wisniewski, "Likwidacja Getta," pp. 400-401. Almost routinely one of the chroniclers of the Lodz Ghetto recorded in 1942, "Two men were hung on the gallows: 16-year-old Grynbaum from Pabianice and 45-year-old Markowski. They were executed for escaping from a labor camp near Poznan." Dobroszycki, *Chronicle of the Lodz Ghetto*, p. 228.

82. Himmler's instructions, May 14, 1940, are quoted in Hrabar, *Fate of Polish Children*, p. 37.

83. Duraczynski, *Wojna i Okupacja*, pp. 234-37, 422-24.

84. *Ibid.*; Madajczyk, *Polityka III Rzeszy*, II, 168.

85. Lukas, *Out of the Inferno*, p. 24.

86. Report, Troniak's interview with Sister Cassiana, February 5, 1946, in PAG 4/1.3.1.2.10, Box 1, UNRRA/NA.

87. Jozef Garlinski, *Polska w Drugiej Wojnie Swiatowej* (London: Odnowa, 1982), pp. 225-26.

88. Jan Karski, *Story of a Secret State* (Boston: Houghton Mifflin, 1944), p. 308; Henri Michel, *The Shadow War: European Resistance. 1939-1945* (New York: Harper and Row, 1972), p. 144; Interview with Korbonski.

89. Kazimierz Smolen, "Dzieci i Mlodziez w Obozach Koncentracyjnych," in Pilichowski, *Dzieci i Mlodziez*, pp. 131, 139; Krzysztof Dunin-Wasowicz, *Resistance in the Nazi Concentration Camps. 1933-1945* (Warsaw: PWN-Polish Scientific Publishers, 1982), pp. 333-42; Sybil Milton, "Non-Jewish Children in the Camps," *Simon Wiesenthal Center Annual*, V (1988), 56.

90. Madajczyk, *Polityka III Rzeszy*, II, 160-62; Tadeusz Bednarczyk, *Obowiazek Silnieszy Od Smierci: Wspomnienia z Lat 1939-1944 o Polskiej Pomocy dla Zydow w Warszawie* (Warsaw: Spolecznie Wydawnictwo Grunwald, 1986), pp. 44-45.

91. Eisenberg, *Lost Generation*, p. 66.

92. Huberband, *Kiddush Hashem*, pp. 175ff.

93. Dworzecki's account was translated into English and published in Eisenberg, *Lost Generation*, pp. 58-62.

94. *Ibid.*

95. Birenbaum, *Hope Is the Last to Die*, pp. 12-13.

96. Nir, *Lost Childhood*, p. 71.

97. Eisenberg, *Lost Generation*, p. 60.

98. Judith Kestenberg, "History's Role in Psychoanalyses of Survivors and Their Children," *The American Journal of Social Psychiatry*, III (1983), 26; Betty Jean Lifton, *The King of Children: A Biography of Janusz Korczak* (New York: Farrar, Straus and Giroux, 1988), p. 303; Zofia Szymanska, *Bylam Tylko Lekarzem* (Warsaw: Instytut Wydawniczy Pax, 1979), p. 143.

99. Zofja Rosenblum, "Jewish Children in Ghettos, Camps, and Woods, 1939-1945," *American OSE Review* (Spring, 1947), IV, 30.

100. Witold Bokszczanin, "Zabawa w Powstancow," in Turski, *Byli Wowczas Dziecmi*, pp. 98-99.

101. Dobroszycki, *Chronicle of the Lodz Ghetto*, p. 374.

102. *Ibid.*, pp. 360-61.

103. Adam Slomczynski, *Dom Ks. Boduena, 1939-1945* (Warsaw: Panstwowy Instytut Wydawniczy, 1975), p. 118.

104. Dwa Lata Okupacji Niemieckiej w Polsce [1941], in PRM 45c/23, PI/GSHM.

105. Teresa Prekerowa, *Konspiracyjna Rada Pomocy Zydom w Warszawie, 1942-1945* (Warsaw: Panstwowy Instytut Wydawniczy, 1982), p. 189; Barski, *Przezycia i Wspomienia*, pp. 27-28, 43.

106. Genia Silkes Papers in YIVO Institute for Jewish Research, New York, New York. Hereinafter cited as YIVO.

107. *Ibid;* Barski, *Przezycia i Wspomnienia*, p. 30.

108. Silkes Papers.

109. Theresa I. Cahn, "The Diary of an Adolescent Girl in the Ghetto: A Study of Age-Specific Reactions to the Holocaust," *The Psychological Review*, LXXV (Winter, 1988), 589-617.

110. *Ibid.*, p. 616.

111. Silkes Papers.

112. Lukas, *Forgotten Holocaust*, pp. 104-06.

113. Silkes Papers.

114. Tory, *Kovno Ghetto Diary*, p. 255.

115. Silkes Papers.

116. Lukas, *Forgotten Holocaust*, pp. 106ff: *Polish Fortnightly Review*, November 15, 1942.

117. Gutman, *Fighters Among the Ruins*, pp. 87-88.

118. Duraczynski, *Wojna i Okupacja*, p. 421.

119. Korbonski, *Fighting Warsaw*, p. 41.
120. *Polish Fortnightly Review*, June 1, 1942.
121. Karski, *Secret State*, pp. 270-71.

Chapter III

Concentration Camps

THE MAJOR DEPORTATIONS from and liquidations of the Jewish ghettos began in 1942. The Germans would virtually complete the process over the next two years. Unlike earlier deportations, these transported Jews to concentration camps where the Germans murdered their victims, mostly by poison gas. Young children and their mothers, along with the elderly and sick, were the first victims of the gruesome platform selections at these camps. The Nazis sometimes spared older children and adult males who looked healthy enough to work until, they, too, either died of hunger or hard labor or ended up in the gas chamber. There were also hundreds of children who were selected, not for the gas chamber, but for medical experiments. Few Jewish children survived the Final Solution.

The Germans began the deportations of Jews from the Warsaw Ghetto, the largest concentration of Jews in Europe, on July 22, 1942. Only a few months earlier, the Nazis had practiced emptying a large ghetto by deporting 40,000 Jews from Lublin in eastern Poland and sending most of them to the death camp at Belzec. Warsaw would be even a greater challenge. Assisted by Jewish police and security units of Lithuanians, Letts and Ukrainians, the Germans did not deport all Jews from Warsaw to the death camp at Treblinka. They dragged many adults and children from their homes and shot them. In some cases, they drowned children in clay pits or threw them into sewers.[1]

The diary entries of one eyewitness reflect the impact of these horrible events during the summer of 1942: "Weeping. The Jews are weeping. They are hoping for a miracle. The expulsion is continuing. Buildings are blockaded. 23 Twarda Street. Terrible scenes." The next day, he noted, "The turmoil is like it was during the days of the bombardment of Warsaw. Jews are running as if insane, with children and bundles of bedding.... Mothers and children wander around like lost sheep: where is my child? Weeping.... The huge round-up on the streets. Old men and women, boys and girls are being dragged away.... A pogrom and a killing the like of which has never been seen."[2]

The killing in the ghetto was random. One young woman returned from work and saw two teenage boys lying in the street, one of whom was left dying for an hour.[3] It was a daily occurrence to see 30 to 40 corpses lying on the street. Even people standing at windows became targets for the bullets of the Germans and their allies.[4]

Many Poles on the Aryan side of the city saw Jewish children shot, pregnant women killed, and fugitives hunted down in the streets. A Christian woman, who saw a gendarme kill a Jewish boy, stood on Nowy Swiat Boulevard and openly prayed for God's retribution on the Germans. Another Pole who showed her defiance was not so fortunate. She was shot to death. "To shoot a victim on the spot is accounted a humane act," one Polish report sent to London at the time stated. "As is also throwing him out of a sixth-floor window... facts of this sort are observed every day in dozens [sic]."[5]

One young survivor recalled how her aunt saved her and three other children in a closet in the attic of an apartment. She stuck two children on each shelf, locked the closet and then barricaded it with broken planks. "We children lay with bated breath," she said. "The Hitlerites were running up and down the stairs, smashing in doors, shouting, laughing, firing shots...." They even broke into the attic where the children were hiding. Almost anything could have given them away. Two of the younger children on the top shelf urinated out of fear. Five grueling hours later, the young girl's mother opened the closet and embraced her child. But the girl's aunt and the mother of two of the little children weren't so lucky: the Germans seized them for deportation to the death camp.[6]

The depth of despair and helplessness was so great that there

A young Polish boy joins adults on a patrol of the Vistula River during the early days of the Warsaw uprising, 1944. (Pilsudski Institute of America)

THIS PAGE & THOSE FOLLOWING:
Jewish children, hungry and
dying, in the ghettos.
(AGKBZH w Polsce)

Dr. Janusz Korczak and some of his children. (AGKBZH w Polsce)

BELOW: A smuggler caught by Jewish police. (AGKBZH w Polsce)

A young smuggler caught by a German guard. (AGKBZH w Polsce)

RIGHT: A small Polish boy on forced labor. (Polish Underground Movement Study Trust)

A young Polish girl weeps over the body of her sister, killed by a German plane during the invasion of Poland in September 1939. (Pilsudski Institute of America)

BELOW:Polish boy engaged in small sabotage. (Polish Underground Movement Study Trust)

was a large number of suicides. Not only did individuals commit suicide, but also entire families. Sometimes one found 10 to 20 victims of suicide in one apartment. To prevent suicides by poisoning, the Germans ordered all pharmacies closed. Some Jews even begged their tormentors to shoot them, but even that had to be paid for in cash or valuables and was not always granted.[7]

Almost two months after the Germans began their *Aktion* in Warsaw, Abraham Lewin recorded sadly in his diary that the terror continued "with all its atrocities and animal savagery, a slaughter the like of which human history has not seen...." Exhausted by the unmitigated horror, almost a month later he wrote, "The human hand and pen weary of describing all that has happened to the handful of Jews who are for the time being still alive, myself among them. The cup of our sorrows has no parallel in our history."[8]

Among the victims of the deportations from Warsaw were the children of several orphanages and homes, the most famous of which was headed by the legendary Polish-Jewish physician, writer and educator, Dr. Janusz Korczak. Born in the late 1870s, Korczak was the son of Jozef Goldszmit, a prominent lawyer. Before the war, Korczak introduced progressive orphanages into Poland and was an advocate of children's rights in Polish courts. He pioneered in the field of child psychology with his books, *How to Love a Child* and *The Child's Right to Respect* in which he argued that children should not be molded to suit adults, but should be allowed to develop and grow as individuals in their own right.

He also wrote children's books, best known of which was *King Matt the First* that described the life of a boy ruler who tried to bring reforms to his people. A classic, the book was as well known in Poland as *Peter Pan* and *Alice in Wonderland* was in the West. The audience for his children's works was not confined to Jews; they were avidly read by Polish children too.[9]

When the Germans established the ghetto, Korczak and his close colleague, Dr. Stefania Wilczynska, had to move their orphanage inside the ghetto. They were so devoted to the care of their children that "It is difficult to determine," wrote Emmanuel Ringelblum, chronicler of the Warsaw Ghetto, "where Korczak begins and where Wilczynska ends."[10] At first, Korczak was optimistic concerning the safety of his home. "Don't worry, the Germans won't harm us," he declared. "They wouldn't dare. I'm much too well known here and abroad." That optimism would soon change to pessimism. During Rosh Hashanah and Yom Kippur, Korczak held religious services for the children. Prayer, he believed, was important for the children and adults because it gave them strength, something they would need to cope with the horrors that awaited them.[11]

In the darkest days of the Warsaw ghetto, Korczak's children did not want for food, an extraordinary feat for Korczak and his loyal staff to accomplish. Always a rebel, he wore his army uniform as an officer of the Polish Army which, he asserted, released him from the obligation of wearing the Star of David. The Germans did not see it that way and threw him into jail from where his friends and colleagues managed to get him released. Abraham Berman, who headed CENTOS, the principal Jewish relief agency in Poland, remonstrated with him about his appearance which only irritated the Germans. "As far as I am concerned, there is no German occupation," Korczak stubbornly replied. "I am proud to be a Polish officer and I shall go about as I wish."[12]

Stubborn and courageous, Korczak spurned several offers from Polish friends to hide him, refusing to leave his orphans for even a minute. At the head of a contingent of 192 children and 8 staff members, Korczak, erect, his eyes looking off in the distance, held the hands of two children as he led them in a silent march to the railroad platform where trains took them to certain death. Further back, Wilczynska led another group of children. One of the older orphans carried the green flag of King Matt, Korczak's story book hero. On the other side of the flag, the Star of David in blue was set on a background of white. According to one eyewitness, it was a scene he would never forget. "This was not a march to the [railroad] wagons but an organized silent protest against banditry."[13]

Within one month, the Germans succeeded in emptying 100 institutions where children received care. During early August, CENTOS officials received a heart-rending note from Maria Rotblat, who ran a boarding home for girls: "Save us. We find ourselves with our children on the road to death." The note mobilized Jozef Barski and other CENTOS members to try to save many girls who had already been sent to the *Umschlag-platz*, the assembly point for adults and children scheduled to be deported, to the death camps. "Our joy, when it was possible to extricate even one child from the *Umschlagplatz*, knew no bounds," Barski later wrote. Indeed, he and his colleagues on this occasion saved several of Rotblat's girls by telling the SS man in charge that the girls had been wrongfully selected for deportation. When the German inquired further, Barski claimed the girls were seamstresses who worked in a ghetto factory producing clothes for the Germans. He released them.

Most children were not so fortunate. They went silently, often holding hands, to the *Umschlagplatz*, fully aware of what was in store for them. During one of these silent marches, some younger children asked fearfully, "Will they drown us?" a death they seemed to fear the most. Out of 400,000 Jews taken to Treblinka between July and September, 1942, 90,000 were children.[14]

The 5,000 children who escaped deportation from Warsaw were mostly older and connected with the remaining labor force the Germans had spared. But even they could not be certain when their turn would come next. One girl, who did not make the trip to Treblinka, said, "At home everyone slept clothed, ready to go down in a minute. We each had our little bundle packed. The only food we had was what we received at work. The little bit that was left at home was for those who did not work. There were no more stores. All had been closed, robbed or vandalized. More and more homes stood empty."[15]

Understandably, those who worked in factories near the ghetto feared going back there. One teenage Jewish girl who survived three "selections" in the factory where she worked, commented that even Polish workers who worked along side Jews in some of these enterprises were afraid to go out and stayed in them over night.[16]

Passes to those who worked in German factories, which were to afford protection to so-called "productive" Jews, proved to be ephemeral. These survivors quickly learned that it was safer to go into hiding as the Germans periodically resumed the deportations to the death camps. In a real sense, there were no children left in Warsaw after the major deportation campaign in 1942. Despite their chronological age, they were adults who tried desperately to stay alive. A small number managed to do so.

After the deportations of the summer of 1942, there were few children's homes left in Warsaw. In December, Karl Brandt, head of the Department of Jewish Affairs for the Gestapo in Warsaw, inspected one of them on Dzika Street, and cynically told its administrator, "It is well that you care for your children." The next day SS trucks rolled up to the home and took all the children to the railroad platform where they were sent, as others had been before them, to Treblinka.[17] The same month, the chronicler of the Warsaw Ghetto mused why 10 percent of Warsaw's Jews still remained alive. "When will they finish us off?" he asked rhetorically.[18]

The events in Warsaw confirmed the growing awareness of Poland's government, in exile in London, of the enormous tragedy that had been going on in Poland since the Germans occupied the country. Ever since 1940, the government of Wladyslaw Sikorski had informed the United States and Great Britain of the German persecution of Poles and Jews. Fed a constant stream of messages and reports from the Polish underground, one of the most effective in German-occupied Europe, the Sikorski government was the first Allied government to recognize that the Germans planned to destroy the Jews of Europe, a view that was not shared either by Great Britain or the United States, or for that matter, Jewish leaders in the West in the summer of 1942.

During the deportations from Warsaw, the *Armia Krajowa* (Home Army) and the civilian section of the Polish underground sent regular reports to London about what was going on in Warsaw. Stefan Korbonski, head of the Polish underground's Directorate of Civil Resistance and later decorated by Yad Vashem, sent daily reports in which he described in detail the appalling activities of the Germans in Warsaw.

It wasn't until December, 1942, however, before the Sikorski government was able to persuade the British and American governments to join it and other Allied governments to declare officially that the Germans were "now carrying into effect Hitler's oft-repeated intention to exterminate the Jewish people in Europe." The Allies finally, if belatedly, condemned the "bestial policy" of the Germans and promised retribution on those responsible for the crimes. "The fact that such a declaration with its concomitant obligations upon its authors, was made at the end of the year [1942] in which the *Endlosung* programme was thoroughly organized in Germany and elsewhere says much for the nature of the underground networks, especially the Polish one, by which such information was sent out from occupied Europe," one scholar has accurately observed.[19]

Other ghettos experienced a fate similar to Warsaw's. About the same time the Germans reduced the Warsaw Ghetto, they liquidated several ghettos near Warsaw—Nowy Dwor, Rembertow, Falenica, Kaluszyn. In Kielce, the Germans seized children from the Jewish orphanage and sick Jews and killed them before others were deported. The Germans spared a small group for labor purposes.[20] A young Polish woman and her sister who brought food every day to Jews in the Radom Ghetto recalled how they were compelled to stand and watch from across the street as SS men shot into a mass of people in the ghetto as they forced Jews into a death march. She saw a Jewish woman with a crying baby in her arms trying to quiet it by attempting to breast feed the child. But the baby kept crying. A Gestapo officer tore the baby from the mother and threw it, head first, to the ground. The baby died. "But you know," the Polish woman said, "I will never forget the inhuman, shrilling scream that the mother let out as she jumped to reach the child. With one bullet to her head she was lying next to her child."[21]

In Lodz, except for the deportation of some ill children in May, 1942, the first major deportation came in September. One distraught father, who blamed himself for the deportation of his 5-year-old daughter, insisted that he had her blood on his hands for apparently deserting her: "What punishment awaits me for killing my own daughter? There was no need to do anything heroic to save her, protect her. On the contrary, I made this offering myself, without being asked. I killed the child with my own hands." In Krakow, the Germans closed the Jewish orphanage which at various times accommodated about 200 children. On October 28, 1942, the director, Anna Fenerstein, and her husband led the children out of the orphanage. The Germans immediately seized them, and murdered them outside of the city. There was an ironic twist: among the dead was a 7-year-old girl who wore a swastika on her dress. She was the daughter of an SS man, killed in the war, and a Jewish mother, who had been arrested.[22]

"To that hundred-times accursed *Umschlag*, drenched in blood and tears, filled with the whistling of railroad locomotives, the trains that bore away hundreds of thousands of Jews to the ultimate destination of their lives," a Jewish girl wrote.[23] Beaten and shoved into a railroad car which held 40 people, the Germans thrust as many as 100 victims. The Germans sometimes placed unslaked lime on the floor of the car and, in order for the lime to do its work, they ordered the people to remove their shoes.[24]

The luck of the Birenbaum family had finally run out when, after avoiding earlier "selections," they, too, ended up at the railroad platform. They knew what awaited them. They seemed almost serene as family members embraced one another before the train arrived. Halina, the young daughter, remembered how her mother whispered, "Don't be afraid, everyone must die sometime, we only die once.... And we shall be together, so don't be afraid, it won't be so terrible." Like most teenagers who believe they are somehow immortal, Halina did not fully understand what death meant.[25] In these dismal circumstances, she affirmed her belief in life and in the end, she survived.

Long before the Nazis established permanent sites at concentration camps to gas their victims, they had experimented for some time with the use of mobile gas vans to kill Jews and non-Jews in western Russia during the Russo-German phase of World War II. "The fall of 1941 and the spring of 1942, when the gas van was being developed and produced, spanned a crucial period in the evolution of Nazi Jewish policy when systematic mass murder of Jews outside Russia was just getting underway," one historian has observed. Originally, the Germans used the gas van as part of the German euthanasia program to eliminate the mentally ill. They decided to employ it on the eastern front in 1941 as a more efficient method to kill people than the firing squads they had been using. SS chief Heinrich Himmler had seen a mass shooting involving women and children and allegedly was so shaken by what he had seen that he ordered one of his henchmen to explore whether improved results might be derived from explosives or poison gas. "The motive behind developing the gas van," says Christopher Browning, "sprang from the desire to alleviate the psychological burden upon the firing-squad murderers, many of them middle-aged family men who were disturbed most of all by the endless shooting of women and children.[26]

Ultimately, 15 mobile gas vans were employed on the eastern front but the most effective use of them from the Nazi point of view was in a stationary setting—principally Chelmno, Poland, where the Germans gassed approximately 152,000 Jews; Semlin, near Belgrade; and Trostinez near Minsk. In Yugoslavia, for example, the Germans shot men but initially spared women and children until they later gassed them at Semlin.[27]

According to Major General Otto Ohlendorf, the dapper articulate commander of the Einsatzgruppe D, the mobile gas vans his group used were similar to family trailers, complete with painted windows on the sides with curtains blowing in the breeze. Even a flowerpot on the windowsill created a serene homey impression. When the vans drove up, mothers and children believed the Germans who told them they would be transported to their fathers and husbands, who allegedly preceded them to another land. The victims entered the vans without hesitation; mothers held children by the hand or in their arms. They were excited about the prospects of a better future with their fathers and husbands. After the women and children entered the vans, the doors closed shut, the driver pressed the accelerator and carbon monoxide killed them in about ten minutes. The van became a traveling mortuary as it reached a deep ditch outside of the city where the corpses were dumped. There mothers and children joined their fathers and husbands who had been machine-gunned to death earlier by the SS.[28]

For all their efficiency, gas vans still had several problems. It enabled the executioners to kill their victims without seeing them die. But the corpses had to be removed from a van that still had traces of gas in them. One German official opined that the process resulted in "immense psychological injuries and damage to the health" of the SS men who unloaded the bodies.[29] For these reasons, German policy had evolved by 1942 in developing stationary gas chambers where the gas of choice was hydrogen cyanide (Zyklon B).

The most notorious death camp, of course, was Auschwitz-Birkenau. Long before it became known as a slaughter house for Jews, it was a penal camp for Poles, later joined by Russian prisoners-of-war. The first mass execution of Polish prisoners occurred on November 22, 1940, when the Germans shot 40 people, a practice that was repeated every week. Poles, who along with Russians, were the first Auschwitz prisoners to be gassed,[30] constituted the largest number of inmates at Auschwitz until 1942 when the Jews became the largest group. Even so, being gentile did not spare one from being selected for the gas chamber either at Auschwitz or anywhere else. There were numerous cases of Polish children and those of other nationalities who died from gassing and other means.[31]

When the trains arrived at Auschwitz-Birkenau, the Germans separated children under 14 years of age from older ones and sent them with their mothers, the aged and the sick to the gas chambers. Those capable of working—men, women and children—were temporarily spared.[32] Dr. Bertold Ebstein remembered how children who did not meet the height requirements of 120 cm. were slated to die. Youngsters stretched to meet the criteria, crying "We don't want to be gassed, we want to live."[33]

One day Dr. Joseph Mengele appeared on the parade ground at Auschwitz where 2,000 Jewish boys had gathered. It was the eve of Yom Kippur. Mengele approached a young, blond-headed boy who was almost 14-years-old and asked him how old he was. The boy told him he was 18. Mengele, furious at the obvious lie, shouted, "I'll show you. Get me a hammer and some nails and a plank." He approached a tall boy in the first row of boys and ordered that the plank be nailed above the boy's head so that it was like the letter "L," only inverted. Then he ordered the boys to file past the board. It was clear to everyone that those who failed to reach the board would be murdered.

"We all began stretching. Everyone wanted to get another half inch, another centimeter," one survivor said. "I also stretched as much as I could but I despaired. I saw that even taller boys than myself did not attain the necessary height...."

Faced with certain death, he picked up stones, opened his shoelaces and stuffed little stones into his shoes, adding about an inch to his height. But that wasn't enough to pass Mengele's test; so he tried and ultimately succeeded in mixing with the group of taller boys who had passed the test. He was one of the fortunate ones; 1,000 boys did not attain the height requirements. Two days later, the Germans took them to the gas chambers.

Mengele, whose contempt for Jews knew no bounds, often selected children for execution during Jewish religious holidays. The West German indictment against him charged:

> Thus it is alleged that he selected Jewish children on the Friday before the Jewish New Year Festival 1944 from camp section B2D in Birkenau; he sent 328 children to their death in the gas chambers on the Jewish New Year festival 1944 from section B2D in Birkenau....[34]

Rudolf Hoess, Auschwitz's commandant who lived with his wife and five children at the camp, described the scene prior to the gassing of women and children:

> I noticed that women who either guessed or knew what awaited them found the courage to joke with the children to encourage them, despite the mortal terror visible in their own eyes.
>
> One woman approached me as she walked past and, pointing to her four children who were manfully helping the smaller ones over the rough ground, whispered: "How can you bring yourself to kill such beautiful darling children? Have you no heart at all?"[35]

One courageous Jewish woman caught Hoess's attention. She scurried between the youngest children and the old women, helping them to undress. "She waited until the end, helping the women who were not undressed and who had several children with them, encouraging them and calming the children," Hoess wrote. "She went with the very last ones into the gas chamber. Standing in the doorway, she said: 'I knew all the time that we were being brought to Auschwitz to be gassed. When the selection took place I avoided being put with the able-bodied ones, as I wished to look after the children. I wanted to go through it all, fully conscious of what was happening. I hope it will be quick. Goodbye!'"[36]

Hoess, a dedicated Nazi party member since 1922, admitted

his own discomfort when he witnessed the gassing of prisoners. "It made me feel uncomfortable and I shuddered, although I had imagined that death by gassing would be worse than it was," he said. For all his discomfort, his excuse for supervising the appalling operations, in his words, at "the greatest human extermination center of all time," was "I was a soldier and an officer." The consummate bureaucrat, who executed, but did not question the order to murder hundreds of thousands of people said, "Whether this mass extermination of Jews was necessary or not was something on which I could not allow myself to form an opinion, for I lacked the necessary breadth of view." For all of his postwar expression of sympathy with the victims of Auschwitz, he never did anything to ease the horrible conditions of the prisoners and blamed SS guards for the ill-treatment the victims experienced.[37]

The SS men, screaming, yelling and hitting their victims with truncheons, forced them to undress and then chased them inside the gas chamber. In order to stifle the cries of adults and children going to their deaths, an orchestra of inmates played songs; one of the favorites was "Rosamunda." From time to time, some women would tear their hair and shriek loudly. They would be immediately led away and shot in the back of the neck. The executioners crammed hundreds of people into one chamber. It wasn't long before the sounds of screaming, coughing and yelling for help came to an end. When the Kapos opened the door, they saw a pile of bodies massed toward the ceiling. The reason was because gas filled the lower layer of air and rose slowly toward the ceiling. People trampled one another, frantically trying to escape from the poison gas. One eyewitness recalled seeing bodies of women, children and the aged at the bottom of the pile; the strongest were on the top. Fighting to survive, they scratched and bruised one another until the gas overtook them. When it was over, one observer said, "their faces, bloated and blue, were so deformed as to be almost unrecognizable."[38]

Then the Sonderkommando, made up of prisoners whose lives were extended temporarily for a few months, had the grisly task of removing the bodies before the arrival of the next convoy of victims. The Sonderkommando, wearing rubber boots, flooded the chamber with water to clean the bodies and the chamber because those who died involuntarily defecated. After that, the bodies were burned.[39]

The Germans killed so many people the crematoria of the death camps could not keep up with the number of bodies to be burned. At Majdanek and the nearby Krempiecki Forest, the Germans placed planks across railings or automobile chassis which served as fire bars. The Germans placed the corpses on one layer of planks, then added another layer of planks and another layer of corpses. In this way, they disposed of 500-1000 bodies in what became a huge bonfire, which burned for two days.[40]

"Someone would grab a child's arm," a Jewish nurse who survived Auschwitz said, "another his legs, and thus little babies were hurled through the air like a length of wood, to land in the blazing pit, while the murderers watched the results of their bravery with great pleasure." Another survivor claimed he saw Hoess himself grab a child by the leg and throw him into the fire, something SS men apparently routinely did, when the five crematoria and 52 ovens of Auschwitz became overtaxed by late 1942. Killing young children by bashing their heads against a wall or pole apparently was a regular occurrence at places like Treblinka, Sobibor and Majdanek.[41]

One day Dr. Miklos Nyiszli, a prisoner-physician at Auschwitz, recalled how one of the Kommandos summoned him to the gas chamber where he had found a young girl who somehow managed to survive. Nothing like this had occurred in the history of Auschwitz. Nyiszli carried the frail girl, who was about 14 years of age, to an adjacent room where the Kommando changed their clothes. He administered intravenous injections to revive the girl while someone ran to the kitchen to get something warm for her to eat. "Everyone wanted to help," Nyiszli said, "as if she were his own child."

After the girl had regained consciousness, the problem was what to do with her. No one had come out of the crematorium alive. Nyiszli, hoping to use his place in the medical hierarchy as leverage—the infamous Dr. Mengele was his boss—appealed to the SS supervisor to spare the girl's life. The SS man believed that if word spread that the girl had survived, he and everyone else responsible for saving her would pay with their own lives. He ordered one of his henchmen to shoot her in the back of the neck.[42]

The Germans deported Chaim Hirszman, his wife and baby boy from Janow to Belzec concentration camp. When they arrived, he and his family joined others in the same barrack where the Germans ordered them to disrobe. "Immediately I knew what that meant," Hirszman said. But when he got to the gas chamber, he discovered he would be part of a squad of Jews to retrieve the bodies after they had been gassed. He saw how the Germans forced women into the chamber and later literally threw in the children on the heads of their mothers. Hirszman's grim job was to shave the hair from the bodies of the women and children for later use by the Germans. Little did he expect to discover his wife among the bodies.[43]

S. Israel was in a group of 390 Jews sent to Majdanek. As was true of other death camps, children and old and sick Jews were sent immediately to the gas chamber. Israel was one of the fortunate adult males to be sent away to mine coal, and because of that survived the war.[44]

According to estimates of the camp resistance movement, 1,000 people died every day in the gas chambers at Majdanek. That estimate meant that 50 percent of the new arrivals at the camp were selected to die. Even Jewish children who were allowed to remain with their mothers, and presumably worked for several weeks at the camp, were killed. One survivor remembered how after the Germans ordered a roll call in June, 1943: "The children, guided by some instinct, instead of assembling, scattered all over the compound. The SS men, aided by the *Blockfuhrers* and *Stubendiensts*, gave pursuit and caught the children, like dog catchers catch stray dogs." The Germans led 100 boys to the gas chamber.[45]

"I almost went insane on the day when I first saw men, women and children being led to the house of death," Yankel Wiernik, a survivor of Treblinka, said. "I pulled my hair and shed bitter tears of despair. I suffered most when I looked at the children, accompanied by their mothers or walking alone, entirely ignorant of the fact that within a few minutes their lives would be snuffed out under horrible tortures."[46]

The Germans originally established Treblinka as a penal camp for Poles, where many died. Early in 1942, they constructed a special death camp there, mostly for Jews. Located near the village of Treblinka, which was near the main Bialystok-Warsaw railroad line, the camp was in a wooded area of the country, isolated from the rest of the outside world. It was there, an enclave of several thousand acres surrounded by barbed wire fences and entanglements, where the Germans deported condemned Jews from Warsaw and other cities and towns.

After the line of naked children, women and men arrived at the gas chamber, two Ukrainians, named Ivan and Nicholas, who operated the machinery of death, came out and beat the people as they entered a chamber that measured 125 square feet. Packing up to 450-500 people inside the chamber, according to Wiernik, "Parents carried their children in the vain hope that the latter would thus escape death." On their way to death, Wiernik saw how "they were pushed and beaten with rifle butts and the gas pipe. Dogs were set on them, barking, biting and tearing at them. To escape the blows and the dogs, the crowd rushed to its death, pushing into the chamber, the stronger ones shoving the weaker ones ahead. The bedlam lasted only a short while, for the doors were shut tightly with a bang." They turned on the motor, gas filled the chamber and in no more than twenty-five minutes, everyone was dead.[47]

And so the destruction of Jews continued at German death camps. There was no let up even as Soviet troops made deep inroads into Poland. In late 1944, just months before Germany's defeat, the Germans sent 600 Jewish boys, aged 12 to 18, to Auschwitz. As soon as they disembarked from the trucks, the Germans told the boys to strip. They realized immediately they were going to their death. Frightened, the youngsters broke into tears:

> The boys' high-pitched voices grew louder and louder in a bitter lament. Their keening carried a great distance. One was completely deafened and overcome by this desperate weeping. With satisfied smirks, without a trace of compassion, the SS men triumphantly hailed savage blows on the children and drove them into the gas chamber. On the stairs stood the *Unterscharfuhrer*, still wielding his club and giving a murderous crack to each child. A few lone children were, all the same, still running back and forth in search of a way out. The SS men chased after them, lashing out at them

and forcing them at last into the chamber. The glee of the SS men was indescribable. Did they never have children of their own?[48]

Children, including Polish youngsters, met death in many ways other than poison gas. In addition to those who died of hard labor and malnutrition, the Germans killed thousands of children in pacification and reprisal operations. The Polish underground reported an increase in the Nazi reign of terror against Poles toward the end of 1942, characterized not only by roundups for forced labor, but also by executions. The head of the *Armia Krajowa*, General Stefan Grot-Rowecki, told his superiors in London on January 21, 1943, "A new wave of terror embraces the entire country."[49] The manhunts conducted by the Nazis in the middle of January alone were so extensive that Poles began to believe the Germans intended to exterminate the entire Polish population just as they were doing to the Jews.[50]

The intensity of the terror campaign reached a high point in the autumn of 1943 when Governor Frank ordered public executions in Warsaw. His decree allowed the Gestapo to shoot anyone who even looked suspicious. Public executions continued until early 1944, but were replaced by secret executions of Poles in the ruins of the Warsaw ghetto. Teenage Poles were among the victims.[51]

In the Polish countryside, one authority estimated that there were 359 villages where children were murdered in pacification operations. In a village near Lublin, for example, on February 2, 1944, in a rather typical pacification, the Germans killed 98 Poles, 39 of whom were children.[52] In the Bialystok region, Nazi efforts to Germanize the area and to eliminate the level of partisan activity resulted in huge losses of children. In that area alone, almost 20 percent of the casualties were children and teenagers.[53]

Before the development and emplacement of the gas chambers in concentration camps, the Germans executed their prisoners, most of whom were Poles before 1942, by shooting them. This practice, of course, continued throughout the war. One former inmate of Montelupich testified that the Germans imprisoned 10- to 14-year-old Polish boys because their fathers had refused to reveal to what military contingents they had once belonged. The Germans shot the boys.[54]

In the first transport of Jewish children who arrived at

Majdanek from the ghetto of Majdan Tatarski, the Germans took young children from their mothers and forced them to die of cold and hunger while older children, considered unfit for work, were shot in the Krepiecki Forest. The largest execution in Majdanek's history occurred on November 3, 1943, when the Germans shot 18,400 people, including children, in pits near the crematoria.[55] "The worst thing happened when a group of mothers with small children were ordered into the pits filled with still twitching bodies," Mieczyslaw Panz, a former prisoner remembered. "The poor women were begging the executioners for mercy for their children. Attempting to prevent the little ones from being drowned in the blood that collected in the pits, they held them high in the air, thus lengthening their lives by a brief moment. The SS-men put an end to their hopeless efforts by machine-gun fire."[56]

When the Germans eliminated the Trawniki labor camp which along with Poniatowa were sub-camps of Majdanek, they shot men, women and children who had been forced to take off their clothes.[57] At Poniatowa, the Germans first took several thousand men from their wives and children and killed them. Then came the turn of the women and children. One survivor remembered how the SS-men arranged the women in groups of fifty and took them out of the building. Her 10-year-old daughter was with her. As the Germans escorted them down the road to ditches which the women themselves had dug earlier, the SS-men yelled, "Gold, silver, jewels, watches! Those who fail to hand them over will be shot!"

In the distance she saw young naked women in a circle, their arms raised as though they wanted to show their beauty to the soldiers in order to spare them. She thought she might do the same thing but even if she passed their examination, the SS-men would not allow her child to remain with her.

The women and children arrived at the ditches, already full of naked bodies. The SS told them to lie down and then:

> Shots were fired; I felt a sharp pain in my hand, and the bullet pierced the skull of my daughter. Another shot was heard very close nearby. I was utterly shaken, turned giddy and lost consciousness. I heard the groaning of a woman nearby, but it came to an end after a few seconds.
>
> I realized that I was still alive, and expected another bullet to hit

me, but I did not move. After a few moments, an SS man brought a woman with a child. I heard her imploring him to permit her to kiss the boy, but the murderer did not permit it and so the unfortunate woman lay down close to myself, her head near my head. A shot was heard and blood splashed on my head and neck. Apparently, I made the impression of being dead. More shots were heard for some while, and then silence descended.

She lay there as SS men walked among the bodies. Those who were not dead yet now received the *coup de grace*. She remained quiet until after the Ukrainian auxiliaries finished covering the graves with foliage. She joined two other women, who also managed to survive, and hurriedly left the area.[58] This was the bloodbath at Poniatowa.

By the summer of 1944, Warsaw was the last major city between Soviet forces and Berlin, the capital of the Nazi empire. Soviet annihilation of twenty-five divisions of German Army Group Center sent a wave of panic and despair among German soldiers and civilians in Warsaw.[59] The moment Varsovians had waited for had finally arrived—the liberation of their capital.

German residents sold their possessions for almost nothing and clogged the roads leading westward to their own country. A German sergeant wanted to sell a Pole three truckloads of sheets and blankets on condition that he also take the trucks too. When the Pole asked why he wanted to get rid of the trucks too, the sergeant told him that it gave him the excuse he needed to explain away to his superiors the disappearance of the sheets and blankets. He would simply report that the trucks had been bombed by enemy planes.[60] Stas, a baldheaded member of the Polish underground, managed to acquire an entire truckload of vodka from a German soldier, who desperately wanted to get rid of it quickly and cheaply. Stas stored the vodka in a friend's cellar where a secret printing press had operated for the Polish underground.[61]

By July 31, 1944, the leading German occupation newspaper stopped publication. Even the Nazi governor of Warsaw, Dr. Ludwig Fischer, panicked and scooted out of the city only to return a few days later, no doubt reprimanded and chastened by his superiors, with orders to defend the city.[62]

Scared German patrols fired aimlessly at civilians. One day

an elderly woman was hit by a stray bullet from an SS patrol which unloaded its bullets at a tram. On one of these days a tram conductor, who made a living selling soap and cosmetics on the black market, told his passengers: "Please, ladies and gentlemen, please hurry up, because the firm is departing, the firm is closing down and going into liquidation!" The passengers laughed and applauded.[63]

Meanwhile, General Tadeusz Bor-Komorowski, head of the *Armia Krajowa* (Home Army), or, *AK* and his lieutenants, believed that in view of the closeness of Soviet troops, the *AK* should take possession of Warsaw before the Red Army arrived. In this way, the *AK* would become the de facto landlords of the Polish capital which the Soviets, when they entered the city a few days later, would have to recognize. This would be a bold political statement to Joseph Stalin, the Soviet dictator, because the *AK* was loyal to his nemesis—the pro-western Polish government, then in exile in London. Stalin had his own plans for the Poles—namely, to install in power a group of Polish Communists which he planned to recognize as the government of Poland. The most effective way to do that was to allow the Germans to destroy the *AK*, the military arm of the Polish government-in-exile. Cynically, Stalin ordered the Soviet military advance on Warsaw to halt and he even refused to give any meaningful assistance to the Varsovians who found themselves fighting the Germans in a 63-day bloodbath.[64]

When the Polish underground launched the Warsaw Uprising in August, 1944, the Germans made no distinctions between Polish children and adults any more than they had between Jewish children and adults in suppressing the Ghetto uprising a year earlier. Units under the command of Oskar Dirlewanger and Mieczyslaw Kaminski, a Russian renegade, perpetrated some of the worst crimes of any enemy units in Warsaw. What transpired in Wola and Ochota, the western and southwestern districts of Warsaw, ranks as one of the worst tragedies in a tragedy-filled war. On August 5 alone, 10,000 Polish civilians were murdered.[65] The combination of atrocity and plunder prolonged the struggle which probably could have ended sooner had disciplined German troops been used from the outset.

Alexandra Kreczkiewicz and 500 of her neighbors on Gorczewska Street had to evacuate their apartments. Children and women cried as several people were shot at the exits of the buildings. Driven by the Germans under a bridge, Kreczkiewicz remarked, "There was no doubt about our fate." When one woman asked where they would be taken, a soldier grimly answered, "German women and children are perishing by your fault; therefore, all of you must perish." The Germans divided the Poles into ranks; Kreczkiewicz's group ended up against a wall and were shot. She fell down wounded and lost consciousness. When she recovered her senses, she feigned death until she was able to inch her way slowly from the area which became an inferno of heat and smoke as the soldiers burned the houses in the neighborhood.[66]

The next day in Wola, the Germans ordered everyone out of No. 18 Dzialdowska Street. A pregnant Polish woman and her three children were among the last to leave the cellar where they had been hiding, hoping to save themselves. The Germans marched the people to the Ursus Factory where they proceeded to execute men, women and children. A 12-year-old boy went hysterical as he saw the bodies of his parents and little brother through a half-opened door. He wasn't even allowed to grieve as German soldiers beat him.

The pregnant woman deliberately hovered in the background of the mass of people who were being slaughtered. She frantically hoped that the SS would not kill someone who was going to have a baby. Such considerations did not apply to the SS or for that matter to a substantial part of the Wehrmacht. They pushed her into a courtyard where she saw corpses at least three feet high. Bodies were everywhere. Then the Germans pushed her into an inner courtyard with a group of twenty people, which included children not much older than 10 or 12. There was a paralyzed old women whose son-in-law had been carrying her all the time on his back. Her daughter was at her side. The Germans murdered the entire family. The old lady was literally killed on her son-in-law's back, and he along with her.

The Germans summoned people in groups of four and led them to the end of a second yard where there was a pile of bodies. There the Germans shot them through the back of their heads with revolvers. The pregnant woman was in the last group of four. She begged the soldiers to save her and her children, offering a large amount of gold to spare them. She breathed easier when they took her gold. Hope turned to horror when the officer in charge refused to free her. Pushed to the place of execution, she held her younger children by one hand and the older boy by the other. The children cried and prayed. Seeing the mass of bodies, the older boy cried out, "They are going to kill us!" The first shot hit him, the second one the mother, and the next two killed the two younger children. The mother fell wounded to one side. The bullet penetrated the back of her head from the right side and exited through her cheek. She remained conscious and witnessed the endless executions of men, women and children. She lay there until the orgy of killing finally came to an end. She managed to crawl away to safety.[67]

Maria Bukowska was one of hundreds of women herded into an area where the SS spotted young Polish girls, some no more than 12 or 13, and raped them while the older women were sent to Pruszkow, the camp outside Warsaw set up by the Germans for Polish survivors of the bloodbath.[68]

The SS also followed a pattern of murdering, looting, and raping in Ochota, another western district of Warsaw. On August 4, fifty of Kaminski's mob surrounded some houses on Grojecka Street. Under the pretext of looking for arms, they looted homes and then took 160 unarmed men, including 12-year-olds, led them into a cellar and shot them in the back of their heads. They poured gasoline over the corpses, then threw grenades. The SS repeated the same grisly scene early the next morning at another house, this time killing 40 men and boys. When the enemy arrested the wife of General Bor, Commander of the *AK*, she asked the German if he shot children. Shrugging his shoulder, he curtly replied, "We had orders."[69]

The murdering reached such intensity by August 7, 1944, that one eyewitness thought everyone in Warsaw would be killed, repeating on a larger scale what had been done earlier to the Jews in the ghetto:

> When we passed No. 9 Gorczewska Street (a house which belonged to nuns), we were called into the house and ordered to carry out the corpses which were there. The courtyard was a dreadful sight. It was an execution place. Heaps of corpses were lying there;

I think they must have been collecting there for some days, for some were already swollen and others quite freshly killed. There were bodies of men, women, and children, all shot through the backs of their heads. It is difficult to state exactly how many there were.

There must have been several layers carelessly heaped up. The men were ordered to carry away the bodies—we women to bury them. We put them in anti-tank trenches and then filled these up. In this way we filled up a number of such trenches in Gorczewska Street. I had the impression that during the first days of the Rising everybody was killed.[70]

There is no way of knowing precisely how many child casualties there were out of the 200,000 estimated losses[71] during the two-month inferno that was Warsaw during August and September, 1944. Since there were no evacuations of Polish civilians prior to the uprising, it can be assumed that the number of children who died was substantial.

If the Germans discovered that women gave birth to children in a concentration camp, the standard procedure was to send the mother and child to the gas chamber. Only if the baby were stillborn did the mother have a chance to survive. The Germans succeeded in making murderers out of inmates, including prisoner-nurses and physicians, who either drowned the newborn in a pan of water or pinched the baby's nostrils to suffocate it. Witnessing the drowning of a little Jewish boy by someone else, a prisoner-nurse said, "I wanted to shout 'Murderess!' but I had to keep quiet and could not tell anyone. The baby swallowed and gurgled, its little voice chittering like a small bird, until its breath became shorter and shorter. The woman held its head in the water. After about eight minutes, the breathing stopped."[72]

Prisoner-physicians often lied to German authorities concerning the pregnancies of women who sometimes, incredibly, managed to conceal their condition until the time of delivery. These physicians injected chemicals into the mothers to induce premature birth. "What could we do?" asked one inmate, "Wherever possible, the doctors resorted to this procedure, which was certainly the lesser horror for the mother."[73] At Ravensbruck, it was common for German doctors to abort women in the eighth month of pregnancy. The equipment and the conditions were so unhygienic that in most cases both mothers and children perished. Approximately 800 children were born at Ravensbruck in the last two years of the war but only 29 newborn Polish children survived.[74]

Until May, 1943, newborn children of all pregnant women—Jewish and gentile—were murdered at Auschwitz. After that, gentile children with blue eyes and blond hair were spared for possible Germanization. In the hope that these children, separated from their mothers, might one day be reunited, a Polish midwife recalled how they developed a way of marking the babies with a tattoo that would not arouse the suspicion of the SS. In this way, mothers had some hope at least that one day they might find their lost child.[75]

In a race-obsessed state like Nazi Germany, one would expect to find physicians who had no reservations about experimenting with human beings to advance Nazism's pseudoscientific theories concerning the so-called master race. Despite the incredible number of experiments performed on hundreds of adults and children without adequate controls, these German doctors failed to add anything of genuine significance to the body of medical knowledge.

Best known of these practitioners was, of course, Joseph Mengele, who managed to escape from Europe after World War II and died of drowning in Latin America in 1979. Described by two biographers as looking "less like a Nazi official than a Hollywood version of one," Mengele was born on March 16, 1911, into an affluent German Catholic family. Bright, but no genius, Mengele desperately wanted to become famous by making some extraordinary discovery in medicine.[76]

He attended the University of Munich where he was influenced by racist studies. He decided to become a eugenics scientist. After earning a Ph.D. and later his medical degree, he did research at the Institute for Heredity, Biology and Racial Purity at the University of Frankfurt. SS membership came in 1938. Thanks to the influence of Dr. Otmar von Verschuer, who provided much of the pseudoscientific rationale for Nazi racial theories, Mengele received an appointment as an SS physician at Auschwitz, which gave him an opportunity to use prisoners, especially twins, as guinea pigs for his research.[77]

When the convoys of Jews, Gypsies, Poles and other Slavs arrived at Auschwitz, Mengele, dressed in a dark green uniform and shining boots, prowled the railroad platform, shout-

ing "*Zwillinge, Zwillinge, Zwillinge!*" ("Twins, Twins, Twins!")
Sometimes in the confusion at the platform, twins escaped his
scrutiny and ended up in trucks that hauled the prisoners to
the gas chamber. One twin who survived the ordeal of Auschwitz remembered: "I was scheduled to go to the chambers. I
knew I was going to lose my life. We were being loaded onto
trucks when this car comes up. A convertible. That's when I
saw Mengele. We were taken off the truck. He stopped the
whole procession because they were going to kill his twins."[78]

"Mengele's twins" included Jews and gentiles of different
ages, including many children whom he housed in special
quarters with better food, beds and sanitary conditions than the
rest of the prison population. Often doting on his twins, who
called him "Uncle Pepi," or "Uncle Mengele," he gave them
sweets. "He brought chocolate for them, the most beautiful
clothes, white pants, even aprons, and the girls had ribbons in
their hair," one former inmate said. "One day he shouted at me
because one girl had one ribbon lower than the other. He told
me, 'How did you do it? They are not as I like them.'"[79]

Surprisingly, one finds survivors today who claim that
Mengele loved children; yet, as one added, "even though he
was a murderer and a killer."[80] This points up the bizarre
duality of Mengele and other SS physicians who displayed
empathy and gentleness toward their victims and yet were
sadistic killers. Robert Jay Lifton, professor of psychiatry, explains this duality as "doubling," a way by which Mengele and
others like him adapted to the bizarre world of Auschwitz; their
"Auschwitz self" subsuming their "doctor-healer self."[81]

The major purpose of Mengele's experiments was to see to
what extent the birth rate could be increased by medically
manipulating the birth of twins. He wanted to preserve the
desirable features of the Aryan race—blue eyes, blond hair,
healthy lithe bodies.[82] He hoped to unlock the key to a prolif-
eration of Aryan twins which would result in overtaking the
prolific Poles and other Slavs whose birth rate before the war
exceeded that of the Germans. Meanwhile, through various
means, the Nazis were succeeding in fulfilling their dream of
reducing in substantial numbers Poles and other Slavs who
would no longer be a threat to the German nation after the war.

Being overtaken by the fertile Poles and other Slavs was a

major concern of Hitler's. "We are obliged to depopulate, as part of our mission of preserving the German population, and we shall have to develop a technique of depopulation," Hitler declared. He had a right, he said, "to remove millions of an inferior race that breeds like vermin!" He said he didn't necessarily mean that all Poles and Slavs had to be destroyed because there were "bloodless" ways "to damn their great natural fertility."[83] By 1942, Nazi methods had already paid dividends: there was an 80% drop in the birth rate among Poles compared to the prewar period.[84]

Mengele subjected children to ceaseless examinations—anthropological, morphological and X-ray. Naked sometimes for up to 2 to 5 hours, the children were cold, scared and cried. "I cried with the children," said one nurse-prisoner who knew of 50 children who had died during the summer of 1944.[85] They drew blood from the children every day. Apparently not all the blood was for blood tests; some of it apparently was sent to German soldiers at the front.[86] One twin who survived commented:

> We were always naked during the experiments. We were marked, painted, measured, observed. Boys and girls were together. It was all so demeaning. There was no place to hide, no place to go.
> They compared every part of our body with that of our twin. The tests would last for hours.
> And Mengele was always there, supervising.[87]

To Mengele one of the most important aspects of his research was to change the color of the eyes of his victims by injecting different colored dyes into them. Often this resulted in infections and blindness. One Jewish doctor, an inmate at Auschwitz, remembered seeing in the Gypsy camp a wooden table with samples of eyes, each meticulously catalogued. Another inmate remembered seeing a wall of eyes, "pinned up like butterflies." She thought she had died and was "already living in hell." When the children and adults involved in these experiments had served their purpose, death by gas or gunshot often awaited them.[88]

For studies of a pathological nature, Mengele obviously needed bodies. "Since it was necessary to perform a dissection for the simultaneous evaluation of anomalies," Dr. Miklos Nyiszli, an inmate physician who worked for Mengele at Auschwitz, said, "the twins had to die at the same time. So it was that they met their death in B section of one of Auschwitz's KZ barracks, at the hand of Dr. Mengele." Nyiszli, ordered to perform dissections of twins, recalled performing them on twins as young as two years old. After dissection, their young bodies were burned.[89]

Mengele even tried to change the sex of twins. Simon Wiesenthal, the famous Nazi hunter, said that he met a man after the war whom Auschwitz physicians had turned into a woman. He was 13-years-old when the operation took place. Although physicians restored him to his former self after the war, the man's emotional health was ruined.[90] There are also claims that Mengele had twins mate with other twins to see if twins reproduced twins.[91]

Even before Mengele arrived at Auschwitz, experiments to sterilize young Jewish and Polish boys and men were underway. Some of the experiments in castration resulted in the genitals of some of the young Polish victims rotting away as they writhed in agony. The Nazi doctors subjected women and young girls to sterilization too. Based on these experiments, one Auschwitz physician reported elatedly to Himmler in June, 1943, that 1,000 women could be sterilized every day.[92]

German physicians at other concentration camps—Ravensbruck, Neuengamme, Buchenwald, Dachau—were also engaged in pseudoscientific research that subjected children and adults to various experiments. They ran the gamut from sterilization to innoculation with infectious diseases.[93]

At Ravensbruck, Nazi doctors subjected 79 Polish women, many of them in their teens, to a number of bizarre experiments. One of these involved injecting the bone marrow with diseased bacilli. One 17-year-old Polish girl, named Krysia, had a large section of bone removed from her legs which were later injected with bacteria. She was one of the few who was not scarred for life. Mostly using young Polish women, the experiments involved not only procedures on bones, muscles and nerves, but also sterilization by X-rays, surgery and chemotherapy. Many of the "Ravensbruck Lapins," or human guinea pigs, survived the war, crippled and weakened by these horrible experiments.[94]

Thirty-eight-year-old Dr. Kurt Heissmeyer, who apparently believed there was no difference between animals and Jews, wanted to complete research to develop a serum to fight tuberculosis. Like Mengele, he was extremely ambitious and wanted to become famous. Although his own colleagues disputed his dubious theories, Heissmeyer had highly placed friends and relatives, including an uncle who knew Himmler personally, who helped him get the green light to conduct his experiments at Neuengamme.

On November 29, 1944, approximately 20 children, mostly Jewish children from Poland, arrived at Neuengamme. The youngest was 5 and the oldest was 12 years old. Heissmeyer innoculated them with tuberculosis bacilli. Just days before Germany's defeat, authorities in Berlin ordered the children put to death. In the middle of the night, they awakened the children who dressed and carried their toys and other personal possessions with them. Taken to a cellar of a school near Hamburg, the children were hanged. Their bodies, along with their personal effects, were burned.[95]

There were also institutions in Upper Silesia, notably the *Medizinische Kinderheilanstalt*, formerly an insane asylum, where they experimented on Polish children, giving them heavy doses of luminal, a phenobarbital used as a hypnotic and sedative, from which most of them died. At another institution, one of the children recalled, "Most of the children at Loben were Polish and they were given spinal injections after which they had to lie in bed for a week and could not keep food down."[96]

Those children who survived selections for the gas chamber or medical experiments when they arrived at a concentration camp were not as fortunate as one would imagine because as one survivor of Auschwitz said, "He was still a candidate for death with a difference—that for three months, or as long as he could endure, he had to submit to all the horrors that the KZ had to offer 'til he dropped from utter exhaustion."[97] That is what awaited most Jewish and Polish children condemned to slow death from disease, starvation, exhaustion and brutality at German concentration camps. There were those, albeit not many, who managed to defy the incredible odds and survived the appalling conditions of camp life.

Jewish and Polish children could be found everywhere in the network of 2,000 Nazi camps that webbed German-occupied Poland. Major camps built exclusively to exterminate people included Belzec, Chelmno, Sobibor and Treblinka. The Germans also built three major concentration camps—Auschwitz-Birkenau, Majdanek, and Stutthof—which also served as extermination centers. Gross-Rosen, located in western Poland today, was used primarily as a labor camp. In addition, there were literally dozens of sub-camps affiliated with the main camps.[98]

After children survived selection to the gas chamber, they joined others in working either in or near the camp or sub-camp. At Majdanek, there were labor units consisting of children as young as 8 years of age who carried ashes from the crematoria to pits. Others worked in the camp's garden and kitchen. In April and May, 1943, transports arrived almost every day at Majdanek with women and child survivors of the Warsaw Ghetto Uprising. Some were gassed, others were spared for a time to work.[99]

In Silesia, thousands of Polish families, mostly of peasant background, found themselves in *Polenlager*, camps surrounded by barbed wire, which were in reality vast pools of slave labor. The child population in these camps sometimes exceeded 40 percent of the prisoner population. The postwar Nuremberg Court considered *Polenlager* fundamentally similar to concentration camps.[100]

Many Polish children whose parents were involved in the Warsaw Uprising of 1944 ended up in concentration camps. This was how 17-year-old Barbara Czuruk found herself at Bergen-Belsen. Thirteen-year-old Jan Konilowicz, who helped insurgents during the uprising, ended up in Mauthausen. The Germans sent 16-year-old Henryka Koperska, who had been wounded in the uprising, to Ravensbruck.[101] The Germans caught 15-year-old Franciszek Kopec, who had been a messenger for partisans operating in the vicinity of his village, and sent him first to Auschwitz and later to Gusen, part of the Mauthausen complex, where conditions were so bad for him that he considered throwing himself against an electrified fence to end his life. Kopec was more fortunate than many other

Polish children sent to Gusen after the Warsaw Uprising of 1944. The Germans bludgeoned many of them to death.[102]

Stutthof, which had the dubious distinction of being the oldest concentration camp in German-occupied Poland, had a large number of children imprisoned there. As in other camps, the Germans treated them as adults and they suffered the same barbaric conditions. The Germans exterminated some children and forced others to work. For still others, Stutthof served as a transition camp for prisoners on their way elsewhere. Ravensbruck also absorbed thousands of children deported from Auschwitz when it closed down operations in the face of the advance of Soviet armies.[103]

The Germans confined "J. A." and her mother at Plaszow where they worked in a factory. At first, she was in a children's home at Plaszow when one day she realized the Germans were going to deport the children to Auschwitz and almost certain death. She managed to run away from the group, joining three other Jewish children who were the last children to survive Plaszow:

> As they were pushing me toward a truck with the other children, a German guard stopped a moment to light his cigarette. He stood spread-eagled. In a second, me and three other children—a boy and two girls—dropped out of line and, running low to the ground, we shot through the German's spread long legs. We broke for the latrine. The German whirled around and fired but he didn't hit anyone because we dropped to the ground as soon as we heard the first of his many shots. He couldn't come after us because he was afraid if he left the other children, they'd break away, too.[104]

Just as "J. A." managed to remain at Plaszow and joined the work force there, 13-year-old Witold Jakubowicz worked at Gliwice, a sub-camp of Auschwitz. The alternative was death. "We tried very hard not to get sick," Jakubowicz said. "We knew that when someone was ill, he would be sent to Birkenau where he could be completely 'cured' with gas."[105]

Some of the children who were spared the gas chamber at Auschwitz ended up in a school for hundreds of youths—Jews, Poles, and others—in bricklaying. When the children completed the training, they marched out to work not to the tune of *Deutschland uber Alles* but, curiously, to *Colonel Bogey* and the

Stars and Stripes. Apparently, the Nazis had declared these marches to be German.[106]

As construction projects were completed and new convoys of children arrived at Auschwitz, the Germans reduced the number of children by selecting some for the gas chamber or killing others with phenol injections. Some boys worked in the garden at Auschwitz where ashes from the crematoria were used "as human manure."[107] One 15-year-old Polish youth unloaded vegetables from a train ramp. While unloading turnips one day, he threw some of them to hungry Soviet prisoners-of-war on their way to work. For that, the Germans took the boy to a block where he was hanged on a post, a form of punishment usually resulting in severe injury or death.[108]

Another Polish boy, who was 10-years-old, told an inmate-physician at Auschwitz that he knew he was near death from starvation. "I still have good clean shoes," the boy told him. "Perhaps you could find someone who will exchange a piece of bread for them. The shoes are no longer of use to me. Definitely not. But I would so much like to have plenty of food before I die."[109]

Leon Wells, a Jewish teenager from an Hasidic family who survived the war to testify at the Adolf Eichmann trial, spent a long time at the Janowska camp where he was in one of the brigades which worked outside the camp. Shortly after his arrival at Janowska, he recalled:

> Tired, emaciated figures moved slowly through the yard. One could hardly believe that these people who just a few weeks ago had gone about well dressed, healthy, and full of strength, tending to their respective jobs. Now their feet were wrapped in straw, held in place by pieces of cloth and string, their clothes ragged and torn, around their waists were cords with dirty eating utensils attached to them. So they trudged along toward the mess hall, where they joined the already waiting breakfast line. The bitter-cold weather had driven all human expression from their faces.[110]

The Germans sent hundreds of Polish boys and girls to special children's camps. There were three main camps—Moringen in Hanover, Uckermark in Brandenburg and Lodz in German-occupied Poland. Although some Polish youth were in Moringen, where they worked in German war industries, they sent most Polish youngsters to Lodz, described as "a small Auschwitz," and to its branch at Dzierzazn.[111]

Polish children at Lodz came from homes where either parents or children themselves had been arrested for involvement in the Polish underground movement. Many children were orphans, without homes or close relatives. Others, in the eyes of the Germans, were criminals and ended up in Lodz. The Germans sent Jozef Cholewa to Lodz for selling matches, considered a crime by the Germans. They sent Stefan Marczewski, who was 13-years-old, to Lodz for picking up pieces of coal from a railroad siding.[112]

Bordering the Jewish Ghetto on three sides, the Lodz camp was surrounded by wire. Consisting of several brick buildings and two wooden barracks, the children, ranging in age from 1 to 16, lived like concentration camp inmates. Maria Wisniewska, confined at Lodz when she was 15-years-old, recalled how primitive life was. Ill fed, the children received coffee and dry bread in the morning. Thin soup, often with bugs in it, was lunch. Usually coffee and bread served as supper. Children got sick from the poor diet and had to be taken to the Jewish hospital in the Lodz Ghetto where Jewish physicians looked after them. One survivor recalled how on one occasion the children were so hungry they ate a pot of glue used to size leather.[113]

Conditions were so appalling that epidemics became commonplace. Young children had no care, and usually suffered from typhus and scarlet fever that took their lives quickly. In one month, out of 273 children in the hospital, 73 died. When epidemics struck, nothing was done to protect healthy youngsters from infected ones. Historians estimate that during the existence of the Lodz camp, 8,000-12,000 children died out of the 13,000 who were confined there.[114]

Discipline at Lodz and Dzierzazn was as barbaric as in any concentration camp. Overseers routinely beat the children, breaking bones, knocking out teeth and even eyes, and hanging children on racks. One of the overseers, known as a "Cat in Boots," was especially sadistic in his treatment of the young inmates. He may have been the one who cut off the testicles of a boy with a pocket knife. The boy died. Teresa Jakubowska, 10-years-old, stole bread and for that received 100 blows that killed her. "A boy working in the footwear workshop failed to accomplish his quota," one former inmate of Lodz remembered. "The guard beat him until his skin cracked and blood was streaming. The beaten boy probably died because he did not return and I never saw him again."[115]

The work day ran 10-12 hours. Girls worked in the laundry or in trades like tailoring. Boys often did heavier labor on the farm, in construction, or worked in a trade. Jewish specialists in various trades from the Lodz Ghetto taught in the camp's school,[116] thus forging a link between the Jewish residents of the ghetto and Polish child-prisoners.

Children were forbidden to use Polish, and at first wore whatever clothes they had when they arrived. But later, even this concession to individuality was forbidden, and all inmates had to wear a gray uniform. They lived in largely unheated rooms with 2 or 3 children assigned to one bed. There was one outside water pump for washing and little or no soap. In these conditions, many children attempted to escape and some succeeded. It wasn't easy, considering the children could be readily spotted by their prison grays.[117]

Child survivors of German camps were remarkable individuals. They were usually highly intelligent and resourceful boys and girls who quickly understood what they needed to do in order to survive. Kitty Hart, the youngest member of Poland's prewar national swimming team, learned what it took to survive Auschwitz: "I was... to know that 'organize' was *the* most important word in the Auschwitz language. It meant: to steal, buy, exchange, get hold of. My very first lesson was that anything here could be used for currency. Even water. I learned fast."[118]

Children at Auschwitz, orphaned or separated from their parents, at first wept for their mothers and talked about going home, but soon the stronger ones stopped crying and understood the reality of the situation and pursued the major task of finding food to supplement their meager diet in order to survive.[119]

One of the most revealing aspects of the life of children in prison camps was the camaraderie that often developed among them. A young survivor remembered how easy it would have been for him to steal food from a younger boy who slept near him. "All I had to do was reach over. It was mine to eat. No, not today. I myself do not understand why I didn't do it. Perhaps it was pity...."[120] The youngsters seemed to face their fate as a group without absorbing the prejudices and hatreds their elders often brought with them into the camp environment. "We could not help being impressed by this hopeful atmosphere that youth created for itself among the holocaust [sic] of its elders," one young survivor later wrote.[121]

Most camps had a network of mutual aid groups who sought to alleviate some of the worse aspects of concentration camp life for children. Women prisoners were especially active in helping and saving older children of different nationalities. Although most Jewish children were usually gassed upon arrival at concentration camps, there were instances where prisoners tried to save them and Gypsy children from death. Aiding children at Majdanek and Auschwitz was made a little easier by the help of Poles who lived in the area and smuggled food and drugs to the inmates, helping to reduce child mortality. Even at that, child mortality at these camps averaged 25-35 percent.[122]

Halina Birenbaum remembered that in the women's barracks it was customary for Kapos and block overseers to pick out a favorite, "a kind of pet servant" on whom these "foster mothers" lavished affection. According to Birenbaum, "A 'little pet' had to be on call all the time, ready to flatter, faun, and inform on her companions, so as to remain as long as possible in the favor of their usually capricious and changeable patronesses."[123]

Sometimes an adult's interest in a young girl or boy was not always benign. At Janowska, one former inmate recalled how Germans rounded up young girls, had sex with them and then killed them. At the Seventh Fort, Lithuanian soldiers in the SS selected pretty young Jewish girls and raped them before shooting them. They called this atrocity, "Going to peel potatoes." To be sure, there were young girls who willingly sold their bodies to survive.[124]

Young good-looking boys were also vulnerable to sexual exploitation. Often they became prey for guards or others who had sex with them.[125] "Homosexuality was an open secret," Thomas Geve, a teenage survivor of Auschwitz recalled. Geve's friend, who became a lover of a Kapo, told him: "What else could have saved me from hard work, hunger and illness?" One senior camp prisoner, a German criminal, had a reputation for pursuing young boys whom he demoralized. When the Germans sent Geve to Buchenwald, he said there were several boys, mostly Polish and Russian, who became male prostitutes for camp leaders.[126]

The same situation existed at Majdanek where a number of boys, mostly Jewish, survived and received special privileges. They did light work, running errands and shining shoes. Some even took charge of labor gangs. Known as *piepels*, these young male prostitutes sometimes tried to match their masters in cruelty toward other prisoners. Others used their privileged position to help less fortunate inmates.[127]

Generally, it appears that under the terrible conditions that characterized concentration camp life, the need for sex either disappeared or diminished substantially among prisoners. However, there were exceptions: healthy young boys and girls had an active interest in sex and participated in heterosexual and homosexual activity.[128]

Chapter Notes

1. Report, Massacre of Polish Jews and Liquidation of the Warsaw Ghetto (September, 1942), in FO 371/31097 C 12185/954/55 PRO.

2. Lewin, *Cup of Tears*, pp. 136-37.

3. *Ibid.*, 141.

4. Report, Massacre of Polish Jews.

5. *Ibid.*; Lewin, *Cup of Tears*, p. 141.

6. Birenbaum, *Hope Is the Last to Die*, pp. 48-49.

7. Report, Massacre of Polish Jews.

8. Lewin, *Cup of Tears*, pp. 157, 176.

9. Lifton, *King of Children*, pp. 3-4, 13.

10. Ringelblum, *Kronika Getta Warszawskiego*, p. 605.

11. Lifton, *King of Children*, pp. 263, 283.

12. *Ibid.*, p. 252.

13. *Ibid.*, p. 340; Ringelblum, *Kronika Getta Warszawskiego*, pp. 606-07. There were also other Jewish leaders of children's homes whom the Germans deported to Treblinka. Aron Koninski chose to go with his children to Treblinka rather than to abandon them. *Ibid.* 617-18.

14. Jozef Barski, *Przezycia i Wspomnienia z lat Okupacji* (Wroclaw: Wydawnictwo Polskiej Akademii Nauk, 1986) pp. 31, 41; Report, Adolf Berman, December, 1942, in Silkes Papers, YIVO.

15. Zuker-Bujanowska, *Liliana's Journal*, p. 39.

16. *Ibid.*, p. 39, 54.

17. Barski, *Przezycia i Wspomnienia*, pp. 33-34.

18. Ringelblum, *Kronika Getta Warszawskiego*, p. 421.

19. Lukas, *Forgotten Holocaust*, pp. 153-61; Korbonski's messages are quoted in *Ibid.*, pp. 156-57.

20. Sinai Leichter, "Kielce," *Encyclopedia of the Holocaust*, II, 801; Isaiah Trunk, *Jewish Responses to Nazi Persecution: Collective and Individual Behavior in Extremis* (New York: Stein and Day, 1979), pp. 122ff. Deportations from the Lublin Ghetto occurred in March

and April, 1942. A major deportation involving children and old Jews from Lodz took place in September, 1942. From Czestochowa, the Germans deported approximately 40,000 people in September and October, 1942. Jews of Mlawa experienced the liquidation of their ghetto by November, 1942.

21. Eva Fogelman, "Psychological Origins of Rescue," *Dimensions*, III (1982), 9-10.

22. Adelson and Lapides, *Lodz Ghetto*, p. 348; Aleksander Bieberstein, *Zaglada Zydow w Krakowie* (N.C.: Wydawnictwo Literackie, 1985), pp. 208-15.

23. Birenbaum, *Hope Is the Last to Die*, p. 28.

24. Report, Massacre of Polish Jews.

25. Birenbaum, *Hope Is the Last to Die*, pp. 29-30.

26. Christopher R. Browning, *Fateful Months: Essays on the Emergence of the Final Solution* (New York: Holmes and Meier, 1985), pp. 57-59.

27. *Ibid.*, pp. 57ff; Shmuel Spector, "Gas Vans," *Encyclopedia of the Holocaust*, II, 543. The Germans also used gas vans in Lublin to kill Poles and Jewish prisoners in the fortress there. The bodies were later burned in Majdanek's crematoria.

28. Michael A. Mussmano, *The Eichmann Kommandos* (New York: Macrae Smith, 1961), pp. 112-21.

29. *Ibid.*

30. Patricia Treece, *A Man for Others: Maximilian Kolbe Saint of Auschwitz in the Words of Those Who Knew Him* (San Francisco: Harper and Row, 1982), pp. 129-31.

31. Maria Jezierska, a former inmate of Auschwitz, said, "Not being Jewish did not at all protect one from being selected for the gas." International Auschwitz Committee, *Nazi Medicine: Doctors, Victims, and Medicine in Auschwitz* (New York: Howard Fertig, 1986), p. 198.

32. Mikols Nyiszli, *Auschwitz: An Eyewitness Account of Mengele's Infamous Death Camp* (New York: Seaver Books, 1986), pp. 23-24.

33. Jozef Wnuk, *Dzieci Polskie Oskarzaja* (Lublin: Wydawnictwo Lubelskie, 1975), pp. 108-09.

34. Gerald L. Posner and John Ware, *Mengele: The Complete Story* (New York: McGraw Hill, 1986) pp. 49-51.

35. Rudolf Hoess, *Commandant of Auschwitz: The Autobiography of Rudolf Hoess*, trans. by Constantine Fitzgibbon (London: Pan Books, 1961), pp. 167-68.

36. *Ibid.* 168.

37. *Ibid.* 22, 164, 186, 201-02.

38. *Ibid.*, p. 168; International Auschwitz Committee, *Nazi Medicine*, p. 31; Nyiszli, *Auschwitz*, p. 46; Filip Muller, *Auschwitz Inferno: The Testimony of a Sonderkommando*, trans. by Susanne Flatauer (London: Routledge and Kegan Paul, 1979), pp. 32-33.

39. Nyiszli, *Auschwitz*, pp. 46-47.

40. *Soviet Monitor*, September 17, 1944, in FO 371/39345, PRO.

41. Judith Sternberg Newman, *In the Hell of Auschwitz: The Wartime Memories of Judith Sternberg Newman* (New York: Exposition Press, 1963), p. 52; Wnuk, *Dzieci Polskie Oskarzaja*, p. 109; Hrabar, *Fate of Polish Children*, p. 66; Paul Lisiewicz, "Wyrafinowane Metody Zaglady Dzieci," in Glowna Komisja Badania Zbrodni Hitlerowskich w Polsce, *Zbrodnie Hitlerowskie na Dzieciach i Mlodziezy Polskiej*, 1939-1945 (Warsaw: Wydawnictwo Prawnicze, 1969), p. 48.

42. Nyiszli, *Auschwitz*, pp. 88-92.

43. Zeznanie Chaim Hirszman, in Eyewitness Accounts, Series I, YIVO.

44. Zeznanie S. Israel, in Eyewitness Accounts, Series I, YIVO.

45. Jozef Marszalek, *Majdanek* (Warsaw: Interpress, 1986), pp. 137-38.

46. Yankel Wiernik, *A Year in Treblinka* (New York: American Representation of the General Jewish Workers Union of Poland, n.d.), pp. 14-15.

47. *Ibid.* 15.

48. Eisenberg, *Lost Generation*, pp. 141-42.

49. Meldunek Zbiorowy, Rowecki do N.W. i Mikolajczyka, December 20, 1942 and Meldunek Zbiorowy, Rowecki do Centrali, January 21, 1943, in Studium Polski Podziemnej, *Armia Krajowa Dokumentach*, 1939-1945 (London: Gryf, 1973), II, 382-87, 406.

50. Interview with Korbonski; Interview with Edward Raczynski, June 21, 1986.

51. Janusz Gumkowski and Kazimierz Leszczynski, *Poland under Nazi Occupation* (Warsaw: Polonia Publishing House, 1961), pp. 123-30.

52. Pilichowski, *Zbrodnie Hitlerowskie*, pp. 28-29.

53. Waldemar Monkiewicz and Jozef Kretowski, "Hitlerowska Polityka Eksterminacyjna Wobec Dzieci w Bialostockiem," in *Wo-*

jna i Okupacja a Medycyna: Materialy (Krakow: Akademia Medyczna im. Mikolaja Kopernika w Krakowie, 1986), p. 145.

54. Wnuk, *Dzieci Polskie Oskarzaja*, pp. 122-23.

55. Hrabar, *Fate of Polish Children*, p. 68.

56. Quoted in *ibid.*, pp. 68-69.

57. Report, Jewish National Committee, February 10, 1944, in FO 371/42790, PRO.

58. Bulletin, Jewish Agency Committee for the Jews of Occupied Europe, February 8, 1945, in FO 371/51112, PRO.

59. Adam Borkiewicz, *Powstanie Warszawskie* (Warsaw: 1957), pp. 38-39.

60. Korbonski, *Fighting Warsaw*, pp. 346-47.

61. W. Zagorski, *Seventy Days*, trans. by John Welsh (London; Frederick Muller, 1957), p. 19.

62. Korbonski, *Fighting Warsaw*, p. 350; Gunther Deschner, *Warsaw Uprising* (New York: Ballantine Books, 1972), p. 22.

63. Korbonski, *Fighting Warsaw*, p. 347; Tadeusz Bor-Komorowski, *The Secret Army* (New York: Macmillan, 1951), p. 207.

64. See Lukas, *Forgotten Holocaust*, Chapter VII.

65. Hanns von Krannhals, *Der Warschauer Aufstand*, 1944 (Frankfurt am Main: Bernard and Graefe Verlag fur Wehrwesen, 1962), p. 134.

66. U.S. Counsel, *Nazi Conspiracy and Aggression*, Supplement A, 800-01.

67. Whitney Harris, *Tyranny on Trial: The Evidence at Nuremberg* (Dallas, Tx.: Southern Methodist University Press, 1954), pp. 201-03.

68. U.S. Counsel, *Nazi Conspiracy and Aggression*, Supplement A, 803-04.

69. Jozef K. Wroniszewski, *Ochota: 1944* (Warsaw: Wydawnictwo Ministerstwo Obrony Narodowej, 1970), pp. 149-50. Leslaw M. Bartelski, "Dzieci w Powstaniu Warszawskim," in Pilichowski, *Dzieci i Mlodziez*, p. 452.

70. Quoted in Harris, *Tyranny on Trial*, pp. 203-04.

71. Krannhals, *Der Warschauer Aufstand*, p. 215.

72. Newman, *In the Hell of Auschwitz*, p. 43.

73. Olga Lengiel, *Five Chimneys—Story of Auschwitz* (Chicago: Ziff Davis, 1947), pp. 99ff.

74. Wanda Kiedrzynska, "Dzieci w Obozie Koncentracyjnym Ravensbruck," in Pilichowski, *Dzieci i Mlodziez*, pp. 147, 151.

75. International Auschwitz Committee, *Nazi Medicine*, III, 188-90.

76. Lucette Matalon Lagnado and Sheila Cohn Dekel, *Children of the Flames: Dr. Josef Mengele and the Untold Story of the Twins of Auschwitz* (New York: William Morrow, 1991), pp. 31-34.

77. *Ibid*. 38-52.

78. Quoted in Posner and Ware, *Mengele*, p. 29.

79. *Ibid*., p. 35.

80. Lagnado and Dekel, *Children of the Flames*, p. 9.

81. Lifton, *Nazi Doctors*, Chapter XX.

82. Posner and Ware, *Mengele*, p. 31.

83. Quoted in *Polish Fortnightly Review*, April 1, 1943.

84. Pilichowski, *Zbrodnie Hitlerowskie*, p. 38.

85. Elzbieta Piekut-Warszawska, "Dzieci w Obozie Oswiecimskim (Wspomnienia Pielegniarki)," *Przeglad Lekarski* (1967), pp. 204-05.

86. Grigorij A. Koltunow, "Przestepstwa Hitlerowskie Wobec Dzieci Radzieckich," in Pilichowski, *Dzieci i Mlodziez*, p. 47; Lagnado and Dekel, *Children of the Flames*, p. 64. Zbigniew Drecki, who grew to adulthood at Auschwitz, commented how physicians took blood from inmates who survived typhus because it was supposed to be disease-free. Drecki, *Freedom and Justice*, p. 47. According to one report, the Germans kidnapped healthy young school children and used them at field hospitals for blood transfusions. Memo, undated, WR/22/18 in PAG-4/2.0.62: Box 15, UNRRA/UNA.

87. Lagnado and Dekel, *Children of the Flames*, p. 64.

88. Posner and Ware, *Mengele*, pp. 34, 39. The West German indictment against Mengele alleged that he was responsible for the deaths of 153 children.

89. Nyiszli, *Auschwitz*, pp. 50ff.

90. Wiesenthal, *Murderers Among Us*, p. 155.

91. Posner and Ware, *Mengele*, pp. 37-38.

92. Lifton, *Nazi Doctors*, p. 283; International Auschwitz Committee, *Nazi Medicine*, III, 69; S. Klodzinski, "Z Zagadnien Ludobojstwa: Sterylizacja i Kastracja Promieniami Roetgena w Obozie Oswiecimskim Dr. Horst Schumann," *Przeglad Lekarski* (1964), pp. 105-111.

93. Dunin-Wasowicz, *Resistance in the Nazi Camps*, pp. 35-36.

94. International Auschwitz Committee, *Nazi Medicine*, I, 137; Wanda Poltawska, *And I Am Afraid of My Dreams*, trans. by Mary Craig (New York: Hippocrene Books, 1989), pp. 10, 34, 39, 85, 87, 99, 109.

95. Gunther Schwarberg, *Dzieciobojca Eksperymenty Lekarza SS w Neuengamme* (Warsaw: Czytelnik, 1987), pp. 5, 33-70, 73ff.

96. Report, Location of UN Children in the U.S. Zone, Germany, in PAG 4/1.31.2.10 Box 1, UNRRA/UNA; R.Z. Hrabar, *Hitlerowski Rabunek Dzieci Polskich, 1939-1945* (Katowice: 1960), pp. 87-88.

97. Posner and Ware, Mengele, p. 26.

98. Madajczyk, *Polityka III Rzeszy*, II, 273; Central Commission, *German Crimes in Poland*, I, 21.

99. Sofia Murawska-Gryn, "Martyrologia Dzieci w Lubelskim Obozie Koncentracyjnym na Majdanku," in Pilichowski, *Dzieci i Mlodziez*, pp. 160, 167.

100. Hrabar, *Fate of Polish Children*, pp. 86-92; Pilichowski, *Zbrodnie Hitlerowskie*, pp. 17-18.

101. Kempisty, *Spraw Norymbergi*, pp. 37-38.

102. Kopec, "Numer 109063," in Turski, *Byli Wowczas Dziecmi*, pp. 552ff; Evelyn Le Chene, *Mauthausen: The History of a Death Camp* (London: Methuen, 1971), p. 216.

103. Janina Grabowska, "Martyrologia Dzieci i Mlodziezy w Obozie Koncentracyjnym Stutthof;" Wanda Kiedrzynska, "Dzieci w Obozie Koncentracyjnym Ravensbruck," in Pilichowski, *Dzieci i Mlodziez*, pp. 168-79; 147-48.

104. Trunk, *Jewish Responses*, pp. 116-20.

105. Lisiewicz, "Wyrafinowane Metody Zaglady Dzieci," p. 48.

106. Thomas Geve, *Youth in Chains* (Jerusalem: Rubin Mass, 1958), p. 98.

107. Ota Kraus and Erich Kulka, *The Death Factory: Document on Auschwitz* (Oxford: Pergamon, 1966), p. 108; Drecki, *Freedom and Justice*, p. 31.

108. Kempisty, *Spraw Norymbergi*, p. 92.

109. Schwarberg, *Dzieciobojca*, p. 28.

110. Wells, *Janowska Road*, pp. 60-61. There are instances where hunger drove some inmates to eat the flesh of corpses in some concentration camps. Stanislaw Sterkowicz," Przyczynek do Zagadnienia Moralnosci Wiezniow Obozow Hitlerowskich," *Przeglad Lekarski*, (1969), pp. 48-49.

111. Franciszek Proch, *Poland's Way of the Cross, 1939-1945* (New York: Polish Association of Former Political Prisoners of Nazi and Soviet Concentration Camps, 1987), pp. 40-41.

112. Kempisty, *Spraw Norymbergi*, p. 41.

113. Protokol Przesluchania Swiadka, Maria Wisniewska, in Z/ot-1057/35-37, AGKBZHP; Hrabar, *Fate of Polish Children*, p. 82.

114. Kempisty, *Spraw Norymbergi*, pp. 65, 73-74; Proch, *Poland's Way*, p. 42.

115. Protokol Przesluchania Swiadka, Wisniewska; Hrabar, *Fate of Polish Children*, p. 81; Tatiana Kozlowicz, "Karny Oboz Pracy dla Dzieci i Mlodziezy w Lodzi," in Glowna Komisja Badania Zbrodni Hitlerowskich w Polsce, *Zbrodnie Hitlerowskie*, p. 31.

116. Kempisty, *Spraw Norymbergi*, pp. 47-52; Protokol Przesluchania Swiadka, Wisniewska; Dobroszycki, *Chronicle of the Lodz Ghetto*, p. 303. When children turned 16 years of age, they were sent as forced laborers to Germany.

117. Sprawozdanie z Wnioskim (Fajychowski) in Kolekcje Z, 1057, in AGKBZP; Protokol Przesluchania Swiadka, Wisniewska; Wnuk, *Dzieci Polskie Oskarzaja*, pp. 90-91.

118. Kitty Hart, *I am Alive: Auschwitz and Birkenau* (New York: Abelard-Schuman, 1961), pp. 49ff.

119. Bogdan Bartnikowski, *Dziecinstwo w Pasiakach* (Warsaw: Nasza Ksiegarnia, 1989), pp. 18-19.

120. *Ibid.*

121. Geve, *Youth in Chains*, p. 69.

122. Dunin-Wasowicz, *Resistance in Nazi Concentration Camps*, pp. 58, 64-65; Alicja Glinska, "Z Badan nad Moralnoscia Wiezniow Oswiecimia," *Przeglad Lekarski* (1967), p. 41.

123. *Ibid.*, p. 101; Birenbaum, *Hope Is the Last to Die*, pp. 121ff. Geve related that a 4-year-old boy staggered around Auschwitz speaking a German-Polish-Yiddish gibberish. Every time the Germans inspected the barrack, inmates hid him under the floor boards. Geve, *Youth in Chains*, p. 203.

124. Wells, *Janowska Road*, pp. 189-90; Tory, *Surviving the Holocaust*, pp. 23-24; Alicja Glinska, "Kierunek Przeksztalcen Moralnych wsrod Wiezniow Oswiecimia," *Przeglad Lekarski* (1969), p. 54.

125. One Allied report, based on information sent to the West by the Polish underground, read: "A great many of the guards choose young good-looking boys and abuse them, as a rule killing them

afterwards." Reports on the Situation in Occupied Poland, No. 6, 1942, in Office of Strategic Services, RG 226, OSS/NA;

126. Wladyslaw Fejkiel, "The Health Service in the Auschwitz Concentration Camp, No. 1 (Main Camp)," *Przeglad Lekarski*, Series II (1962), p. 17; Geve, *Youth in Chains*, pp. 77-78, 87, 203.

127. Eisenberg, *Lost Generation*, pp. 147-49. For a novelistic account, based upon real experiences of *piepels*, see Ka-Tzetnik 135633, *Atrocity* (New York: Lyle Stuart, 1963).

128. This subject is touched upon in several works. See Terence des Pres, *The Survivor: An Anatomy of Life in the Death Camps* (New York: Oxford University Press, 1976), pp. 189-91; Geve, *Youth in Chains*, pp. 127-28, 130; Eugene Heimler, *Night of the Mist* (New York: Vanguard, n.d.), pp. 54-55, 92, 143. Poltawska makes a brief but important reference to lesbian activity at Ravensbruck. Poltawska, *And I Am Afraid of My Dreams*, p. 58.

Chapter IV

Germanization

WHEN THE GERMANS annexed western Poland to the Reich, they deported Poles and Jews to the General Government in order to Germanize the new land. As has already been seen, the Germans forced Poles and Jews out of their homes and businesses and transported them in conditions so appalling that thousands of people, including children, perished even before they got to their destination.

Shortly after Poland's defeat, Himmler received a ponderous forty-page document concerning the problem of the Poles and Jews who lived in the annexed lands and the way the Germans should deal with them. Since many districts in the annexed lands had a very high percentage of Poles and almost as many Jews as Germans living there, the report pointed out, "The necessity arises for a ruthless decimation of the Polish population and, as a matter of course, the expulsion of all Jews and persons of Polish-Jewish blood." Anxious about the potential of Poles overwhelming the Germans, the report went on: "If the transfer of Poles from the Reich territory is not effected in a ruthless manner, it has to be feared that the population will increase more or less at the same rate as before the war and up till now."[1]

While virtually all Jews were sent to the General Government and confined in ghettos there, the Germans were more discriminating concerning the Poles they intended to deport. The Nazis selected Poles for deportation according to their occupational status and their attitude toward Germans. The Polish intelligentsia, defined broadly to include virtually anyone who had an education, and Polish political leaders were prime victims for deportation. Poles, described as "neutrally inclined" by the Germans, were considered possible candidates for Germanization and could remain. Some groups—Wasserpolen, Masurians, and Kashubs—were not deported because of their alleged racial similarity to the Germans. They, along with most of the Poles in Silesia, were automatically Germanized. The Poles who remained in the annexed lands would be denied a Polish cultural life. There would not be any Polish schools, only German ones emphasizing Nazi racist theories. Religious services had to be conducted in German. All Polish corporations, associations, clubs, theaters, cinemas and the press ceased to exist.[2]

As western Poland was de-Polonized, Heinrich Himmler, who already headed the SS and police establishments in Germany, supervised the transfer of German colonists into the new land, now known as the Wartheland. Most of these colonists came from areas annexed by the Soviet Union in 1939-40 and from other areas annexed in eastern Europe. Some also came from Germany itself.[3]

The Nazi colonial experiment on Polish soil did not go very well. Many of the younger colonists did not speak German, or they spoke it very badly. Older peasants were often so completely denationalized, they had to be sent to central Germany to be taught how to be a German before they went to their new homes in the Wartheland. Despite Nazi indoctrination programs and the constant control of the Gestapo to which the new settlers were subjected, German leaders feared that these German colonists would be racially contaminated by the Poles who still lived in the area. Arthur Greiser, head of the Nazi party in the Wartheland, worriedly told his German subjects: "The dangers confronting the very essence of our German community are still overwhelming. So do not let your foreign and alien surroundings have the slightest influence on you." Notwithstanding Nazi claims of German superiority over the Poles, Greiser's lament conceded the advanced cultural level of most Poles over the backward German colonists. That was why Nazi authorities insisted the newcomers from the East settle in tight communities where they lived under constant Nazi police observation and control.[4]

After two years of fanatical efforts, the percentage of Germans living in the Wartheland increased only slightly. The Nazis finally conceded failure by declaring that genuine colonization of Polish lands would not begin until after the war.[5]

As the war progressed, the General Government evolved from the status of a protectorate toward an incorporated area. That meant the Nazis intended to de-Polonize and de-Judaize the area while they increasingly Germanized it. Hitler set the tone for Nazi policy when he declared to his lieutenants in March, 1941, that he wanted the area free of Jews and Poles. There could be little doubt that enslavement and extermination of Jews and Poles were the ways the Nazis intended to Germanize the area. Governor Frank, who saw his mission to make the General Government as German as the Rhineland, echoed Hitler when he said, "There is not a shadow of doubt that the territory of the General Government must be and will be colonized by Germans."[6]

SS General Odilo Globocnik, a fanatical believer in Germanizing the General Government, persuaded Himmler to establish German settlements in the Lublin area, southeast of Warsaw. His plan envisaged a belt of German colonies extending from the Baltic Sea to Transylvania. Globocnik, in fulfillment of Hitlerian aims, wanted to hem in the Poles living between the Wartheland and German settlements in the East. In that way, as one German report opined, Poles would be gradually crushed "economically and biologically."[7]

Himmler liked the idea so much he personally visited the region and decided that the hub of the operation should center on the city of Zamosc, located outside of Lublin, which became in his honor Himmlerstadt. Once the plan evolved, the Germans intended to expel Poles from the region in numbers substantial enough to accommodate 10,000 settlements, each comprising 50,000 Germans transferred mostly from eastern Europe. Making the Globocnik plan his own, Himmler wanted to Germanize completely the General Government in twenty years.[8]

"They began to rap at the windows and the doors... we were surrounded and there was no escape for us," one child survivor of Zamosc said. "At that moment I realized, though I was a child, the immensity of the horror and misfortune befalling us."[9] The expulsion of Poles from the Zamosc area began in November, 1942, and extended to July, 1943. The operation rivaled in fanaticism, though not in the number of people involved, Greiser's expulsion of Poles and Jews from the Wartheland.

The Germans divided people into four groups. They selected Poles with desirable racial characteristics and packed them off to Lodz for racial examinations. Less desirable Poles from a racial point of view, but still exploitable economically, ended up as forced laborers in the Reich. The unfortunate victims condemned to the last category were slated for Auschwitz and almost certain death. Children with racial value to the Nazis were forcibly snatched from their parents and sent away to be Germanized.[10]

The Germans sent adults and children to transit camps where, due to the horrible conditions, the mortality rate was extremely high, especially among children. In one camp, there were 4,000 children; another held 3,500. Some 50,000 prisoners passed through one of the camps, known as the Zamosc Rotunda; 10 percent of them were children. The Zamosc Rotunda earned an infamous reputation for mass executions of adults and children. In one instance, 36 Boy Scouts and a group of boys wearing school uniforms sang the Polish national anthem as the Germans shot them. One Polish peasant recalled seeing the Germans remove 10 corpses of children every day from one of the camps.[11]

Perhaps the most painful experience involved the abduction of children from their parents. "I saw children being taken from their mothers," one eyewitness remembered. "Some were even torn from the breast. It was a terrible sight: the agony of the mothers and fathers, the beating by the Germans, and the crying of the children." In the rail cars carrying the adults and children to various destinations, many died of suffocation in the summer and cold in the winter. Packed into the cars like animals, they were given neither food nor drink.[12]

Once word spread about the pitiful plight of the children, approximately 30,000 of whom had been expelled from the Zamosc area, the Poles tried to help as many of them as they could. "You may have bombed our Warsaw, you may imprison and deport us, but you will not harm our children," one Varsovian angrily affirmed.[13] The reaction of the Poles to the plight of the children was so intense, German authorities lamely denied that anything terrible had happened to them.[14] In the hope of helping the Zamosc children, Polish women waited for hours at railroad stations as trains loaded with children rolled westward across Poland. In Warsaw, residents reacted spontaneously and ransomed many emaciated and terrified youngsters. The same thing happened in other cities. In Bydgoszcz and Gdynia, Poles bought children for 40 Reichsmarks. In some places the German price for a Polish child was 25 zlotys. In Pomorze, women literally stormed trains and carried off hungry and terrified children. In Warsaw, so many women fought so aggressively for the children, the Germans decided to alter their transport routes in the future.[15]

As a result of these rescue efforts, some Polish children were rescued and reared by Polish families until they could be reunited after the war with their parents or relatives. Tadeusz Sokol was 4-years-old when the Germans deported him from Zamosc. Raised by another Polish family until the end of the war, he was reunited with his mother in May, 1945.[16] Sokol was one of the fortunate ones because only a small number of Polish children could be saved from the Germans; most of them either died in freezing trains at Auschwitz or Majdanek or were deported for Germanization to the Reich. Out of the 30,000 children deported from Zamosc, it is estimated that 4,454 of them ranging in age from 2 to 14 ended up in the Reich for Germanization.[17]

Children considered unfit for Germanization found their way to Majdanek and Auschwitz where they died. Kazimierz Wdzieczny, a Majdanek survivor, recalled how the Germans assured mothers that their children would be well taken care of by the Red Cross and other humanitarian agencies. When trucks arrived to haul the children to the gas chambers, mothers sensed that something terrible was about to happen to their children and refused to give them up. Amidst the crying and lamenting of mothers and children, the Germans forcibly took the children into the waiting vans. Wdzieczny remembered seeing one SS man, a certain Hoffman, standing at the door of one of the gas chambers enticing children with candy and dolls to enter.[18]

At Auschwitz, the Germans murdered 200-300 Polish children from the Zamosc area by phenol injections. The victim sat on a stool, sometimes blindfolded with a towel. The executioner placed one hand on the back of the child's neck and another behind the shoulder blade. In that way the child's chest was thrust out. The executioner drove a long needle into the chest, depositing a toxic dose of phenol. Within a few minutes the child died. One former inmate said, "As a rule not even a moan would be heard. And they did not wait until the doomed person really died. During his agony, he was taken from both sides under the armpits and thrown into a pile of corpses in another room.... And the next victim took his place on the stool."[19]

Remembering the fate of one group of 48 boys from Zamosc, one Auschwitz survivor stated: "The Germans started a rumour in the camp that the boys would be sent for training as bricklayers. As I found out, the Germans transferred these boys to the camp at Auschwitz to Block 13 where they remained two days, after which they were killed with injections and cremated. I cannot remember the name of the German doctor who killed the children."[20] In another case, on March 3, 1943, two groups of 121 Polish boys between 8 and 14 years of age were given fatal phenol injections. *"Mamo! Mamo!"* ("Mother! Mother!"), the dying screams of the youngsters, were heard by several inmates and made an indelible haunting impression on them. Apparently there were also a number of Zamosc children who died in the gas chamber.[21]

Between November 1942 and March 1943, the Germans emptied 116 villages in the Lublin region, 47 of them in Zamosc alone. In one month beginning on November 27, the Germans expected to nab 34,000 people from 60 villages, but they succeeded in seizing only 9,771 residents; the remainder escaped into nearby woods. The Germans stubbornly resumed the expulsions in June and July, 1943, clearing 171 villages in the districts of Bilgoraj, Tomaszow, Zamosc, and Hrubieszow. By August, 1943, 110,000 Poles had been expelled, constituting 31 percent of the inhabitants of the Zamosc region.[22]

Pacification raids sometimes accompanied the expulsions,

often resulting in fires that took the lives of many people. In Kidow, the Polish underground reported the murder of 170 farmers by the Germans.[23] So systematic were the Germans in clearing some places that only cattle were left to wander in the fields. Simultaneously with the Zamosc operation, the Polish government reported mass deportations of men, women and children from the Bialystok area. By the end of January, 1943, the Poles claimed that 40,000 residents had been deported from that area.[24]

The majority of Poles, understandably panic stricken that they would be exterminated as the Jews had been in similar deportation operations, abandoned their homes and property and fled to the forests. In one village, two people stayed; all the others fled.[25]

The major Polish underground military organization, the AK, had no partisan units yet in the region and could not respond immediately to the German actions. But the AK chief, General Stefan Grot-Rowecki, ordered a general increase in resistance activity, especially a widening of Polish diversionary operations against the Germans. The Polish government in London feared that these operations would get so out of hand that they might prematurely lead to a general armed uprising, which was supposed to occur only when the Germans were at the point of imminent collapse on the eastern front.[26]

Germanization of the Zamosc region was no more successful than it had been in the Wartheland. Rather than leave anything of value to German colonists, Poles burned their houses, barns and movable property, much like the Russian kulaks did during Stalin's collectivization campaign, and fled into the woods. Other Polish farmers chose to resist; one group attacked German settlers in Cieszyn and killed 30 of them. Polish attacks led, of course, to German reprisals. The Polish attack on Cieszyn so enraged Himmler that he personally ordered the annihilation of entire Polish villages.[27]

German reprisals did not deter the AK and other underground military groups from continuing their attacks on new German settlements. In June, 1943, the AK boldly attacked a German village in which 69 inhabitants died.[28] "If the bloodthirsty occupant intends to try on us the same experiment as on the Jews," one Polish underground newspaper declared, "he will first have to withdraw an army from the front."[29]

Polish retaliatory operations widened to include attacks on railroad, military and government targets. Shortly after the Germans initiated the Zamosc operation, the *AK* attacked a railroad bridge on the Lublin-Lwow line. Within a month, the *AK* had become sufficiently strong to launch 60 sabotage and diversionary operations in the Zamosc area. The People's Guard, known as the *GL* after its Polish name, was a Communist military group which also conducted operations in the area. The Peasant Battalions, known as the *BcH* after its Polish name and later a part of the *AK*, also operated in the area.[30] These operations, combined with the German defeat at Kursk, the greatest tank battle in modern times, forced the Nazis to abandon efforts to Germanize the General Government.

"We used to be Germans. But we are Poles now. In a few weeks you will get to like it too," a young Germanized Polish boy told another youngster at a Displaced Persons camp after the war.[31] His words revealed what had happened to thousands of Polish boys and girls who constituted the largest group of European children whom the Nazis attempted to denationalize during the Second World War.

For all their racist propaganda about the alleged inferiority of the Poles, Nazi leaders were amazed by the number of Polish children who possessed the Nordic features which they regarded as so desirable. "When we see a blue-eyed child we are surprised that she is speaking Polish.... if we were to bring up this child in a German spirit, she will grow up as a beautiful German girl. I admit that in Poland one can find German racial traits among the people and with caring and development will give us Germans in the course of time a possibility to destroy this part of the General Government," Hans Frank said.[32]

To Nazi fanatics like Frank, this alleged Teutonic blood had to be recovered even if it meant kidnapping racially desirable children from orphanages, hospitals, homes and schools. To Hitler and his cronies, Germanization was as important in determining the future of the German nation as military victories against the Allies. "What the nations offer in the way of good blood of our type, we will take, if necessary by kidnapping their children and raising them here with us," Himmler declared. It was all part of the ongoing struggle between German and Slav. "It is a mere nothing today to shoot 10 Poles, compared with the fact that we might later have to shoot tens of thousands in their place, and compared to the fact that the shooting of these tens of thousands would be carried out even at the cost of German blood."[33]

The Nazis established an elaborate classification of persons considered to have German blood, and it contained provisions concerning the rights and duties of people in each classification. Called the Racial Register (*Volksliste*), the list classified people into four categories. Class I included Germans who before the war had promoted the Nazi cause. Class II were Germans who had been passive in the Nazi struggle but retained their German nationality. Class III included people of German extraction who had been previously connected with the Polish nation but were willing to submit to Germanization; this category also included Germans living in a mixed marriage—either with a Polish man or woman—and the children of these unions. Class IV were people of German descent who had become Polonized and resisted Germanization.[34] People eligible for classification on the *Volksliste* but refused inclusion were treated harshly. Usually the Germans deported them to the Reich or to a concentration camp.

Not only were children of ethnic Germans or mixed Polish-German families who met the criteria for the *Volksliste* Germanized but also children of Polish families were subjected to the process. The Germanization of Polish children began but was not limited to the annexed lands. A special Nazi agency for racial matters, the Race and Resettlement Office (*RuSHA*), established branch offices where they screened and classified prospective Poles to be made into Germans.

Himmler, acting in his capacity as Reich Commissioner for the Strengthening of German Folkdom, early in the war talked about selecting racially valuable Polish children for Germanization. Shortly before the German invasion of the Soviet Union, Himmler thought "it right that young children of especially good race belonging to Polish families should be apprehended and brought up by us in special creches and children's homes which are not too large." Acceptable children would be turned over to childless couples "of good race."[35] By February, 1942,

Nazi policy had evolved to the point that Ulrich Greifelt, Himmler's henchman who headed the SS in Poland, authorized taking children from Polish orphanages and foster parents, subjecting them to a series of examinations and tests and Germanizing those "recognized as worthy blood bearers for the *Deutschtum* [Germany]." Those children capable of Germanization, who were 6- to 12-years-old, Greifelt ordered, would be taken to Nazi boarding schools while younger children would be farmed out to German families by the *Lebensborn* [Well of Life].[36]

In a curious contradictory reversal of racist ideology, the Nazis assumed that Polish children with Nordic features were automatically German because the child and his family had been alleged products of the process of Polonization. The same bizarre logic was applied to the Polish intelligentsia, who led the Polish resistance movement. To the Nazis, these leaders were largely Nordic which enabled them "To be active in contrast to the fatalistic Slavonic elements."[37] The implication was obvious: If the Polish elite were re-Germanized, then the mass of Polish people would be denied a dynamic leadership class.

The Nazis culled every available source to gather Polish children who met their racial criteria for Germanization. They abducted Polish children from orphanages, foster parents, parents who refused to sign the *Volksliste*, and parents or guardians who had been either murdered or sent to forced labor or to concentration camps. They also abducted children from unmarried Polish women working as forced laborers in Germany, through periodic roundups and from special operations of the Zamosc type. Moreover, the Germans had an existing pool of candidates for Germanization in the large number of Polish youngsters who worked as forced laborers in the Reich.[38]

Some of the kidnapping operations relied heavily upon the notorious Brown Sisters, women dressed in Victorian style brown uniforms. These women, a female version of the Brown Shirts, were members of the NSV (Nazi Welfare Organization), originally established in 1933 to look after the welfare of the German people. Working through their Youth Office, the Brown Sisters operated throughout Europe. Completely dedicated to

Hitler, these fanatical women, described as "stony-hearted robots," literally robbed Polish women of their children.[39]

They prowled villages and towns in Poland and other eastern European countries where they searched for fairhaired, blue-eyed children. Using candy and even slices of bread as lures to attract boys and girls, the Brown Sisters used the opportunity to question the youngster about his or her parents and siblings. After gleaning all the information they could from the child, the Brown Sisters checked town hall records on the family and if this preliminary search promised racially desirable results, the child would be taken from the home, usually at night, and never heard from again.[40]

The SS and other Nazi agencies also acquired Nordic-looking children in concentration camps. At Auschwitz, the SS selected several children for Germanization. Before being sent to Germany, the children were placed in quarantine. Polish inmate physicians tried to get as many of the children out of quarantine by diagnosing some bogus illness. "We diagnosed whooping cough or some nasty rash made its appearance. This was a pink plaster, cut skillfully and glued to the child's skin, that looked like a rash," Dr. Janina Kosciuszkowa said. The chief medical officer at Auschwitz, Dr. Mengele, wasn't easily fooled, but Dr. Kosciuszkowa said, "He was terrified of a rash and to our joy he sent the children back from quarantine." Unfortunately, many Polish children rescued from Germanization died at Auschwitz. But, of those who survived, Dr. Kosciuszkowa said, "When we now meet those youngsters, now already adults, we welcome each other like members of one's family."[41]

After seizing the children, the Germans sent them to one of a number of establishments—located in Poznan, Kalisz, Pruszkow, Bruczkow or Ludwikow—where the children were subjected to a number of racial, medical and psychological tests to determine their suitability for Germanization. The Nazis established a system of eleven racial types. Those who tested the youngsters used forms which contained 62 points. The examination placed heavy emphasis on physical traits: arms, legs and heads were carefully measured. Even the size of a girl's pelvis and the boy's penis was considered important for reproductive purposes.[42]

Ideally, the Nazi racial experts preferred to transnationalize children no older than 8- to 10-years-old, but even this criterion was watered down to include teenagers over 17 years. During the racial selection process, the Nazis placed the children in three categories: they were considered a desirable, tolerable or undesirable increase to the population. The object of the tests was not to establish the German descent of the candidate, but rather to select children with sound physical and mental qualities.[43] That is why Polish and other Slavic children were so vulnerable to the Germanization process.

In addition to racial considerations, the experts attached great importance to the impression the child made. Thirteen-year-old Wojciech Wysocki, described as "Eastern Nordic" by the German experts, was considered "very promising" for Germanization because of his calm, candid appearance. Agnieszka Miszewska was also considered promising because she not only was mentally able but also made a good impression. A Polish child might meet Nazi racial and medical tests but if he or she displayed so-called "negative" character traits—i.e., was unwilling to accept their new nationality—they were dropped from the Germanization program.[44] The feverish pace of these examinations can be seen in the large number of them that were conducted right up to the end of the war. In Lublin alone, between February, 1940, and September, 1941, the Germans conducted over 4,000 examinations.[45]

Children selected for Germanization ended up in schools or institutions run by a number of Nazi organizations before they became available for adoption by German families. Younger children usually came under the supervision of the *Lebensborn* [Well of Life]. Originally established in 1935 to provide maternity facilities for the wives and girl friends of the SS and police establishment, *Lebensborn* broadened its activities to include the Germanization of kidnapped children.

The Nazis tried to conceal what they did by emphasizing secrecy and even taking circuitous routes to Germanization centers to cover their tracks. They repeatedly used euphemisms to try to give respectability to their activity. "Polish children" became "Polonized German children" or "Children of German descent" or even "German orphans." To allay suspicions of parents or guardians, the Germans told them that the children would be sent to schools or rest homes.[46]

The core of the Germanization process was to destroy the Polish identity of the boys and girls. Barbara Mikolajczyk was an adolescent when the Germans took her and her sisters to Bruczkow, where the Nazis forced them to learn German. "The Germans always said that we must forget about speaking in Polish and about Poland," Mikolajczyk said. They beat her and the other children when they spoke Polish. Mikolajczyk now became Baber Mickler. Placed in a German home, she had to address a German woman as "Mama." Like other Polish children doled out to German households, Mikolajczyk received a fraudulent birth certificate and genealogy which the Germans inventively composed for her.[47]

When a child received a German name, often a number of the initial letters of the Polish name were preserved—Sosnowska became Sosemann, Witaszek Wittke, Kawczynski Kancmann. Apparently, the intention was to allow the two names to blend in the memory of the child so that the original name would be forgotten. Often the children got names which corresponded phonetically to their Polish names—Piatek became Pionteck, Jesionek Jeschonnek. Finally, some new names were German translations of the Polish—Ogrodowczyk was Gartner, Mlynarczyk Muller.[48]

The Nazis examined Jan Sulisz, a Polish orphan, at Bruczkow and placed him in a school attended by German children. Forced to join the Nazi youth group *Hitlerjugend*, he, too, was cut off from his Polish roots. Interestingly, Sulisz, whose new name was Suhling, met Barbara Mikolajczyk and her sisters at a Germanization center in Salsburg. The SS gave Suhling to a German business establishment from which he escaped. Unfortunately, he was caught and beaten. He survived the war to be reunited with relatives in Lodz. A similar thing happened to Willi Nililek, who was sent to work in a German factory. When he and his friends were caught speaking Polish, Nililek said, "They stuck us in the arms and back with needles. I was sick. The other two boys went crazy and were given 'death pills.'"[49]

Despite the severe penalties involved, many Polish children continued to speak Polish. Jerzy Stickel, sent to a German institution in Ujazdow where he was treated as a German youth, was one of them. After the war, when Stickel learned he was Polish, German children got so angry with him they beat him up.[50] In one institution, older Polish children used to wake up younger ones at night to use the Polish language and especially to recite their prayers so they wouldn't forget their heritage.[51] "I could not reconcile myself to denying my nationality, so I went on talking Polish," said Sigismund Krajeski, who was 10-years-old when the Germans sent him to Gmunden, Austria. "For this I was often tied to a post and beaten, but as I was strong and refused to give in, I managed to stand it." When German families came to the institution to select a child for themselves, Krajeski deliberately spoke Polish. "Of course the resulting punishment was dreadful, but I preferred it to disgracing myself and going to a Hitler family. They had no success with me." Indeed, they didn't. Krajeski ran away and managed to return to his home in Poznan.[52]

There were several escapes from the Nazi Germanization center at Kalisz, where the Germans appropriated a monastery from Polish monks to set up their racist school. According to Stanislaw Kulczinski, known as "Papa Stanislaw," a handyman there, the Germans brought thousands of children to Kalisz. Those who refused Germanization were beaten and deprived of food. Zygmunt Swiatlowski, stubbornly refusing denationalization, was killed by the woman supervisor of the institution. "The children were always sad," Papa Stanislaw said. "They lived in fear and were homesick, and the German supervisors felt nothing but hatred for them because they were nothing but little 'Polacks' and did not belong to them."

One day he befriended a little girl, Christina, and gave her some candy and homemade toys which she later shared with her friends. Shortly thereafter, Papa Stanislaw met a woman who had traced her daughter to Kalisz. He agreed to help Christina escape from the institution but the problem was how to arrange it. "At last we found a way on the day when the Germans wanted to have a load of waste paper dumped at the public refuse pit outside," he said. He hid Christina under the paper; her mother anxiously waited near the pit to take her daughter home. Christina was the first Polish child to escape successfully from Kalisz. Others would follow, many with the help of Papa Stanislaw.[53]

Unfortunately, most children could not escape from Kalisz. Ryszard Tloczynski was one of several youngsters from Rogoz who, after satisfying the Nazi examiners that he was a promising candidate for Germanization, went to Kalisz and spent several months there. After that, the Germans placed him in an SS kindergarten at Oberweiss where German families selected the children they wanted to adopt. Spared adoption because he worked in the school kitchen most of the time, Tloczynski was liberated by American troops and looked after by Polish-American soldiers at the end of the war.[54]

Bronislawa Ewertowska's daughter, Eufenia, 7-years-old when the Germans kidnapped her, was not as fortunate as Tloczynski. Like hundreds of other Polish children, Eufenia was indoctrinated at Kalisz, and then sent to Austria where she ended up in a German household. She never returned to Poland.[55] A similar fate occurred to Agnieszka Klimczak's 4-year-old daughter, Teresa. Klimczak possessed Category III status on the *Volksliste* but preferred to raise Teresa and her son as Poles. For that, the Nazis took the children away. One day Klimczak spotted her daughter and took her back, but the Nazis seized her again. The Germans imprisoned Klimczak for one year. Meanwhile, all traces of her children disappeared.[56]

Some Polish children were so completely Germanized that after the war, they chose to remain in Germany. Jan Chrzanowski, first examined when he was less than 1-year-old, was an ideal candidate because of his youth and, according to his German examiner, was a "harmonious blend of Nordic and East Baltic types." Chrzanowski's German foster mother wanted his name changed immediately. "She objects to having to register him everywhere under his Polish name," the German medical examiner reported. So completely Germanized, Chrzanowski refused to return to his mother in Poland because the only mother he really ever knew was his German parent.[57]

There were stubborn Poles who managed to hide their children from Nazi kidnappers. After Irena Nowak learned that it was likely the Nazis would take 6-year-old Konrad and his younger brother, Waclaw, she hid one of the boys and sent the other to relatives in Poznan.[58] Janina Kowalska did the same thing. Her son Franciszek had been spotted by the Brown

Sisters who commented how German he looked. When Franciszek told his mother, she hastily left her village and lived with cousins until the end of the war. Zenona Strozyk, an elementary school girl, remembered how Germans would often stop her and comment upon her fair complexion and blue eyes. She never gave any of them a chance to talk very long; she would stick her tongue out at them and run away.[59]

Some adolescents, not adopted by German families, ended up at camps in Grodkow and Cieszyn which housed boys 8 to 19. Intense Germanization of these youngsters was a prelude to their conscription, usually after turning 17, into the Wehrmacht. Discipline was extremely severe. Fifteen-year-old Henryk Kramarczyk recalled being locked up in solitary confinement and beaten to the point of losing consciousness by his Nazi "educators." Younger boys became *Hitlerjugend*. Thus the Nazis prepared to train Germanized Poles as an army of 20th century Janissaries to fight for them.[60]

Polish boys, who were neither adopted nor placed in the *Hitlerjugend* nor the Wehrmacht, were sent to work in German factories. Young Polish girls ended up in the *Bund Deutscher Madel*; some may even have become candidates for breeding children in SS maternity homes.[61]

The Nazis even agonized over how much Jewish blood in a family's line was sufficient to contaminate German blood. As late as May, 1943, when Nazi military fortunes had worsened following the debacle at the Battle of Stalingrad, Himmler wrote to the Nazi Party secretary Martin Bormann, supporting racial examinations "not only in quarter-Jews but also in persons with even less Jewish blood. We must follow a similar procedure to that which is used in breeding plants and animals, but this must remain between us." He believed that children of such mixed marriages had to be racially examined and if the results indicated racial inferiority, the youngsters should be sterilized.[62] Himmler, who followed specific so-called "racial cases," often gave detailed instructions concerning the disposition of the Polish families and children involved. In one case, Brunhilde Muszynska's children, 4-and 7-years-old, were considered possible candidates for Germanization but when Himmler discovered Muszynska had Jewish blood, he ordered her arrest and the sterilization of her children.[63]

There seems to be general agreement that 200,000 Polish children were deported for Germanization purposes. Not all were Germanized. But only 15-20 percent of the children kidnapped by the Germans were recovered at war's end.[64] Some parents and relatives are still looking for their children.

Chapter Notes

1. *Trials of War Criminals before the Nuernberg Military Tribunals Under Control Council Law No. 10. Nuernberg, October 1946-April 1949* (15 vols.; Washington, D.C.: Government Printing Office, 1949-53), V, 91. Hereinafter cited as *TWC.*

2. Kamenetsky, *Secret Nazi Plans*, pp. 51-52; Report, Office of Strategic Services, May 31, 1943, in RG 226, OSS/NA; *TWC*, V, 92-93.

3. Kamenetsky, *Secret Nazi Plans*, p. 55.

4. Polish Research Center, *German Failures in Poland* (London: 1942), pp. 13-15, 28.

5. *Ibid.*, p. 18.

6. Central Commission, *German Crimes in Poland*, I, 33; Madajczyk, *Polityka III Rzeszy*, I, pp. 125ff.

7. *TWC*, 864-65.

8. *Ibid.*; U.S. Counsel, *Nazi Conspiracy and Aggression*, II, 641; Czeslaw Madajczyk, "Generalplan Ost," *Polish Western Affairs*, III, (1962), 397, 399.

9. Hrabar, *Fate of Polish Children*, p. 51.

10. Duraczynski, *Wojna i Okupacja*, pp. 393-96.

11. Memo, undated, in WR/22/18, PAG-4/2.0.62: Box 15, UNRRA/UNA; Hrabar, *Fate of Polish Children*, p. 60.

12. Gumkowski and Leszczynski, *Poland Under Nazi Occupation*, p. 154; Central Commission, *German Crimes in Poland*, II, 81.

13. Pilichowski, *Zbrodnie Hitlerowskie*, p. 17.

14. Aide Memoire, Appendix, August 5, 1943, in FO 371/34550, PRO.

15. *Ibid.*; Meldunek, Rowecki do Centrali, March 12, 1943, and Depesza, Delegat Rzadu i D-ca AK do N.W. i Min. Mikolajczyka, April 3, 1943, in *AKwD*, II, 479, 488; Depesza Prokurator do Komendy Powiatowej Milicji Obywatelskiej, August 21, 1946, in Kolekcja Z, 187/I-178, AGKBZHP; Macardle, *Children of Europe*, pp. 75-76.

16. Raport, CKOS, Alexsandra Swiecka in Kolekcja Z, 187/I-132V, AGKBZHP.

17. Jan Dobraczynski, *Tylko w Jednym Zyciu: Wspomnienia* (Warsaw: Instytut Wydawniczy Pax, 1977), p. 240; Pilichowski, *Zbrodnie Hitlerowskie*, p. 14.

18. Wyciag z Protokolu, Kazimierz Wdzieczny, November 14, 1945, in Kolekcja Z, 187/I-4, AGKBZHP.

19. Kazimierz Smolen, "Dzieci i Mlodziez w Obozach Koncentracyjnych," in Pilichowski, *Dzieci i Mlodziez*, pp. 129-30; International Auschwitz Committee *Nazi Medicine*, pp. 104-105.

20. Gumkowski and Leszczynski, *Poland Under Nazi Occupation*, p. 157.

21. Wnuk, *Dzieci Polskie Oskarzaja*, p. 110; Smolen, "Dzieci i Mlodziez w Obozach Koncentracyjnych," p. 130; International Auschwitz Committee, *Nazi Medicine*, III, 221. According to Polish physicians, 35,000 people died as a result of phenol injections at Auschwitz. *Ibid.* 67.

22. Central Commission, *German Crimes in Poland*, II, 70-73.

23. Depesza, Kierownictwo Walki Cywilnej do Mikolajczyka, December 23, 1942, in *AKwD*, II, 394.

24. Aide Memoire, Appendix, August 5, 1943.

25. U. S. Counsel, *Nazi Conspiracy and Aggression*, IV, 916; Meldunek Zbiorowy, Rowecki do Centrali, January 21, 1943, in *AKwD*, II, 405.

26. There is an extensive correspondence on this subject between underground officials in Poland and Polish government leaders in London. See PRM 76/1, PRM 105/4, and PRM/K 102/54A-J, in PI/GSHM.

27. Depesza, Rowecki do Centrali, January 29, 1943, in *AKwD*, II, 407; *TWC*, IV, 871-72.

28. Komisja Historyczna Polskiego Sztabu Glownego w Londynie, *Polskie Sily Zbrojne w Drugiej Wojnie Swiatowej*, Vol. III: *Armia Krajowa* (London: Instytut Historyczny im. Gen. Sikorskiego, 1950), 478.

29. *Zywia i Bronia*, February, 1943.

30. Duraczynski, *Wojna i Okupacja*, pp. 400-403.

31. Quotations from Returning Europe's Kidnapped Children, (Exhibit 27), History of Child Welfare, in PAG-4/4.2; Box 81, UNRRA/UNA.

32. Pilichowski, *Zbrodnie Hitlerowskie*, p. 18.

33. U.S. Counsel, *Nazi Conspiracy and Aggression*, IV, 559-60.

34. *Ibid.*, I, 103ff; *TWC*, IV, 715-16.

35. Dokument Nr. 3, Himmler do Greisera, June 18, 1941, in Glowna Komisja Badania Zbrodni Hitlerowskich w Polsce, *Zbrodnie Hitlerowskie*, p. 146.

36. Anordung Nr. 67/I, February 19, 1942, Z/Ot, 1056, 282V, in AGKBZHP.

37. *TWC*, IV, 767.

38. Hrabar, *Hitlerowski Rabunek*, pp. 50ff, Wnuk, *Dzieci Polskie Oskarzaja*, pp. 7-8.

39. Clarissa Henry and Marc Hillel, *Children of the SS*. Translated by Eric Mosbacher (London: Hutchinson and Co., 1975), pp. 155-56.

40. *Ibid.* pp. 156-57.

41. International Auschwitz Committee, *Nazi Medicine*, III, 223-24.

42. Hrabar, *Fate of Polish Children*, p. 112; Wnuk, *Dzieci Polskie Oskarzaja*, p. 8; Henry and Hillel, *Children of the SS*, p. 153. Other racial centers included: Buszkowo, Chelm Lubelski, Dzialdowo, Dzierzazania, Glogow, Gorzyce Wielkie, Kietrz, Korfantow, Lubawa, Lubliniec, Oterow, Polczyn, Potulice, Puszczykowo, Raciborz, Rusinowo, Zamosc, Zwierzyny, Zary.

43. Hrabar, *Fate of Polish Children*, p. 135.

44. *Ibid.*, pp. 135-36.

45. Sprawozdanie, December 15, 1941, z/Ot-1050/293-4, in AGKBZHP.

46. Depesza, Bader do Namiestnika Warthegau w Poznaniu, Z/ot-1056/291-92, in AGKBZHP; Gumkowski and Leszczynski, *Poland Under Nazi Occupation*, p. 166.

47. Wnuk, *Dzieci Polskie Oskarzaja*, p. 60.

48. Gumkowski and Leszczynski, *Poland Under German Occupation*, p. 176; Hrabar, *Fate of Polish Children*, pp. 135-37.

49. Wnuk, *Dzieci Polskie Oskarzaja*, pp. 61-62; Quotations from Returning Europe's Kidnapped Children.

50. Wnuk, *Dzieci Polskie Oskarzaja*, p. 31.

51. S. Sawicka, "Zbrodnaia Niemiecka nad Dzieckim Polskim," *Przeglad Zachodni*, No. 9 (1947), 736.

52. Henry and Hillel, *Children of the SS*, pp. 159-60.

53. *Ibid.* pp. 161-63.

54. Protokol Przesluchania Swiadka, Ryszard Tloczynski, May 18, 1946, NTN 27/123-123v, in AGKBZHP.

55. Protokol Przesluchania Swiadka, Bronislawa Ewertowska, May 18, 1946, NTN, 27, in AGKBZHP.

56. Wnuk, *Dzieci Polskie Oskarzaja*, p. 46.

57. Henry and Hillel, *Children of the SS*, p. 170.

58. Protokol Przesluchania Swiadka, Irena Nowak, May 16, 1946, NTN, 27/120-120v, in AGKBZHP.

59. Interview with Pelagia Lukaszewska, September 22, 1992; Zenona Strozyk, "W Krakowie i Gdzie Indziej," in Turski, *Byli Wowczas Dziecmi*, p. 232.

60. Pilichowski, *Zbrodnie Hitlerowskie*, pp. 20-21; Hrabar, *Fate of Polish Children*, pp. 92-93.

61. Konnilyn Feig, "Non-Jewish Victims in the Concentration Camps," in Michael Berenbaum (ed.), *A Mosaic of Victims: Non-Jews Persecuted and Murdered by the Nazis* (New York: New York University Press, 1990), p. 166.

62. Benno Muller-Hill, *Murderous Science: Elimination by Scientific Selection of Jews, Gypsies and Others* (Oxford: Oxford University Press, 1988), p. 53n.

63. Wnuk, *Dzieci Polskie Oskarzaja*, p. 14.

64. Glowna Komisja Badania Zbrodni Hitlerowskich w Polsce, *Zbrodnie Hitlerowskie*, p. xxiv.

Chapter V

Resistance

POLISH AND JEWISH youth played a major role in the resistance movement against the Germans in Poland. That movement was often bitterly divided, reflecting various political and ideological orientations among Poles and Jews. In addition, the prewar differences and suspicions that had divided Poles and Jews continued during the occupation and the forced separation of the two groups by the Germans unfortunately prevented close cooperation between them against their common enemy.

Virtually all Polish and Jewish political and military organizations in occupied Poland had youth groups that actively contributed in the struggle against the Germans. Polish and Jewish children were involved in wide-ranging resistance activities; they did everything from acting as underground couriers and conducting small sabotage to fighting the Germans in military operations.

By far the largest and most important military organization of the underground conspiracy in wartime Poland was the *Armia Krajowa* (Home Army), or *AK*, first headed by General Stefan Grot-Rowecki and, after his arrest by the Germans, by General Tadeusz Bor-Komorowski. The *AK* was an umbrella organization that incorporated a plethora of military groups with different political views. Bor-Komorowski himself described his organization as "a conglomeration of commanders and detachments, whose attitudes to one another are frequently undisguisedly hostile, and who are held together only by a badly frayed thread of formal discipline that may snap at the start of active operations."[1]

Although the *AK* swelled to almost 400,000 officers and men by the first half of 1944, only a small portion of the organization conducted active military operations against the Germans while the bulk of the *AK* was immobile. Limited finances and scarce weapons forced the *AK* command to downsize its operations against the Germans. At one point, only 10,000 out of 250,000 soldiers of the *AK* were armed to a reasonable degree. One high-ranking officer commented in early 1944 that the average *AK* soldier considered himself well armed if he had a personal weapon of any kind; even a few hand grenades counted as a personal weapon.[2]

Because only a small portion of the *AK* engaged the Germans at any time, it is easy to understand why the organization limited itself to intelligence, sabotage-diversionary and reprisal operations. The *AK* could not undertake large-scale operations to liberate great numbers of Poles and Jews from prisons and concentration camps. The *AK*, like the populace at large, was helpless in preventing the Germans from rounding up Poles for forced labor, reprisals and executions. It was even more at a loss to help Jews who were difficult to contact in the ghettos, let alone free. Besides, most Jews in the ghettos followed the leadership of the *Judenrats* (Jewish Councils) which opposed active resistance against the Germans.

The *AK*'s primary role was not to engage the Germans in a series of small operations which invited savage reprisals and sapped the strength of the organization. Rather, the leadership prepared the *AK* for an eventual uprising which would be launched only when German power in the East crumbled and the Poles could assert their military and political authority over their own country.[3]

All shades of political opinion, except the extreme left and extreme right, could be found in the *AK*. The Communists, considered traitors by most Poles, organized the *Gwardia Ludowa* (People's Guard) or *GL*, later known as the *Armia Ludowa* (People's Army) or *AL*. The extreme right rallied around the *Narodowe Siły Zbrojne* (National Armed Forces) or *NSZ*, who not only killed Germans, but also attacked Jews, for which the *AK* was often mistakenly blamed. The *NSZ* also vented their anti-leftist views by killing Poles suspected of left-wing sympathies.

The primary difference between the *AK* and the *GL/AL* was the fact that each group had a different political vision concerning what it wanted to see in Poland after Germany's defeat. The *AK*, loyal to the Polish government-in-exile, expected to fill the military and political void in Poland left by the collapse of the German empire and to establish a moderate democratic government. The Communists wanted to prevent that from happening and instead to pave the way for a Polish government favorable to Moscow which, of course, is what ultimately happened. The differences were so deep and bitter that each side killed members of the other group. "One thing is certain," an American report at the time said, "the Germans are helped by the lack of unity in the underground and by the basic fact that each side has other aims than fighting the Germans."[4]

Polish teenagers constituted the core of the underground resistance in Poland. That there was a conspicuous absence of boys and girls in the 16-20 age bracket in Warsaw was due to the fact that they were involved in conspiracy against the Germans and had to maintain a low profile. Though there were many exceptions, boys and girls under 16 to 18 years of age ordinarily did not participate in combat operations against the Germans.[5] They usually were involved in non-combatant roles—serving as couriers, distributing the underground press, cleaning and storing weapons, and helping escapees from the Germans find hiding places.

These activities carried considerable risks. Maria Radecka, arrested and sent to the Lukiszki prison on suspicion she was an underground courier, remembered how much 16- and 17-year-old couriers of the *AK* suffered in the cell next to hers. "Nothing was pleasant," she wrote about prison life at Lukiszki, "from the poignant graffiti on the cell walls telling of the torture and giving dates of their writers' executions (the Germans never quite succeeded in obliterating them)...."[6] Franciszek Kopec, no more than 16-years-old at the time, served as a messenger for partisans operating near his home. The Germans arrested a member of the underground and under torture revealed Kopec's name. Beaten and deprived of food, Kopec was later sent to Auschwitz.[7]

Prior to the Warsaw Uprising of 1944, the underground activity in which Polish youngsters were most visibly involved was "small sabotage," a euphemism Poles used to describe diversionary-propaganda work. Developed by the head of the Polish Scouting movement, Alexsander Kaminski," small sabotage was primarily, though not exclusively, conducted by hundreds of Boy Scouts, organized in a conspiratorial group called *Wawer*. The group took its name from the village of Wawer where in December, 1939, the Germans murdered scores of Poles. Even though the Germans were responsible for countless other atrocities, Poles never forgot *Wawer*, which became something of a battle cry for Poles never to stop their resistance against the Germans.

Wawer conducted an impressive number of activities against the Germans. Young boys threw acid bombs at the Germans, tore down German flags and replaced them with Polish colors, placed flowers on Polish memorials, painted Polish symbols for resistance on buildings and walls, sent fictitious orders to German units which caused confusion in their ranks, and distributed anti-German leaflets to demoralize German soldiers and civilians in Poland. On several occasions they substituted the word *Verloren* (Lost) where the Germans had written *Victoria* (Won) to describe their military exploits. One time the Scouts rewrote a German propaganda poster that read "Germany conquers on all fronts" to read "Germany is prostrate on all fronts."[8] These young rascals did much to maintain Polish morale and foster the spirit of resistance. Almost every day pedestrians in Warsaw and other Polish cities wryly smiled at some new mischief for which these boys and girls were responsible.

Varsovians chuckled when the Scouts unscrewed a tablet with German writing from a monument of the famous astronomer Copernicus, and replaced it with one that read sardonically, "In retaliation for the destruction of the Kilinski statue (by the Germans), I order an extension of winter for six weeks. Nicholas Copernicus, Astronomer." General Bor-Komorowski remarked, "Strangely enough the winter that year did last much longer than usual and caused a severe setback to the German plans for a spring offensive on the eastern front."[9]

The Scouts targeted the German cinema in Poland and urged

Poles not to attend the low quality, propagandistic and sometimes pornographic films. The slogan "Only Pigs Sit in the Cinema" appeared frequently and there was no doubt who was responsible for it. They extended their campaign to the theaters themselves by exploding stink-bombs during performances. "We worked in pairs," Zbigniew Bokiewicz remembered. "While one dropped a bomb from the balcony into the stalls, the other sat downstairs and tried to create as much panic as possible when the bomb went off, hoping to clear the cinema." During one of these escapades, Bokiewicz, who had just acquired a new hat, went downstairs while his partner went to the balcony. "Unfortunately he threw the stink-bomb straight into my hat. I was furious. I gave such full vent to my feelings that the cinema emptied in three minutes. My hat, of course, was ruined."[10]

It was impossible for the Germans to keep up with the number of children and young adults who were involved in the underground conspiracy against them. The story of Jadzia, a young Polish girl, is rather typical of Polish youth during the German occupation of Poland. By day, Jadzia was a student; by night, a conspirator. Jadzia's apartment had become a "joint," a meeting place for young people involved in the conspiracy where the clandestine press was divided for distribution, arms and ammunition were hidden, and boys who had been forced to leave their homes found temporary shelter.

One evening Jadzia and other young people turned their cares away from conspiracy to partying. They turned up the volume on their record player and the noise brought several armed German soldiers up the stairs to her apartment. Fear gripped everyone in the room because closets and drawers contained enough incriminating evidence of their involvement in the underground for the Germans to execute them.

"Why do you gentlemen want to hurt me?" Jadzia cooed like a child in broken German. "Don't you see, gentlemen, that this is my birthday—aren't we allowed to dance a little on this occasion?" The German officer rebuked her for not having a special permit for such a large gathering of young people. She graciously invited the officer in charge and his men to have some liquor. "We don't have time, we must go elsewhere," he said, tempted by the offer. After a cursory look around the apartment, the Germans left and even wished her and her guests a good time.[11]

There were numerous Polish children who, like Jewish boys and girls, operated with partisans and participated directly or indirectly in combat roles. During school breaks, 14-year-old Henryk Fafara and his school chums used to talk about the fabled activities of guerrilla units operating in the Kielce area and they fantasized about being with them in their operations against the Germans.[12]

Fafara, like many young boys his age, identified with the legendary Major Henryk Hubal (Dobrzanski) who was considered by some to be the founder of the Polish partisan movement. Within a few months following Poland's surrender in 1939, Hubal organized hundreds of peasants and workers in a partisan unit that operated against the Germans. Several children and many teenagers were reported in the group. In the opinion of the *AK*, however, Hubal's operations did more harm than good, provoking savage German reprisals. General Rowecki tried to deter Hubal from continuing his attacks on the Germans, but this fiercely independent leader stubbornly refused to submit to Rowecki's authority. Although Germans killed him in the spring of 1940, Hubal's legend lived on to inspire Polish youngsters like Fafara throughout the war.[13]

Fafara took the first step toward his life as a partisan when he spotted a German motorcycle and destroyed it by throwing rocks at it. Finally, one day Fafara decided to join the partisans. He wrote a note to his parents, cut a piece of bread and salt pork for the road and left home in search of partisans. After two days of wandering aimlessly, he stumbled upon an *AL* unit whose commander introduced him to his soldiers, saying, "See for yourselves, our nation has had enough of the occupier; even children flock to the war. Here we have a new partisan."

Just as Fafara began to learn about weaponry, his mother suddenly appeared and appealed to the commander to release her son because of his extreme youth. Dejected, Fafara was told to return when he turned 16. But he couldn't wait that long. Again he left home, looking for the same unit but instead he found an *AK* group. To his surprise some of the same men in the first unit now fought with the *AK*. In a sense it was like a homecoming. Despite his youth, the *AK* accepted him and gave him the nickname "Little Falcon," by which he was known for the remainder of the war.[14]

The life of Waclaw Milewski, a young teenager and member of the *AK*, reflected the civilian character of most members of the *AK*. Milewski worked in a sugar beet factory in the Kielce region during the week, but on weekends trained with his unit. "On Friday after work, we all set out on a long march to the mountains. About dusk, we reached a village where our weapons were hidden," Milewski said. "And we then marched throughout the night, arriving at the summit of the Holy Cross Mountains at dawn. There, full scale training took place. We participated in drills of all kinds and even shot our weapons on a rifle range." Surprisingly, Milewski and his friends behaved as if there were no German army in Poland. After the completion of maneuvers on Sunday evening, members of the unit returned home, ready to go to work the next morning. Milewski's unit later ambushed some Germans who, in turn, attacked the unit's camp where everyone who was there, including boys as young as 12-years-old, were killed.[15]

"I thought he would become a priest some day. He was so pious," Father Jan Januszewski said about Staszek, who was no more than 15-years-old when he was seized by the Brown Sisters for Germanization. He escaped two times from German schools and managed to return home. When he learned his parents had been arrested for their role in the underground, he sought out relatives in Warsaw where he made contact with the *AK*. By early 1943, he found himself in eastern Poland operating with an *AK* unit. Although Staszek participated in combat missions, the commander of the unit preferred that he use his mechanical ability to repair old and broken weapons which the soldiers were forced to use. Staszek did not survive the war. He was killed in an attack on a German convoy somewhere in the Vilna area.[16]

Jurek Kolarski was barely 16 when in September, 1939, a German motorized unit swept into his town, killing Jews and Poles. Horrified, Kolarski ran away as fast as he could. He met a young Jewish boy and they not only became close friends, a friendship their parents frowned upon before the war, but also members of the *AK*. "I made contact with a small group that had organized not far from the village as a resistance force.

Most of the men were young like me," Kolarski said. "Only after I made sure that my Jewish friend would be welcome in the unit did he reveal himself. He ended up one of the best fighters in the unit, killing ten or twenty Germans with a rifle that was older than he was." Kolarski outlived his Jewish friend to fight the Communists in Poland in the years immediately after World War II.[17]

Older youngsters, usually over 18, formed combat units which distinguished themselves in organizations under the *AK* and the *AL*. Legendary units of the Scouts—*Zoska, Parasol, Wigry*—who fought in the *AK* achieved distinction especially during the Warsaw Uprising in 1944. The *ZWM* consisted of young Poles and Jews who served with the *GL/AL*. One of the most outstanding units of the *ZWM* was a battalion of the *AL* known as *Czwartakow*. The fact that the *ZWM* conducted approximately 50 percent of the diversionary raids of the *AL* in the Warsaw region dramatizes the extent of their involvement in combat.[18]

The high point of the Polish resistance against the Germans came on August 1, 1944, when the AK launched the Warsaw Uprising. The 63-day struggle saw Polish boys and girls performing a number of roles, including combat. One of the most remarkable accomplishments of Polish youth during these dangerous days was to run a postal system for the capital's residents, a unique achievement of which no other besieged city in Europe could boast. Despite the obvious danger, which took many casualties, young boys and girls carried mail through the streets, rubble, and sewers. During the first month of the uprising, they moved 120,000 pieces of mail.[19]

Others served as couriers, carrying messages and newspapers to hundreds of outposts at the city's barricades. Joe was 9-years-old and one of the youngest couriers of the *AK* during the uprising. "One day Joe appeared with a German helmet on his head which would have covered his whole face had it not been supported by his ears," wrote Wanda Jordan, who was associated with the underground press during the uprising. "His most dramatic appearance was the day he came with a big bull terrier at his heels. From then on, the boy and his dog shared the dangers of his daily expeditions." There were very few dogs left in Warsaw; they quickly disappeared as starvation gripped the population of the city," Jordan said. "One day Joe came to the office without his dog. 'What happened? Where is your dog?' I asked. 'They ate him,' Joe said, sobbing."[20]

There were several underage urchins like Tygrys, a pseudonym for a boy whose real name is not known, who destroyed a German tank. The Germans took him and several of his young friends into captivity after the uprising and nothing was heard from them again.[21] Fourteen-year-old Jerzy Swiderski started out as a courier but became a fighter by the end of the uprising. On August 3, as Swiderski accompanied a patrol to deliver a message, bullets whizzed perilously close to his head. A few days later, he again narrowly escaped death from a Luftwaffe bomb. But many of his fellow Scouts weren't so lucky. "Rubble, blood and tears—this is the work of the Germans. Many of our boys perished. At roll call many of our acquaintances, friends... are missing. We are unable to understand, to fully understand this," he wrote in his diary on August 13, 1944, when the Germans had already seized the military initiative from the Poles. Downcast, Swiderski noted how the bodies of his friends could not even be found. But he courageously continued to do his job. "Here, at the barricade, embracing the Nazi blow, creeping with a message, I feel a true son of the fatherland, a true Pole and Polish soldier," he wrote. "I am aware of my family. I know nothing about them except that they are fighting. I know that when we meet after the uprising, none of us will be ashamed."[22]

By August 19, the Germans concentrated their enormous firepower on Old Town, Warsaw's historical centerpiece of narrow winding streets and ancient timbered houses that hugged the Vistula River. Using huge assault guns and howitzers, the kind they used to shell Dover, England, the Germans bombed the Poles in Old Town night and day. They also employed Junker bombers and Stukas which flew ceaseless sorties over the area. In the two-week effort to take this district of Warsaw, the Germans used 3,500 to 4,500 tons of bombs on an area three-quarters of a square mile in size,[23] perhaps the largest amount of steel to be expended in so small an area during the war. Old Town's buildings became the collective graves of thousands of men, women and children who were buried alive. Just three days into the Nazi assault on Old Town,

400 buildings in Polish hands had been completely destroyed and another 300 had been burned.[24]

The first day of the German attack on Old Town, Swiderski wrote in his diary, "We shall remember [this day] until the end of our lives." His diary entries became less frequent and more laconic during the German effort to take Old Town from the Poles.[25] Swiderski was one of 1,500 defenders left in Old Town by September 1. There was only one way out: the sewers. To evacuate the entire detachment would mean leaving Old Town undefended while the men retreated underground. To make matters worse, if the Germans discovered what the Poles were doing, a few well-placed bombs in the sewers would decimate all of them. And how could the 1,500 men, along with several hundred civilians and prisoners, be concealed from the Germans when the manhole they had to use was only a few hundred yards away from them? For General Bor-Komorowski, it was the most difficult decision he had to make during the uprising. On the night of September 1, 1944, hundreds of military personnel, including Swiderski and civilians, made the long journey through the slime and stench of the sewers to safely reach City Center where the struggle continued.[26]

Paying tribute to all of the defenders of Old Town, Colonel Karol Ziemski, the commander of the sector, also noted the courage and determination of Polish youth under his command. "I am very proud of the fact that I had so many splendid sections under my command," he said. "That the men and women, boy-scouts [sic] and boys fought with such enthusiasm for the freedom of the capital of their homeland. It is also the achievement of all that the old city managed to last so long."[27]

There were also a number of young Jewish boys and girls who had earlier fled from the ghetto and had been cared for by sympathetic Poles. Before the uprising, some of them congregated around Three Crosses Square and sold cigarettes. Now they became couriers and fighters in the Warsaw uprising. They were among the estimated 1,000 Jews who took an active part in fighting shoulder to shoulder with the Poles during the uprising. The *Information Bulletin*, the official publication of the *AK*, mentioned the names of several young Jewish boys and girls. In the August 13, 1944, issue, one article was entitled, "Antek the Sprayer."

Antek-the-Sprayer and runner Nina were a well matched pair. He went to 'work,' she cleaned the arms, loaded the magazines and carried ammunition. They were often accompanied by 13-year-old runner 'Mickey.' This tireless trio, always gay and energetic, was the apple of the eye of the whole detachment.... Brought from the hospital on a stretcher to Antek's grave, the commandant, Captain 'Sokol' bade farewell to his favourite in a short soldierly speech ...Little 'Mickey,' brave Warsaw urchin, who had not been afraid to act as a negotiator with the Germans in B.G.K. (the National Economy Bank) cried like a baby. Today, Nina, Mickey and the rest of the group are still in the front line.[28]

The agony for the Poles finally ended when they surrendered to the Germans on October 2, 1944.

The Jewish underground movement began later and was considerably smaller than the Polish resistance. The Jewish conspiracy against the Germans was largely led by young men and women who found themselves in bitter disputes and clashes with the ghetto leadership of the *Judenrats*. Young Jewish leaders associated with youth groups, especially leftist Zionists like the Hashomer Hatza'ir, had a remarkably prescient understanding, even before there was enough evidence to support their view, of the German intention to slaughter the Jews of Europe. To leaders of the Jewish youth movement, the only way to deal with the Germans was to resist.

Leaders of the *Judenrat* disagreed with the assessment of youth leaders, concluding that the German slaughter of Jews in eastern Poland and western Russia in 1941 was not likely to expand to include the annihilation of Jewish ghettos in the General Government. To them, the suggestion of youth leaders to resist the Germans would only invite savage Nazi reprisals. To the *Judenrat* leadership of the ghettos, most notably Mordechai Rumkowski in Lodz and Jacob Gens of Vilna, the correct posture for Jews to follow toward the Nazis was a passive one that emphasized work and productivity which benefited the German war effort. Presumably this would convince the Nazis to stop their oppression and killing of Jews. In a matter of months, the predictions of the leadership of Jewish youth groups proved to be correct.

These Zionist youth groups, composed of youngsters and young adults, were imbued with the idea of settling in communal agricultural settlements in Palestine. To them, Poland was merely a transition to a future life in Palestine. Since Jewish political parties had abdicated responsibility insofar as resistance to the Germans was concerned, these youth groups filled that void during the war.

They organized themselves into cells that spread throughout German-occupied Poland, linked together by couriers, mostly young girls, who transmitted important underground literature. Emmanuel Ringelblum, the historian of the Warsaw Ghetto, wrote of them: "These heroic girls-Chaika Grossman, Frumka Plotnicki, and others—are a subject worthy of a great author: heroic and brave girls who travel to and from the cities and towns of Poland. They have Aryan documents, and they are like Aryans.... One even wears a Cross, from which she is inseparable,... They are in unsurpassable danger."[29]

Among these emissaries was a remarkable Polish Christian, Irena Adamowicz, a leader in the Polish Scout movement. She took enormous risks in her missions to various Jewish ghettos on behalf of Jewish underground organizations. She was the first emissary to reach Kovno to tell the Jews there of the sufferings of their kinsmen in Polish and Lithuanian settlements. Leib Garfunkel, a Zionist member of the Kovno *Judenrat*, said of Adamowicz: "Her tremendous desire to give moral support to the prisoners in the ghettos is what brought her in 1942 to the Vilna, Kovno, and Shavli ghettos. She sat for an entire day with a small circle of Zionist activists in the Kovno ghetto and spread before them the story of the torture of the Jews of Warsaw, Lodz, Lublin, Cracow, Lemberg, Bialystok, Grodno, Vilna, and others." Though pessimistic about the future of Jews in the ghettos, she tried to encourage and comfort the beleaguered Jews.[30]

In addition to Hashomer Hatza'ir, other influential youth groups which played an active role in the growing resistance movement included Dror, Akiva, Betar and Gordonia. Hashomer Hatza'ir and Dror were the largest youth movements in the Jewish underground; they had 1,000 members each in Warsaw alone. In Krakow, Akiva and Dror played a major role in the Fighting Organization of Jewish Pioneer Youth, while Hashomer Hatza'ir and those not connected with any youth group organized *Iskra*, which was under substantial

Communist influence.[31] Thanks to their commitment to the resistance, these and other unaffiliated groups participated in the uprising in Warsaw, the first urban rising in German-occupied Europe, and played a role in resistance activities in Lwow, Bialystok, Czestochowa, and Bedzin. In Warsaw, youths groups either became members of the *Zydowska Organizacja Bojowa* (Jewish Fighting Organization) or *ZOB*, or fielded their own units in the Warsaw Ghetto uprising in April and early May, 1943. Organized late in July, 1942, in the midst of the massive German deportations of Jews from Warsaw to the death camps, *ZOB* expanded its political base by December and was headed by the legendary Mordechai Anielewicz.[32] Approximately 3 to 5 percent of Warsaw ghetto's residents—1,000 to 2,000—were involved as combatants in the courageous but hopeless operation that Ringelblum described as a struggle "between a fly and an elephant."[33]

Prior to the uprising, the *AK* had given a limited number of arms to the Jews, unwilling to jeopardize scarce resources in an operation that was doomed to failure. The *AK*'s position had always been to delay a major strike until the Germans were at the point of military collapse; in 1943, the Germans were still too strong. Notwithstanding obvious political and ideological differences between the *AK* and Jewish groups in the ghetto, the *AK* conducted more than two dozen combat, supply and evacuation actions on behalf of the Jews and lost the bulk of the 55 Polish soldiers in these operations. Scores of Jewish resistance fighters, including young adults and children, were evacuated from the ghetto inferno to the Christian districts of the city.[34]

Unlike more moderate Jews, leftist Zionists saw their future linked with the Communists who were considered, however, "the other enemy" in the eyes of most Poles. When the Nazis and Soviets partitioned Poland by the Soviet German Non-Aggression Pact in 1939, Hashomer Hatza'ir considered the pact justified. Anielewicz, the young hero of the Warsaw Ghetto uprising, was the editor of *Neged Hazerem*, a periodical which embraced communism over capitalism and the Soviet Union over Poland.[35]

Predictably, most of the left Zionist youth leaders had close contacts with the *Polska Partia Robotnicza* (Polish Workers

Party) or *PPR*, and its military arm, the *GL/AL*. The *PPR*, revived in Warsaw by Stalin in January, 1942, had a significant Jewish presence, including one of its notable leaders, Pawel Finder. By early 1943, Jewish leaders, especially Hanka Szapiro-Sawicka, organized the *Zwiazek Walki Mlodych* (Youth Struggle Organization) or *ZWM*, which, as we have seen, was an affiliate of the *PPR* and provided most of the manpower for the *GL/AL*.[36]

Anxious to impress the Polish population that the Communists were the most militant of all underground groups in their opposition to the Germans, the Communists began operations in May, 1942. Though the military value of the targets was often small and the casualties large, these operations popularized Communist activity and made the party a political force that could not be ignored. Though deeply divided and unable to attract a popular following—membership in the military arm of the party was greater than in the party itself in 1942—the Communists went on in December, 1943, to establish the National Council of the Homeland, a challenge to the political legitimacy of the Polish government-in-exile and its representatives in Poland. It even asked for but did not receive recognition from the United States. In July, 1944, the Kremlin created the Polish Committee of National Liberation in Chelm, which later moved its activities to Lublin. Early in 1945, Stalin granted diplomatic recognition to the Lublin Committee, as it was popularly known, as the legal government of Poland.[37]

In view of the close association of many Jews with Polish and Soviet Communists, little wonder there was considerable hostility between Poles and Jews in the partisan movement. Long standing Polish charges of Judeo-Communism were confirmed in the eyes of the Poles who saw Jews collaborating with Poland's second enemy, and this revived anti-Semitic feelings among many Poles.

Joseph Riwash's life serves as an excellent example of how Jews who served with the Soviets were perceived by some Poles. Riwash, raised in Vilna, became a partisan and later a member of the NKVD. He observed how ruthlessly Poles who had doubts about joining partisan units under Soviet command were treated by the Russians. He remembered a young Pole who demurred serving with the Communist-led partisans on the grounds that he was an only son whose parents needed him on the farm. "I also have a father and mother, you know," the Soviet officer shot back contemptuously. "But I'm here, fighting in the woods! I suppose that by your definition I'm a son-of-a-bitch for leaving my parents!" The Soviet told his aide, "Take the slacker away and shoot him!"[38]

Although Jews, including children, could be found in virtually all underground organizations in German-occupied Poland, there were fewer Jews in the AK than in the AL. The primary reason for this had less to do with anti-Semitism, which certainly existed in the AK, especially in the lower ranks, than in the nature, complexion and operation of the AK. The vast majority of AK members were civilians, subject only to mobilization, who went about their jobs and daily routines unnoticed. Most Jews could not function that way. For the most part, Jews were unassimilated; they did not know Polish well or at all. If they managed to escape from the ghettos, they had to hide. The logical place to go was to the forest. When Jews went there, they found and joined partisan units organized by the Soviets and the GL/AL, not the AK, because the AK did not place priority on partisan warfare that it did later in the war.

Obviously, Jews in eastern Poland had an advantage over their kinsmen elsewhere because it was easier to flee from a small town or village and find shelter in a nearby forest than it was to escape from the urban ghettos of Warsaw, Lodz or Krakow where German control and separation from the Polish community was virtually absolute. Moreover, a successful escape to the home of a Christian Pole placed the risk of the death penalty on the Pole as well as the Jew. Then, too, there was always the danger of falling into the hands of *szmalcowniks*, a criminal element that preyed on Jews and even Polish Christians with Semitic features, blackmailed them, and even denounced them to the Germans.

Out of the first nine GL/AL units operating in the Kielce area in the period 1942-43, three were Jewish, one was predominantly Jewish, and Jews constituted a large proportion of the membership of two others. Large numbers of Jews could also be found in the ranks of Soviet partisans—92 Soviet partisan formations had Jewish commanders. Although Jews could be found by the hundreds in the AK and other non-Communist formations, the Jewish partisan movement, which numbered approximately 30 units, was primarily linked with the Communists.[39]

"The ghettos, the camps, and the woods were full of... youthful Jewish heroes," Joseph Tennenbaum wrote. They acted not only as couriers between ghettos but also as resistance fighters. One of the most heroic was 17-year-old Leybka Feldman. He shot a Polish collaborator who had given information to the Germans concerning the hiding places of several hundred Jews. The Germans tortured him to try to extract the information, but he died without betraying his compatriots.[40]

Sixteen-year-old Dawid Alfiner became part of a unit commanded by a Soviet captain and acted as the group's incendiary. He succeeded in blowing up a German train. He also took part in an operation that freed Jewish girls from imprisonment.[41] Another Jewish boy, who looked 18 but was only 14-years-old, related his exploits, perhaps with some hyperbole, as a young partisan after the war: "I had two revolvers, one in each hand and I kept the reins of my horse in my mouth," he said. "When we attacked we would move like lightning and I used to shoot Germans on the left and the right. Sometimes I threw grenades at them. The best thing was the dynamite, though.[42] Thirteen-year-old Eisen Szmul, who was the youngest member of his partisan group, remembered, "Our group was very big. We had infantry and cavalry, tanks and artillery. I was with them for a year. Every day they taught me to ride on horseback and to shoot....It was hard work but I learned to shoot so well that they took me along wherever they went." Szmul recalled a major battle with the Germans who requisitioned supplies from local villagers. "Our patrols signaled to us that the Germans were in the village. We surrounded it and attacked them. Oh, it was a real battle. I was on horseback, the reins in my teeth, and I shot the Germans with my tommy-gun."[43]

Itzhak, who was 13-years-old when he fled from the Germans in Poland to Russia, joined a Soviet partisan unit. He provided for his family and even acquired a reputation as an expert with a rifle. According to one account, "His rifle was bigger than he, but no one dared jest about it. His fame as a valiant fighter spread far and wide. He took part in all the raids, shoulder to shoulder with his elders." He later served with the Red Army in its conquest of Berlin.[44]

Living and fighting in the forests of eastern Poland and western Russia was one of the worst places in Europe. Danger lurked everywhere. There were no battle lines. Germans, Poles, Ukrainians, White Russians and Jews all operated there. No one could be certain who was a friend and who was a foe. Children had to be alert for all sorts of dangers that loomed from Germans and hostile partisans. They had to be patient, often remaining immobile, sometimes for weeks, in a hole, tent or lean-to. They had to accept meager rations of food, often stolen from nearby peasants, and to suffer the illnesses and diseases that accompany filth, malnutrition and poverty. Above all, they had to be courageous in confronting the Germans and hostile partisans. Despite the enormous dangers, fleeing to a forested area and joining up with partisans or becoming part of a family camp was still the best hope for most Jews in the countryside to survive the war. While the principal purpose of partisan groups was to fight the enemy, the family camps were primarily interested in saving Jewish lives. Combat with the enemy was of secondary importance.

When Germans surrounded Moses Romanowski's ghetto, he said, "The Jews understood that this was the end." Approximately 30 to 40 young Jews, armed with gasoline and hatchets, fought the Germans and as many as 150 people fled to the partisans. Unfortunately, many women and children, unwilling to fall into German hands, threw themselves into the river and drowned.[45] Aron Grendeg remembered after he and scores of other Jews fled from their ghetto, they joined a partisan group led by a Russian Jew. The group, consisting of 80 men, women, and children, ambushed Germans and also clashed with unfriendly Poles.[46] W. Saloman recalled life among a group of young Jews, who had run away from the ghetto and organized a partisan unit. Ukrainian bands pursued them and Jewish youths suffered many losses.[47]

There are no accurate figures of the number of children who were members of the fighting organizations of Poland's ghettos and of partisan units which operated in eastern Poland. According to one Israeli historian, there were about 2,000 members of the youth movements who were active in the fighting groups of the main ghettos in German-occupied Poland. As for the partisans, one estimate suggests there were approximately 5,000 Jewish partisans in the *GL/AL* and the Peasant Battalions that operated in the General Government.[48] The leaders of Jewish youth and combat units tended to be young adults while the rank and file was often made up of teenagers and even younger children.

Chapter Notes

1. Quoted in Reuben Ainsztein, *Jewish Resistance in Nazi Occupied Eastern Europe* (New York: Barnes and Noble, 1974), p. 402.
2. Komisja Historyczna, *PS2* III, 119; Letter, Perkins to Alan, May 4, 1944, in FO 371/39425, PRO.
3. This is discussed in Lukas, *Forgotten Holocaust*, pp. 63ff.
4. Office of Strategic Services, "Underground and Guerrilla Warfare in Poland," in OSS/NA.
5. See material in PRM 45c/23, PI/GSHM.
6. Lukas, *Out of the Inferno*, p. 143.
7. Franciszek Kopec, "Numer 109063," in Turski, *Byli Wowczas Dziecmi*, pp. 552 ff.
8. Bogdan Hillerbrandt, "Udzial Dzieci i Mlodziezy w Walce z Okupantem Hitlerowskim," in Pilichowski, *Dzieci i Mlodziez*, pp. 443ff. Hanson, *Civilian Population*, p. 44; Duraczynski, *Wojna i Okupacja*, pp. 247, 384; Wladyslaw Bartoszewski, *Warsaw Death Ring, 1939-1945* (Warsaw: Interpress Publishers, 1968), pp. 28-33, 151-54; Meldunek Organizacyjny, May 16, 1942, in *AkwD*, II, 256; Office of Strategic Services, "Underground and Guerrilla Warfare in Poland."
9. Duraczynski, *Wojna i Okupacja*, pp. 384-85; T. Bor-Komorowski, *The Secret Army* (New York: Macmillan Co., 1951) p. 84.
10. Lukas, *Out of the Inferno*, pp. 24-25. There were other types of sabotage conducted by children. Zofia Kruk was a child laborer on a German farm during the war. She used to leave some old milk in a can so that when fresh milk was later poured into it, the whole churn was spoiled. At least one out of every twelve churns was spoiled. Zofia Kruk, *The Taste of Fear: A Polish Childhood in Germany* (London: Hutchinson and Co., 1973), p. 77.
11. Lukas, *Out of the Inferno*, pp. 168-71.
12. Henryk Fafara, "Dwa Razy w Partyzantce," in Turski, *Byli Wowczas Dziecmi*, pp. 519-26.
13. Duraczynski, *Wojna i Okupacja*, pp. 227-29.
14. Fafara, "Dwa Razy w Partyzantce," pp. 519-26.

15. Lukas, *Out of the Inferno*, pp. 126-27.

16. Interview with the Reverend Jan Januszewski, August 2, 1982.

17. Lukas, *Out of the Inferno*, pp. 97-99.

18. Hillerbrandt, "Udzial Dzieci i Mlodziezy," pp. 444-47.

19. Leslaw M. Bartelski, "Dzieci w Powstaniu Warszawskim," in Pilichowski, *Dzieci i Mlodziez*, p. 456.

20. Lukas, *Out of the Inferno*, pp. 81-82.

21. Bartelski, "Dzieci w Powstaniu Warszawskim," p. 457.

22. Jerzy Swiderski, "Dziennik Powstanczy," in Turski, *Byli Wowczas Dziecmi*, pp. 584ff.

23. George Iranek-Osmecki (trans.), *The Unseen and Silent: Adventures from the Underground Movement Narrated by Paratroops of the Polish Home Army* (London: Sheed and Ward, 1954), pp. 242-43.

24. Bor-Komorowski, *Secret Army*, pp. 286, 289.

25. Swiderski, "Dziennik Powstanczy," pp. 584ff.

26. Bor-Komorowski, *Secret Army*, pp. 316-17.

27. Quoted in Gunther Deschner, *Warsaw Rising*, (New York: Ballantine Books, 1972), p. 119.

28. Quoted in Ziemian, *The Cigarette Sellers of Three Crosses Square*, p. 155. There were also other interesting connections of Jews and Poles during the uprising. Liliana Zuker-Bujanowska was a 16-year-old Jewish girl, who was aided by several Poles. She married a Pole who fought for the *AK* during the Warsaw Uprising. She received false papers and was protected by the *AK*. Zuker-Bujanowska, *Liliana's Journal*, pp. 66-81.

29. Gutman, *Fighting Among the Ruins*, pp. 73-76.

30. *Ibid.* p. 178.

31. *Ibid.*, pp. 109, 146-47.

32. Lukas, *Forgotten Holocaust*, p. 172.

33. *Ibid.*, p. 178.

34. *Ibid.*, pp. 179-80; Proch, *Poland's Way of the Cross*, pp. 112-13.

35. Teresa Prekerowa, "Podziemie Zydowskie a Podziemie Polskie," *Odra*, No. 4 (1991), p. 31-32.

36. *Ibid.*, pp. 33-34; Lukas, *Forgotten Holocaust*, p. 77.

37. *Ibid* p. 77-78; Richard C. Lukas, *The Strange Allies: The United States and Poland. 1941-1945* (Knoxville: University of Tennessee Press, 1978), p. 60.

38. Joseph Riwash, *Resistance and Revenge, 1939-1949* (Quebec: N.P., 1981), p. 60.

39. Ainsztein, *Jewish Resistance*, pp. 410-35; Michael Elkins, *Forged in Fury* (New York: Ballantine Books, 1971), p. 182; Shmuel Krakowski, *The War of the Doomed: Jewish Armed Resistance in Poland. 1942-1944* (New York: Holmes and Meier, 1984), p. 3.

40. Ben Lappin, *The Redeemed Children: The Story of the Rescue of War Orphans by the Jewish Community in Canada* (Toronto: University of Toronto Press, 1963), p. 80.

41. Zeznanie Dawid Alfiner in Eyewitness Accounts, Series 1, YIVO.

42. Quoted in Lena Kuchler-Silberman, *One Hundred Children* (New York: Doubleday, 1961), p. 123.

43. Quoted in Rosenblum, "Jewish Children in Ghettos," p. 32.

44. Eisenberg, *Lost Generation*, pp. 232-33.

45. Zeznanie Mojsze Wolfa Romanowskiego, in Eyewitness Accounts, Series 1, YIVO.

46. Zeznanie Arona Grendego, in Eyewitness Accounts, Series 1, YIVO.

47. Zeznanie W. Salomonego, in Eyewitness Accounts, Series 1, YIVO. The situation in western Belorussia and western Ukraine was similar to that in Poland where most inhabitants were against leaving the ghettos for fear of inviting Nazi reprisals. A Jewish tailor told a young Jewish partisan, "How much better we'd be if you were dead!" Charles Gelman, *Do Not Go Gentle: A Memoir of Jewish Resistance in Poland, 1941-1945* (Hamden, Ct.: Archon Books, 1989), p. 17.

48. Israel Gutman, "Youth Movements," *Encyclopedia of the Holocaust*, IV, 1702; Lukas, *Forgotten Holocaust*, p. 79.

Chapter VI

Hiding

SAVING A JEW in most European countries was easier than it was in German-occupied Poland. Yet most published accounts have emphasized what the authors consider to be the favorable records of these countries in saving Jews and usually draw invidious comparisons with Poland. One of the ironies is that the countries which saved a high percentage of Jews were usually collaborationist regimes which had comparatively few Jews to worry about and experienced relatively mild German occupation policies compared to Poland.

Much that has been said about the efforts of many of these countries either has been exaggerated or is even fraudulent. The legend of the good Dane, symbolized by the fanciful story of King Christian X wearing the Star of David to display his solidarity with Danish Jews, obscures the fact that several thousand Danish Jews had to pay most of the cost of their rescue by ship to Sweden. Collaborationist regimes like France, Romania and Bulgaria may have tried to protect their own Jewish citizens but they had no compunctions about turning over thousands of foreign Jews to the Nazis or, as in the case of Romania, to massacre almost all of the Jews of Bessarabia and Transnistria. Poland and the Netherlands were non-collaborationist countries which experienced extreme severity from the Germans in the occupation of their countries. The consequence was that the percentage of Jewish losses in these countries was high.

Unlike other European countries, a gentile in Poland automatically ran the risk of losing his life if he gave assistance—even a piece of bread—to a Jew. Unlike their kinsmen in western Europe, Polish Jews and those Jews deported to Poland from other parts of Europe had to live in ghettos, effectively isolating them from the Polish community. The Jews of Lodz, for example, were so isolated from the gentile section of the city, there was only one case of a Jew surviving the war on Aryan territory.[1]

Citizens in France, Denmark, Norway and the collaborationist countries of the Balkans obviously did not have to deal with the degree of terror and persecution the Nazis visited upon the Poles, who were the first victims of Hitler's racial policies between 1939 and 1941, when the Jews became his primary victims. The misery and impoverishment most Poles experienced made it extremely difficult for them to aid a Jew, notwithstanding the death threat that hung over their heads for doing so.

Not the least of the obstacles in inhibiting Polish assistance to Jews was the past history which Poles and Jews shared, especially the difficult and divisive years of the Second Polish Republic from 1919 to 1939. These years saw the expression of Polish and Jewish nationalism, sometimes in extreme forms, which inevitably led to tension and animosity between the two communities. One of the leading Polish political parties, the National Democrats, wanted to create a "national" Poland, appealing to the growing Polish middle class which felt frustrated with the number Jews in the professions and businesses in Poland. The National Democrats were anti-Semitic and spearheaded discriminatory practices against Jews during the interwar years. Likewise, Zionists cared little for Poland. They wanted to create their own national homeland in Palestine. To be sure, there were moderate groups among Poles and Jews, such as the Polish Socialists and Jewish Bundists, both of whom shared a common goal of working for socialism in Poland.

Except for a small assimilated group of Jews, most Polish Jews remained unassimilated, preferring to distance themselves from the Polish gentile community around them. Before World War II, 80 percent of Polish Jews declared Yiddish to be their mother tongue and few of them could speak Polish very well, if at all. Almost half of Polish Jews were sympathetic with Zionist political views which, of course, had nothing to do with working for the benefit of Poland. Thus the bulk of Polish Jewry had their own newspapers, schools, businesses, and cultural institutions. Though they lived side by side for centuries, Jews and Poles clung to their own lifestyles and value systems.

For the most part, Poles and Jews tolerated each other, a toleration that was marred by anti-Semitic incidents, comparatively rare until the years immediately prior to World War II. Jews in prewar Poland had to contend more with economic and bureaucratic discrimination than with physical assaults. The Polish government did not enact Nuremberg-type laws as the Germans did. Nor did Poland have a large anti-Semitic fascist party as many countries around it.[2]

Since most Polish Jews were unassimilated, it is easy to understand why some Poles remained indifferent to them during the German occupation. Most Poles, preoccupied with Nazi terrorism aimed against them, simply did not know the Jews any more than the Jews knew the Poles. They were strangers inhabiting the same land.

Enemies are an obvious necessity to ethnic, religious or national myths. Poles stereotyped Jews and Jews did the same to Poles. Both Poles and Jews had many myths about each other to fan the flames of misunderstanding, suspicion and even hatred at a time they desperately needed each other. These mythologies constituted obstacles in drawing the two communities together in the face of the horrors of Nazi occupation and especially in sheltering Jewish children in Polish homes and institutions. Few Jews considered giving up their children to Polish protectors until the Germans began to liquidate the ghettos and to exterminate them. As one eyewitness to the liquidation of the Warsaw Ghetto said, the priorities of the Jewish relief agencies obviously had to change. "Forget education, rehabilitation, and other such irrelevancies," she said.[3] But it was rather late to save many children when the Germans were already deporting thousands of young boys and girls to the death camps. "Parents were now pleading, begging the institutions to take their tots and hide them. The terror and panic multiplied hourly," she added.[4]

Some Jews wanted guarantees from Poles concerning the

safety of their children. Obviously, no such guarantees could be given. "I couldn't even guarantee that I would get them [Jewish children] past the sentry," said Irena Sendler, a courageous Pole who played a critical role in saving the lives of many Jewish children.[5]

Many Jews were reluctant to turn over their children to Polish Christians because they feared that they would be Christianized and therefore lost to Judaism. Emmanuel Ringelblum, the historian of the Warsaw Ghetto, apparently subscribed to the myth, widespread among Jews, that the Catholic Church wanted to take advantage of the plight of the Jews to win over Jewish children to Christianity.[6]

The stereotypes and misunderstandings about Poles fatefully took its toll as many Jewish parents refused to give up their children to the safety of Polish homes and institutions. One Jew, a boy at the time, summed up how many Jews viewed Poles, "They were always seen as strangers, *goyim*, the people on the other side of the fence."[7] One former Polish underground soldier, obviously offended by Jewish attitudes toward him, put it this way. "Before the war, Jews called me *goy, goy!* They didn't want to have anything to do with me. But during the German occupation, they wanted my help."[8]

While Jews often sneered at Poles for their alleged poor business sense, Poles stereotyped Jews for allegedly being too lazy to do manual labor. While unassimilated Jews frowned on having social relations with Poles, some assimilated Jews justified hiring Jews while excluding Poles because they felt more comfortable with their own.[9]

No doubt the myths about all Poles being anti-Semites and victimizers of Jews prevented many ghetto Jews from considering giving up their children to them. No one knows how many Poles had anti-Semitic views any more than how many Jews were Polonophobic. But contemporary sources do reveal there were anti-Semites—often young Polish thugs and *Volksdeutsch*—who persecuted and blackmailed Jews. These disreputable elements constituted a small fraction of the Polish population—7,000, according to the Israeli War Crimes Commission—who actively collaborated with the Nazis.[10]

This corresponds closely to what contemporary Jewish observers said about Polish anti-Semites who victimized Jews during the war. Jewish historian Emmanuel Ringelblum, not always friendly to the Poles, stated during the war, "No one will accuse the Polish nation of committing these constant pogroms and excesses against the Jewish population. The significant majority of the nation, its enlightened working-class, and the working intelligentsia, undoubtedly condemned these excesses,...." He went so far as to say that by late 1942, "Polish organizations combated and did away with blackmail." Adolf Berman, head of CENTOS and respected in the Jewish and Polish communities, agreed with Ringelblum's assessment, "Accounts of martyrdom of Poland's Jews tend to emphasize their sufferings at the hands of blackmailers, the 'blue' police and other scum. Less is written, on the other hand, about the thousands of Poles who risked their lives to save the Jews. The flotsam and jetsam on the surface of a turbulent river is more visible than the pure stream running deep underneath, but that stream existed."[11]

Jews were no different than gentiles in defining a nation by their worst elements. Even a well-educated former member of *Hashomer Hatza'ir*, who was aided by Poles, thought nothing about stereotyping Poles by saying, "After all, every Pole hates Jews." To her, Poles "delighted in the sport of sniffing out runaway Jews."[12] It took confinement in a concentration camp to challenge the prejudices of a Jewish teenager about Poles. "The... Poles I knew... had led me to generalizations similar to those they themselves had arrived at about the Jews," he said.[13] Unfortunately, today one reads astonishing statements, ostensibly from well-informed individuals who suggest that somehow Poles were not as moral or humane as other Europeans.[14] No doubt many who write such things are still mourning their past, unable to make the careful distinctions and differentiations that are necessary to evaluate fairly controversial aspects of the history of the war.

On the other hand, there are individuals, like Rabbi M. Schulweis, who offer a way for Jews and Poles to understand and appreciate each other's perspectives of the past. Taking his inspiration from Spinoza's *Ethics*, Schulweis makes the point that rescuers of Jews blur the line between "us" and "them." As he says, "Heroes convince me how facile generalizations about 'them' are. They can also help others to overcome the thinking that 'we always suffer at their hands and they always hate us.'"[15] Obviously, anti-Semitism no more defined Poland in the past than extremist Zionism defines Israel today.

Many ghetto Jews simply did not want to part with their children, even though there was a good chance they could be saved by Polish friends and acquaintances. The wife of one of the leaders of the Bund in Warsaw refused to give up her son to Polish friends. "In spite of everything, maybe we will manage to survive or we will die together," she said. Mother and son died in the Warsaw Ghetto Uprising. If this well-informed, assimilated woman was reluctant to give up her son to Polish friends, it is not too difficult to understand why other Jewish women from less fortunate socio-economic circumstances and less knowledgeable about Poles preferred to keep their children and to die with them.[16]

Some Jewish parents placed their children with Polish families or representatives of Polish humanitarian organizations before the Germans deported them to the death camps. Other children, orphaned or abandoned by family and relatives, sneaked over to the Aryan side of the city and Poles took them into their homes or found other homes or institutions to look after them. Some Jewish children also found their way to the Polish side through the Jewish resistance movement; in Warsaw, for example, Jewish boys and girls entered the Polish section through walls of the ghetto or the sewers during the course of the Warsaw Ghetto Uprising.

Despite the many obstacles in getting Jewish children from the ghetto into Polish homes and institutions, thousands of boys and girls were hidden, fed and clothed by Poles during the war. In the Warsaw region alone, approximately 2,500 Jewish children were placed in homes and institutions by *Zegota* (Council for Aid to Jews). There were other children who were sheltered by families and groups that had no connection with *Zegota*. There were also a number of youngsters who moved about on their own, usually scavenging for food wherever they could and finding a barn, hole or clearing to spend the night. One former member of the Polish underground estimated that 5,000 Jewish children were saved by Polish convents and monasteries during the German occupation.[17]

What were Polish attitudes toward the Jews during the war?

It is impossible to generalize about how Poles felt toward the Jews because there was no uniformity. The vast majority of Poles, themselves victimized by the Germans, were understandably preoccupied with their own lives and survival, and were inactive as far as the Jews were concerned. Within this group, there were many Poles who felt compassion for the Jewish people. They might be described as passive humanitarians who either feared becoming actively involved in aiding Jews because of the risk of death or were so pauperized by the war they simply could not help anyone else, Pole or Jew, without jeopardizing the survival of their own families. There was another group, a minority of Poles, who were hostile or indifferent to the plight of Jews and some of them, often young thugs or *Volksdeutsch*, as well as some members of the Polish Blue Police, engaged in blackmailing Jews or otherwise collaborated with the Germans. But even within this group, the anti-Semitic National Democrats changed their traditional views about Jews as the bizarre logic of German racism became apparent in the extermination campaign and some National Democrats personally aided Jews. Finally, there was an extraordinarily active group of Poles who expressed their sympathy and compassion for Jews by risking their lives to help Jewish adults and children.[18]

There are no definitive statistics concerning how many Poles aided Jews during the German occupation, let alone how many specifically aided Jewish children, and it is unlikely there ever will be. After all, aiding a Jew had to be a clandestine operation and in activities of this sort, the fewer the files and records the better for all concerned. Poles who aided Jews often preferred not to know who their charges were. When the Polish aid organization, *Zegota*, did not inform Polish families who the children were that they cared for, it was not because the rescuers could not be trusted. Rather, *Zegota* operated on a universal principle of the underground—the less people knew the better it was for them and the organization.

Emmanuel Ringelblum, from his vantage in the Warsaw Ghetto, estimated that in Warsaw alone 40,000 to 60,000 Poles were involved in hiding Jews, a figure which did not include Poles who tried but, despite their best efforts, had been unable to save Jewish adults and children because the Nazis murdered them and their Polish protectors. Polish historian Wladyslaw Bartoszewski says that "at least several hundred thousand Poles of either sex and of various ages participated in various ways and forms in the rescue action."[19]

Bartoszewski's estimate is probably too conservative in view of the fact that usually many people—often as many as 10 or 12—were involved in the painstaking process of providing shelter, food, clothing and false documents for one Jew. In a typical convent, for example, there might be 50 or 60 or 80 nuns who were directly involved in rescuing a handful of Jewish children. Jews who found refuge with Polish families frequently moved from temporary shelters to more permanent hideouts during the course of which several Polish families, usually consisting of two adults and two children, were involved in sheltering and feeding them. The operation was so dangerous that some Jewish children are known to have had to change their hiding places every week, even every day. The N. Gross family lived in 43 different Polish households during the German occupation![20]

Every apartment building was collectively responsible for its inhabitants. Designed by the Germans to keep track of all people in the building, the system made it extremely difficult to hide a Jew. Yet Polish families who did so obviously needed the help or at least the silent acquiescence of the caretaker, his family and neighbors.

When Jews who had been children during the war assembled at an international gathering in New York in May, 1991, the *Hiding Experience Directory* dramatically revealed that many Polish rescuers were usually involved in helping one Jewish child. The directory, noting those responsible for aiding one former Jewish child, is peppered by such references as "Various People," "Various Polish People," "Various Poles," "Polish Families," "Sisters of Charity."[21]

If one accepts the usual estimate of 100,000-120,000 Jewish survivors in Poland (excluding those who fled to the Soviet Union and returned after the war), then a reasonable estimate of the number of Poles who aided Jews would be approximately 1 million. Since there were more Jews sheltered by Poles than survived the Holocaust—one estimate is 450,000[22]—the number of Poles who aided Jews could possibly have reached 3 to 5 million.

Variables of education, sex, class and social and economic background were not major factors in motivating people to rescue Jews. Polish rescuers came from different classes and backgrounds. Their decision to aid Jews at the risk of their own lives was a personal choice, based upon the inheritance of values they received as children. These values emphasized independence, compassion, tolerance and humanity.

Zofia Lewin, an assimilated Polish Jew who had been aided by many Polish families, including those with children, summed up the Polish response by saying, "The overwhelming majority of the people with whom I came in contact—and they belonged to all strata of the population, to various social and political circles—expressed, by their attitude towards me, their protest against this stand adopted by the Nazi occupants.... They did not let me feel that my presence was dangerous, they also treated me as one of themselves."[23]

"I know of hundreds of peasants in the Polish and White Russian countryside who provided Jews—sometimes complete strangers—with a chance of survival, though they knew that if they were discovered by the Germans, their farms would be burned to the ground and they themselves would be gunned down together with their wives and children," said Joseph Riwash, a Jewish partisan and later a member of the Soviet NKVD.[24]

Among the Polish peasants who helped Jews in the town of Radoszyce, inhabited by approximately 1,500 Poles and 2,000 Jews, was Maria Zielinska, mother of two little boys. Zielinska had provided a hiding place to a Jewish man who, upon his arrest by the Germans, informed on her. The Germans led Zielinska, followed by her weeping sons, to a courtyard where she was publicly executed in the presence of 50 spectators. "Everyone was stunned. Nobody could move," said Zdislaw Rurarz, at the time a 12-year-old Polish boy, whose family also helped the Jews in the local ghetto. "Only after some time, when the Germans were about to leave the scene, her sons rushed to the body. Soon a horsedrawn cart appeared and Mrs. Zielinska was carried away."[25]

Much peasant help to Jews was spontaneous and took the

form of giving food and drink, for which Poles were shot. Sometimes Jewish men, including young boys, could not bear the gnawing hunger they suffered while working in a labor camp in the Kampinos area and risked beating and death by seeking food in nearby villages. "As it turned out, all the local Christians, without exception, treated us very kindly and deeply regretted our situation," Rabbi Shimon Huberband recorded in his memoirs. Thanks to the fiery sermons about the plight of Jewish inmates, which included Jewish teenagers, Huberband said, "The peasants began to bring various food items to the labor sites. Any inmate who could manage to steal himself over to a peasant while at work received all sorts of delicious foods from him and several dozen Jews owed their survival to the humane acts of the priest." One day, when Jewish prisoners completed their work at the labor camp, Huberband recorded one of the most touching scenes of Polish compassion for the tormented Jews:

> We marched through the village. We were given a warm farewell by the entire Christian population. Dr. Kon told us that when we passed the home of the Christian priest, he would greet us, and that we, in turn, should tip our hats. And that is what occurred. The honorable priest came out of his house with a bouquet of white roses in his hand. He did not say a word, because there were Germans in his home. As we passed by his house we tipped our hats. He answered by nodding his head.
>
> We owe him, the priest of Kampinos, a great deal. Many of us owed our lives to the warm and fiery sermons of this saintly person. His unknown name will remain forever in our memory.[26]

Scenes like this have been recorded by other Jews. When the Germans forced-marched Thomas Geve, a Jewish teenager at the time, from Auschwitz to Gross Rosen, he remarked about the "stubborn old women [who] stood at the kerb [sic] handing out milk—even at night. That they were beaten by the guards, who were infuriated at not receiving such favours for themselves, did not deter them at all."[27]

In the village of Cycow, where the Germans had shot many Jews, Iccek Gerstein approached his Polish friend, Antoni Symoniuk, to care for his 1-year-old daughter, Marysia. Symoniuk had four children of his own. Gerstein promised to reward the

Pole for the risk he took but Symoniuk later never asked for money nor did Gerstein give him any. He took the child because, as he said, Gerstein "was my friend." Symoniuk's wife, Marianna, fully supported her husband's commitment and for that suffered a brutal beating from the Germans who accused her of hiding a Jewish child in her home. She denied Marysia was Jewish, claiming that she was one of her own daughters. "If one of the girls was Jewish," she told the Nazi inquisitors, "then she too was a Jew." Marysia survived the war but Marianna Symoniuk never fully recovered from the beating she had received and died shortly after the war.[28]

Polish women of Warsaw and its environs showed extraordinary courage in sheltering Jews. Leokadia Jaromirska and a friend found two abandoned Jewish babies near a convent wall a few miles from Warsaw. Jaromirska took one baby, whom she named Bogusia. Her friend, who already had several children to care for, gave the other baby to another Polish family. Jaromirska, who had difficulty supporting herself, Bogusia, and two Polish friends who looked after the child when she was at work, took on the additional burden of sheltering a Jewish woman, who sometimes took incredible risks of discovery by strolling in broad daylight in full view of the public.

Someone informed on Jaromirska but the local Polish police warned her to leave town before the Gestapo arrived. "It is more than a blood tie. I wouldn't have loved my own offspring more. She was the only one for me, and my beloved one," Jaromirska said about Bogusia. The little girl gave her protectress a scare one evening when they met a Wehrmacht officer who offered a biscuit to Bogusia. The child told Jaromirska in Polish that she would not take it from him because he was a German. The officer, who did not understand Polish, asked Jaromirska what the girl had said. "I got worried," the woman related. "Perhaps he understood. I said to him in German, 'She's not hungry.' So he put the biscuit in my pocket." When they walked away, Bogusia remonstrated with Leokardia, saying, "Mother, throw that biscuit in the water. The Germans kill people. I don't want their dirty cookies." Leokardia was astonished by the girl's wisdom.[29]

Jewish children from the Warsaw Ghetto who begged for food on the Polish side of the wall often received a warm reception from Poles. Sometimes there were Poles who spurned them. Sofia Kalot's door was always open to Jewish children, who came to know her quite well. She gave food and shelter to several of them. One day Polish blackmailers broke into her apartment, expecting to find them. But she had hidden the children too well. However, the incident revealed the jeopardy in which the children and Kalot found themselves. The children decided on their own to leave Kalot's apartment. After the children thanked the woman for her help, Kalot wept and handed them a birth certificate of her deceased daughter. "Take it, it may come in useful," she said to one of the Jewish girls. As the children left, Kalot made the sign of the cross over them. The children walked slowly in order not to arouse the suspicion of nosy neighbors. "They went without knowing where; four small figures creeping along the shadow of the houses," according to one account.[30]

Ewa Brzuska was a tough old shopkeeper who fed Jewish children in her Warsaw shop. She also allowed them to sleep there. One day a member of the Polish Blue Police came into Brzuska's store and accused her of hiding Jews. She hurled so much verbal abuse at him in the presence of her customers that the intimidated policeman left without pursuing the matter any further. Brzuska's feats were matched by Janina S., whose apartment on 11 Wielka Street was intersected by the walls of the ghetto. She allowed 53 Jewish families, including many children, to find refuge there for varying lengths of time.[31]

The Polish middle class also aided Jews. An actress, Wanda Olbryska, saved 20 Jewish women, men and children from the Nazis. One of the children, 5-years-old at the time, is now a physician in Israel. "She was a great person, phenomenal," recalled one Jewish friend about Olbryska. For two years, Olbryska and her brother risked being executed by concealing Jews and partisans in their Warsaw suburb home located in Zielonka, an especially dangerous area which the Germans intended to make free of Jews. Ten of the individuals, including children, left her to join partisan bands. The remaining 10 people stayed with her until the end of the war. Asked why she risked so much, Olbryska said, "It was from the heart. I just thought I was supposed to do it. I didn't think about it. I just did it." Olbryska, who died in Canada in 1986, was appropriately buried in Powazki Cemetery in Poland, resting place of many of Poland's great men and women.[32]

Pero, an officer in the Polish underground army who worked during the day as a hotel clerk, helped save the lives of Mala Piotrkowska and her 13-year-old daughter, Bronka, by direct confrontation with the Gestapo. Piotrkowska, forced to leave her hideout one day, wandered around the streets of Warsaw with her daughter. Obviously Semitic-looking, she was quickly spotted by a gang of hoodlums and denounced to the Germans. Piotrkowska stubbornly maintained she was Christian. Disbelieving her, the Gestapo said she and her daughter would be executed unless a Pole could vouch that they were Christian. She contacted Pero, whom she knew, and in fluent German he convinced the Gestapo that the family was indeed Christian. The Germans released them and mother and daughter lived with Pero. The Pole's bold action in defense of the Piotrkowskis enabled them to function as Christians and if future denunciations occurred, all they had to do was to go to Gestapo headquarters and be cleared by them![33]

A professional nurse paid with her life for sneaking out Jewish children from the Krakow Ghetto and placing them in the homes of friends on the outskirts of town. "She would walk with a child hidden between her legs under the large hoops of her dress. Once this walk was mastered, she could take the child through the ghetto, past the German militia-staffed guard post and on to safety with an adoptive family," according to one account. The nurse had performed this routine six or seven times when she attempted to take out a youngster with tuberculosis from the ghetto. Just as she and the child were leaving the ghetto, the child coughed. That alerted the militiaman who knocked the nurse to the ground and, along with other guards, shot the child and then murdered the woman.[34]

Polish landowners were among the righteous gentiles too. Halina Martin's family, who were well-to-do landowners, also owned in partnership with several Jews the town mill in Tarczyn. Martin, seeing early in the war that the Germans intended to murder Jews, urged her friends and acquaintances in Tarczyn to hide among Polish farmers in the area. She was even willing to assume the cost of their upkeep. But most Jews, as elsewhere in Poland, refused to believe they were doomed unless they hid themselves. "The Germans were clearing the area of Jews but a torpor had set in on Tarczyn. A stubborn, hypnotic faith persisted that nothing could possibly happen here," Martin said.

Then one day it happened. The Germans surrounded Tarczyn and began the deportation of Jews. Martin, aided by laborers from her estate and the local Polish police, including their chief Jarzabek, ran interference for Martin as she tried to help as many Jews as she could. They created enough confusion to enable Martin to reach a few unfortunate people. "Amid the lamentation, the prayers, and the swearing that was going on in German, Polish and Yiddish," Martin said, "We managed to thrust an eiderdown at some old woman or a blanket to wrap up her child. We drew the Germans toward an empty doorway, shouting, '*Jude, Jude!*' while at the other side of the house we pulled a terrified girl through a broken window. A hand over the child's mouth, a sack covering her, and then her rescuer ran with his human bundle into some quiet alley to look for safety." Martin's colorful shawl was used to wrap up one of the babies. "The colored shawl was important," she said. "Later it would be cut into pieces by people from the ghetto who came to me for help."

Laborers on Martin's estate later found a Jewish boy lying unconscious in a potato field. Martin recalled how slight he was. "The bony arm that protruded from his tattered threadbare coat showed that he had been starved to the limit. His huge, grown man's shoes were well-worn. Flies settled around him," she said. "I gently rolled the boy on his back and lifted his hand from his face. The whites of his eyes were visible under the half-closed lids. The parted lips hardly took in any air." They brought the boy to Martin's villa where he recovered enough to transport with the assistance of the local Polish police to a safe haven.

None of this escaped the notice of the Gestapo who interrogated Martin. While her Nazi inquisitor tried to pry out of her where the boy was, Martin lost her temper which, curiously, may have saved her. She shot back at the Gestapo officer:

> Listen, you. I'm a mother. For me, a child's a child whether it be German, Turkish, Jewish, Chinese, or Polish. If I find one lying in a ditch, I'll always feed it. You threaten death? Fine! I'd rather not

live in a world where a woman, a mother, can't help a child. You can shoot me, hang me. Do you have children? Where? Are they in Berlin? Under the falling bombs? Who's going to help them when they're lying wounded in a ditch somewhere?

Shocked by Martin's sincere outburst, the Gestapo officer, in a rare display of Nazi magnanimity, allowed Martin to leave his office unharmed, but not without a threat. "This is the last time," he declared. As she left the Gestapo prison, Martin saw a young member of the Polish underground who watched to see what the Germans intended to do with her. It was a young boy, who took off his cap, looked up to the sky, and as if he pointed to something, raised his thumb in a gesture of success.[35]

Barbara Makuch was an 18-year-old high school graduate when the Germans invaded Poland. Later employed as an instructor in a local school, Makuch became aware that its principal, a certain Mr. Polowicz, looked after a Jewish boy and also harbored a Jewish physician, Dr. Olga Lilien. Little did Makuch and her mother realize that their courage and compassion would soon be tested as Polowicz's had been.

One day a Jewish woman from the ghetto implored Makuch to take her little girl, Malka. She and her husband knew they were doomed. Makuch agreed, changed the child's name to Marysia, a typical Polish one, and moved to another city because of German searches in the area. Eventually, Marysia ended up staying with the Felician Sisters while Makuch joined *Zegota*, the clandestine aid organization on behalf of Jews. Makuch collected and distributed money and forged documents, found refuge for Jews and transferred them from one hiding place to another. But the Gestapo caught up with her after they discovered her carrying large amounts of documents and money. Arrested and tortured, Makuch ended up in Ravensbruck, where she remained until American soldiers liberated her in May, 1945. Marysia survived in the convent. Marysia's mother also survived. Both became lifelong friends of Makuch.[36]

The Julian Rys family were rather typical of most Poles of modest means. Yet that did not prevent them from sheltering and caring for Felicja Markiewicz and Leopold, her 2½-year-old son. "Our food was not more than modest," Rys said. It was so difficult that Mrs. Rys had to sell her coat to buy chickens to eat. To make matters worse, the Germans quartered two soldiers in their home, forcing the Ryses to hide Felicja and Leopold in the garret where they had to be covered with straw. Only when the soldiers left the home for the day did the woman and her son have freedom of movement.

The stress on everyone was sometimes unbearable. One day the Germans had to go through the garret, where the Jews were hidden, to erect a radio antenna. Fortunately, they did not find the Markiewiczs. By the winter of 1944-45, Rys declared, "We were exhausted, hungry and frightened." Then one day as Rys returned from the post office, where he was employed, he thought the end for him, his family and the Markiewiczs had come when he spotted a pack of Gestapo men in front of his home. They barked out orders and tried to push away Mrs. Rys and their children who blocked the entrance to the home. But when the Gestapo spotted Mr. Rys in the uniform of a postman, they suddenly called off the inspection, apparently impressed by Rys's official status.

The irony was the Gestapo intended to search for suspected underground operatives who had derailed a German train, not for Jews in hiding. "When I look at the situation from the perspective of time, it was downright hopeless. I am amazed we were able to survive," said Rys, who personally knew another Polish family, including a child, who was killed for hiding Jews. Like other Poles who had to endure the stress associated with the rescue experience, the health of all members of the family deteriorated to the point that they all ended up with heart disease after the war.[37]

One of the most extraordinary cases of Polish aid to Jewish children involved Anna Zwarycz, who took the remarkable step of giving a home to a Jewish child but did not make a secret of what she did. Tried by a court, she was acquitted on the grounds that she did it openly. But Dr. Jozef Ganser, a senior official in the German Ministry of Justice in the General Government, challenged the court's decision. "It would be most unjust," he declared, "if one granted shelter openly and audaciously should go unpunished, while one who does the same thing secretly incurs the death penalty." Ganser's challenge resulted in Zwarycz's execution.[38]

Rare was the Pole who could hide and feed a stranger without the help of other Poles, either private individuals or representatives of various humanitarian organizations. Since the war had impoverished the Poles, many of them needed financial aid from Polish organizations or from the Jews they sheltered, if they could afford it. Poles in poverty received up to 1,000 zlotys a month from *Zegota* to help sustain them and a Jewish child. Some Poles refused financial help when it was offered. One Polish woman told a *Zegota* representative, "Madam, give this allowance to someone who really needs it. Our child [Jewish] lacks for nothing."[39]

It was more difficult to hide a young child than a teenager or adult. Young children, especially those under 6-years-of-age, were the most vulnerable to danger because at that age they did not control their thoughts. In a public place, streetcar or on the street, they could and sometimes did blurt out something that betrayed their Jewishness. One inadvertent remark was sufficient to jeopardize the child and the family who sheltered him. Olesh Blum was a 6-year-old boy whose mother wanted Poles to look after him. On his way to a temporary shelter, the youngster incessantly asked the woman who escorted him questions about the busy bustling part of Warsaw that contrasted so sharply with the ghetto. "Olesh and I boarded a trolley to go [to] the home where he was to stay. I was disturbed by his incessant questions. The passengers began to smile and exchange meaningful glances. I had to get off with him. I was afraid that the youngster would give himself away by a word or act. The child's innocent babbling could bring disaster to us both," his Jewish escort said.[40]

One Polish woman, who was active in rescuing Jewish children, was on a streetcar with a little Jewish boy who suddenly awakened from sleep and started to scream in Yiddish. As some of the passengers began to panic, the streetcar operator handled the situation brilliantly. He requested all passengers to disembark, claiming the streetcar was broken and that he needed to take it to the garage for repairs. Instead he drove the Polish woman and Jewish boy to the outskirts of the city where she lived.[41]

That is why it was necessary to keep young Jewish children indoors, especially in the cities. In the countryside, especially in convents, youngsters had more freedom to go outside, play and live a more normal life, under the watchful eye of a Polish protector who would snatch away the child before the arrival of suspicious strangers or the Germans.

Those confined all day frequently lay quietly in bed. Some children were isolated for so long they forgot how to walk, or worse contracted a form of rickets. Because of the dangers of talking within earshot of neighbors, all of whom could not be trusted, talking was discouraged. "The small four-and five-year-olds forgot how to talk," one Jewish physician who survived the war recalled. "Their development went into reverse. They were like tiny animals looking with their enormous eyes, and letting out intermittent cries. They did not even know how to play."[42]

Unless they were in hiding, children with obvious Semitic appearances usually were at greater risk than those who could pass for gentiles. For girls, sometimes all that was necessary was to change hair color or the style to make the girl a convincing Pole.[43] One Jewish boy's hair was too dark to pass for a Pole. In order to make him appear more Aryan-looking, he applied so much peroxide to his hair that he turned out a redhead rather than a blond. Then he was worse off than before because red hair in Poland was associated with Jews. He panicked. He decided to use another bottle of peroxide. This time it worked and he became a blond. Still he was not the picture of the typical Polish boy. "We continued desperately working on my appearance," he said. "Nothing could be done about the color of my eyes or their sad expression. There were no plastic surgeons available to improve the curvature of my nose."[44]

Since Jewish boys were circumcised and Polish gentiles were not, it was easy for Germans to check to see if a boy was a Jew. "Circumcision was the amazing stroke of history," Julius Streicher, the Nazi editor of *Der Sturmer*, said.[45] To remove the mark of cicumcision involved an expensive and risky operation by a physician who had experience performing them. One boy acquired a substance which dentists applied to shallow incisions to make skin heal without the use of sutures. He used the substance to try to hide the circumcision by gluing foreskin to the glans of his penis His attempt to remake himself failed.[46] Sometimes young boys were dressed up as girls to hide their gender. One boy walked and swayed like a girl and even carried a doll with him to avoid being identified.[47]

Children rescued from the ghetto usually went to temporary quarters on the Polish side of the city before a permanent home could be found for them. They had to be given false identification papers, printed by the thousands by the Polish underground and provided without cost to Jews, and new Polish names. One teenage girl who passed for a Pole was admonished by her father to avoid false documents with a name ending in "ski." "Every Jew is becoming a 'ski,'" he said. "You don't want any part of that. It's the first thing they'll look for."[48]

Jadwiga Piotrowska, who ran a temporary way-station for Jewish children, remembered how the Germans conducted a search of the houses in her neighborhood at a time when she had several Jewish youngsters in her care. She had a list of names of Jewish children, their new Polish names and the places where they lived. She anticipated having to burn the list if the Gestapo entered her apartment but fortunately, they didn't.[49]

Unless a boy or girl could speak Polish without Yiddish inflections, it was wiser for them either to remain silent when they were in a public place or to avoid contacts with people not known to them. Children from assimilated Jewish families had few problems in this regard and most of them spoke Polish fluently.[50]

Jewish children in hiding had to be taught the fundamentals of Catholicism, not to proselyte them but to help save them, because the Germans frequently stopped suspicious youngsters, especially girls, and ordered them to recite prayers routinely said by Catholics. A suspicious looking boy was simply ordered to drop his trousers. Understandably, sometimes the youngsters resisted learning about another religion because of its unfamiliarity or because of admonitions from their parents or guardians.[51]

Everyone had to be wary of *szmalcowniks* (blackmailers) who, though not numerous, betrayed Jews and the Poles who aided them. Historian Bohdan Vitvitsky makes the excellent point, "A single Ukrainian or Polish collaborator could easily brutalize a hundred Jews in a couple of hours while it might require an extended commitment by several Ukrainians or Poles to shelter a single Jew." He suggests this might be the origin of the popular notion that "every second Slav was a collaborator."[52]

Under the threat of being revealed to the Germans, blackmailers threatened Jews to pay for their silence. Some of the blackmailers managed to acquire the addresses of where the Jews had hidden. "They used to come to the flats and take everything from people—right down to their wedding rings," one survivor remembered. "The arrival of extortionists at a flat was the ultimate disaster, as after the first plundering there would come another, until the moment when the helpless people, stripped of everything, were handed over into the hands of the 'appropriate authorities.'" Once the blackmailers made contact, then it was critical for Jews to change their residences and acquire new identification papers. This was called "burning" a place.[53]

Sometimes *szmalcowniks* sought out their youngest and most vulnerable targets for questioning if they suspected them to be Jewish. Often the youngsters passed the test, but sometimes they protested their Polishness too much and only aroused greater suspicion. When questioned by one inquisitor, a little Jewish boy said, "I'm not Icek, I'm Jacek." Then he conscientiously made the sign of the cross and quickly recited a Catholic prayer.[54]

Often ghetto Jews inadvertently incriminated their own friends by seeking them out on the Aryan side of the city, hoping to find shelter. All blackmailers had to do was to watch and wait for such contacts. Then, too, there were a number of Jewish informers who preyed on their own people. "The activity of their own informers, renegades, and traitors was a greater plague to the people of the ghetto than with similar types among the Poles," Wladyslaw Bartoszewski, a respected historian, said.[55]

Poles who sheltered Jews were not exempt from the exactions of blackmailers because if they were reported to the Germans, they could be expected to be executed. Most Poles despised the *szmalcowniks* for the low lifes they were, preying on poor vulnerable, persecuted people. Andrzej Jus, a Pole, and his Jewish wife, Karolina, recalled how they hid in a Polish village that, he says, was typical in organizing "a united front against the Nazis." The village produced one 18-year-old informer who was shot by units affiliated with the Polish Home Army.[56]

Polish underground authorities condemned blackmailers and pronounced death sentences on over 2,000 of them during the period January 1943 to June 1944. Hundreds of executions were carried out.[57] A young Polish boy, Edmund Golecki, personally witnessed the executions of Polish traitors by the Polish underground.[58]

But it was not an easy matter to investigate and bring blackmailers to justice. It was difficult to acquire evidence. Agents were unable to interrogate the blackmailer because as soon as the suspect learned he was under investigation by underground authorities, he would place himself under German protection or even betray the agents working on the case.

The problem of blackmailing Jews and the Poles who helped them was part of the larger question of collaboration with the Germans. Although the number of people involved directly in collaboration with the enemy was small, the damage they did was enormous. The Polish Home Army, for example, lost 15 intelligence agents because of the treasonable activities of one collaborator. Polish collaborators were even responsible for the arrest and execution of the first commander of the Home Army, General Stefan Grot-Rowecki.[59]

Jews who could pass for Poles in public were able to walk freely, to buy things at stores and in some cases, even to work. Yet, as "Poles," they ran the same risks that characterized the life of other Poles during the German occupation. They never knew when they went outside that the Germans might cordon off a busy intersection or square and seize them for forced labor in Germany or worse, send them to prison to be executed in retaliation for an act of sabotage by the Polish underground.

A teenage boy or man caught in labor roundups could be subjected to medical examinations if the Germans suspected he was Jewish. If the Jew had the good fortune of having a humane prison-physician at Pawiak or Gesia, and there were some, his secret would be kept. But others promptly informed the executioners of the discovery. Thus the irony was that Jews likely to survive the occupation were often those who looked Semitic, had little or no knowledge of Polish and had to be confined most of the day in a Polish home.

Not only Polish men and women were involved in aiding Jews, but also children of rescuers played an important role in the household. Often they had to gather extra food, empty waste, and act as messengers. Like their parents, they always had to be wary of what they said and to whom they said it because even an innocent remark could lead to a German search of the premises and possible disaster.

In 1939, Zofia Ryszewska Brusikiewicz was 12-years-old. She lived with her parents and two younger brothers in Warsaw. Prior to sheltering a Jewish journalist, Zofia's father consulted with his daughter about the matter. "In spite of my young age," Brusikiewicz said, "I was able to understand how the Germans treated Jews and the tragic destiny of our tenant if he did not find shelter with us." Over time, thirteen Jews, including a 4-year-old girl, found a home with Zofia's family. It was a major problem to feed so many people without attracting attention but Zofia helped her mother to buy groceries, bought by the Polish family and those Jews who could afford to contribute. "The way we lived completely excluded us from any social life. We were not allowed to visit anyone or to have visitors. This concerned us children too. For our own safety and the safety of the thirteen people we sheltered, we were alert all of the time. We did not want to give away our secret," Zofia said. Her passive attitude in school and her refusal to join adolescent friends in the Polish resistance movement brought disapproval from her peers. Living a reclusive life in fear of being killed by the Germans was not easy for the children of rescuers. But from the perspective of time, Zofia admitted, "I am able to appreciate how exceptional was the behavior of my parents, who endangered their lives and the lives of their children to save strangers."[60]

Sometimes children took their own initiatives to help Jews. Nine-year-old Wladyslaw Milewski lived with his parents in a small village near a forest in the area of Bialystok. One day two Jewish girls approached him and asked for food. Milewski fed the girls who sheltered themselves at the edge of the forest. Somewhat later, two Russian prisoners-of-war joined the girls, one of whom soon had a child. Local peasants took care of the baby until the Germans discovered it was Jewish and murdered it.[61]

The initiatives taken by Polish children on behalf of Jewish children and their families made them genuine rescuers themselves. Frieda Saperstein was 11-years-old when she asked 15-year-old Marisia Szul to help her and her family. Szul readily agreed, hiding Saperstein, her mother, a baby brother, and a family friend in a covered hole under a barn. Saperstein and the others remained in the hole during the day and moved about and bathed only in the evening. When Saperstein's baby brother cried, her mother stuffed cloth in his mouth to keep him quiet. Saperstein's mother never considered killing the child as others had done to keep from being discovered by the Germans. The Gestapo arrested Szul on suspicion of her harboring Jews. Despite severe torture, she never revealed where the Jews were hidden. "I tell you the truth, I don't know why I did it," Szul said later. "If I live, why couldn't somebody else? God gave life to everybody; why take away that life? Everybody has a right to live in this world." The gratitude and bond that Saperstein feels toward Szul to this day is very deep. "She's in our hearts. Her life is my life. My life is her life," Saperstein said.[62]

One of the most remarkable examples of Polish children aiding Jews concerns 16-year-old Stefania Podgorska and her 6-year-old sister, Helena. It all began when the son of Stefania's former employer, Joseph Burzminski, managed to escape from a train that carried him, his brother and cousin to Belzec and certain death. He found his way to Przemysl where Stefania and Helena lived. The young girls ended up sheltering not only Burzminski but also 12 other Jews, including 4 children, from the ghetto.

One day the girls and their Jewish charges thought the end for all of them was at hand when the SS ordered the girls to vacate their home within two hours in order to accommodate German nurses and soldiers. The Jews urged the Polish girls to save themselves because it was clear the Germans would execute them if they were found with the Jews. Stefania never lost hope that everything somehow would turn out well. Her prayers were answered when the SS returned and only requisitioned one room instead of the entire home, allowing Stefania and Helena to hide the Jews in the attic behind a false wall.

Life in the attic was cramped, forcing adults and children

most of the time to lie head to foot like sardines in a can. When the Soviets liberated the city and discovered what Stefania had done, they hailed her. "Hero! Hero! She is a bigger hero than we.... We had our country behind us!" one Soviet excitedly exclaimed. Another soldier, making a pointed reference to Stefania's younger sister, yelled, "Not 2 girls but 1½!" To this day, Stefania, who married Burzminski in 1945, refuses to call herself a heroine. "Some people say I'm a hero. I just did what I should do," she said modestly.[63]

Young Aniela Narozniak shares credit with her mother for saving many Jews who had run away from the Krakow Ghetto. The Narozniak family cared for many Jews, including two young Jewish sisters and a cousin. Aniela's responsibility was to act as a sentry to warn the household when anyone approached the home. So effective was she at her work that the Germans never found anyone hiding in the home, even though many Jews found temporary shelter there at various times during the war.

But the Germans were always suspicious of the Narozniaks and believed that the best way to find out what they were looking for was to intimidate Aniela and her younger brother by subjecting them, not the mother, to intense interrogation at Gestapo headquarters. It didn't work. Aniela never broke under the pressure. Her brother, frightened by the experience with the Gestapo, cried most of the time. The Germans threw up their hands in despair. Despite the terrifying experience with her inquisitors, Aniela served as a courier for the Polish Home Army.[64]

Leonard Lukaszuk, an adolescent boy who lived in eastern Poland, helped his grandmother hide Jews in their home. In his town, a large number of Poles helped Jews in the ghetto by giving them food and medicine and later by hiding them. Like the Narozniaks, the Lukaszuk's had a close call: The Germans broke into their home, expecting to find Jews. Finding none there at the time, a German militiaman shot Lukaszuk and his grandmother but he was so drunk, he missed both of them. Fortunately, both scurried off to safety.[65]

The rescue experience often bound in friendship the rescuer's children with the Jewish youngsters who were rescued. The example of the Alexsander Roslan family is illustrative.

Roslan, who had a son and daughter of his own, smuggled two Jewish brothers from the Warsaw Ghetto while a third boy, hidden in a village, joined the Roslans and his brothers a short time later. The youngest boy, David, had been terrified during his separation from his older brothers because, as he said, "I had been told not to let anyone see me naked. I couldn't sleep and I would not let anyone touch me, especially to change my clothes. All I ever wondered was 'What did I do wrong?'"

David's infectious personality charmed the Polish family and he even became Roslan's favorite. Roslan's daughter, 7-years-old at the time, admitted, "The rest of us were jealous of the extra fruit and vitamins that father gave to David." The Jewish boys could not play outside but, said Roslan's daughter, "We all had fun at home. We played together, they were like my brothers."[66]

There were many such bonds between Polish and Jewish children and some of them have maintained contact for the past half-century. As Judith Kestenberg said, "The sibling bonds that developed between rescuer children and the Jewish children... were marked and have consistently endured.... The loving family atmosphere created by the rescuer parents fostered normal relations between the children. The rescuer children were made to feel a part of the meaningful and humane act of rescue."[67]

To be sure, the experiences of some Jewish children in Polish homes were not so loving or caring as in the Roslan home. One-year-old Krysia Klog ended up with a poor Polish family in Pludy, near Warsaw. The toddler was not cared for very well. She wandered through the house barefoot and dirty. The Polish woman distributed Krysia's clothes and shoes to her own children. Eventually another Polish family was found for the little girl.[68]

During the German occupation Jews received aid from Polish secular and religious groups. One of the major Polish relief organizations which the Germans allowed to operate under their close scrutiny was the *Rada Glowna Opiekuncza* (Central Welfare Council), which provided a variety of social services to adults and children. Under the leadership of Adam Ronikier, it operated over 1,000 facilities—soup kitchens, nurseries, day-centers, hospices—that benefited 200,000-300,000 people in the period 1941 to 1943. A large part of the *Rada*'s activities focused on children. In 1941, Polish children up to the age of 15 constituted 42 percent of those who received help, mostly food and clothing, from the organization. By 1942, the number of children given food by the *Rada* had decreased because the Germans ordered a curtailment of these supplementary allocations, which were banned completely in schools beginning in January, 1943.[69]

Jewish representatives regularly participated in the meetings of the *Rada* prior to the organization of the *Zydowska Samopomoc Spoleczna* (ZSS) (Jewish Self-Help Society), which was supported by the *Rada*. Even after the Nazis closed down the operations of the *ZSS* late in 1942, the *Rada* continued to give financial aid to the Jewish Welfare Bureau. On several occasions, Ronikier spoke in defense of the Jews to the German authorities, especially during the deportations from the Warsaw Ghetto.[70]

For some time *Rada*'s operatives, Irena Sendler, who was connected with the Social Welfare Department of the Municipal Administration of Warsaw, and her associate, Irena Schultz, had contact with the Jewish relief agency, CENTOS, and brought money, food and medicine to the Jews of Warsaw. Sendler wore an armband with the Star of David to show her solidarity with Warsaw's Jews. It also enabled her to move around the ghetto without the Germans and the Jewish police interfering in her work. When the ghetto was sealed off by the Germans, Sendler, using her position in Warsaw's municipal administration, obtained documents to allow her and her associate legal entry into the ghetto and to continue their relief efforts. Approximately 3,000 Warsaw Jews were beneficiaries of their work.[71]

In January, 1942, the Gestapo complained to Polish relief officials about the large number of poor and homeless children in the streets of Warsaw. Jan Dobraczynski, who headed the *Rada*'s children's branch and whose wife personally hid two Jewish girls, took the initiative to gather as many of the youngsters as possible from the streets and to take them to *Rada* facilities where they were fed. In this operation, 50 percent of the children picked up from Warsaw's streets were Jewish. Since the children were on the Polish side of the ghetto wall, they ran the risk of being executed by the Germans. Dobraczynski contacted Dr. Janusz Korczak who volunteered to take the homeless Jewish children and house them in his orphanage in the ghetto. To return Jewish children to the ghetto in January, 1942, was not considered especially dangerous. "No one yet talked or thought of mass murders," Dobraczynski said.[72]

After the deportations of Jews from the Warsaw Ghetto began in the summer of 1942, Dobraczynski's group increasingly expanded *Rada*'s operations to include Jewish children in obvious defiance of Nazi orders. When the Germans started to deport Jews from the ghetto, Irena Sendler said, "We had a new job to do—to get as many Jews as possible out of the ghetto, particularly children." The *Rada* operated several homes which hid Jewish children. Jadwiga Strzalecka, an energetic and selfless woman, looked after several Jewish children in one of the *Rada*'s homes. One day the Gestapo checked the establishment, frightening everyone as they scrutinized several of the Jewish children. Almost miraculously, even though several of the children had Semitic appearances, the Gestapo was satisfied the home was free of Jews. There were numerous apartments in Warsaw which were called the "emergency care service," where children could stay at least temporarily until false documents were prepared for them and permanent shelters could be found.[73]

"The number of Jewish children who needed help rose every day," Dobraczynski said. A number of his closest associates, all women, who had already taken personal initiatives in helping Jewish children appealed to him to have the *Rada* expand its operations in behalf of Jewish children even further. Dobraczynski then contacted several convents which accepted a large number of Jewish children. "I selected those institutes— all religious ones—whose heads I could trust completely and laid my case before them quite openly," Dobraczynski said. "I said that we would be sending a certain number of children to them and they had to know that these were Jewish children who would be coming to them with false records. They would recognize them by the fact that the letter directing them to a particular institute would be signed by myself permanently." As Jaga Piotrowska, one of Dobraczynski's close associates, remarked, "Records were written by trusted welfare workers.

Many Catholic parishes were willing to provide false certificates and the letters...."[74] As one participant involved in placing Jewish children in convents observed, "This could be, after all, a death sentence for the entire convent."[75]

Unfortunately, not all of the *Rada*'s establishments escaped harm from the Nazis. Adina Szwajger, a young Jewish woman who passed for a Christian, worked in a child day care center of the *Rada*, housed in a monastery of the Salesian Fathers in Powisle. Everyone in the center was young and connected in some way with the Polish underground. One day when Szwajger came to work, she found the center deserted. The previous day the Germans had taken away the priests and the secular staff. Szwajger remembered, "I am sure that those who lived in Warsaw at the time still remember those bodies hanging in black priest's habits, on the empty ground of the ghetto, visible from beyond its walls, in Leszno Street. That is where, in the spring of 1944, the Nazis hanged the Salesian Fathers."[76]

The Poles were unique among the people of German-occupied Europe to form a clandestine organization exclusively devoted to aiding Jews. In late September, 1942, following the first major deportations of Jews from the Warsaw Ghetto, Zofia Kossak, chairperson of the Front for Reborn Poland, and Wanda Krahelska-Filipowicz, an activist leader in the Socialist Party, had a major role in forming the Provisional Committee for Assistance to the Jews. During its brief existence, the committee helped approximately 200 Jews, mostly children, in the Warsaw region.[77]

Three months later, the Provisional Committee gave way to the Council for Aid to Jews (*Rada Pomocy Zydom*) or better known as *Zegota*, a cryptonym derived from the Polish word for Jew, *Zyd*. The executive board of *Zegota* represented the moderate-left of the Polish political spectrum: Julian Grobelny, a Socialist, chaired the group; Tadeusz Rek, representing the Peasant Party, was vice-chairman; Dr. Leon Feiner, member of the Bund, was second vice-chairman; Dr. Adolf Berman, representing the Jewish National Committee, was secretary; and Marek Arczynski of the Democratic Party was treasurer. The Front for Reborn Poland was initially represented by Ignacy Barski and later by Wladyslaw Bartoszewski. Even Jews under the care of groups not represented in *Zegota*—the Polish Syndicalist Union and the Polish Workers Party—received help from it. With headquarters in Warsaw, *Zegota* established regional groups in Krakow and Lwow and cooperated with groups in Lublin and Zamosc. The representative of the Polish government in Poland, the *Delegatura*, played a critical role in the establishment of the Provisional Committee and later *Zegota*.[78]

Zegota carried out an impressive program of aid that webbed the entire country. It was involved in finding shelter, providing food and medical assistance, and giving proper documents to Jews under its care. It also carried out an active campaign against blackmailers, informers and the anti-Semitic propaganda of the Nazis. *Zegota* never lacked for personnel, many of whom were connected with other organizations, such as the *Rada* and the *Armia Krajowa*.[79]

As for Warsaw itself, it is estimated that there were 15,000 to 30,000 Jews hiding in Warsaw during the period 1942-44 and that 4,000 of them were beneficiaries of the work of *Zegota*. Approximately 40,000-50,000 Jews, almost half of the Jews who survived the Holocaust in Poland, benefitted from some form of aid from *Zegota*.[80]

One of the important aspects of *Zegota's* activities was to forge documents which Jews needed to survive. Using the printing presses of the Democratic Party, *Zegota* produced an average of 100 forged documents every day. In less than two years, *Zegota* was responsible for making available 50,000 documents, 80 percent of which reached Jews without any cost to them.[81]

The Polish government provided most of the funds for *Zegota's* operations. Until June, 1943, *Zegota*, in turn, provided money to Jewish organizations involved in relief work. After that, a small amount of money came to *Zegota* from the Jewish National Committee and Jewish organizations abroad. The Government Delegate's initial grant to *Zegota* in January, 1943, was 150,000 zlotys and this increased to 2,000,000 zlotys by August, 1944, and eventually it went as high as 4,000,000 zlotys.[82]

What *Zegota* received from the Polish government and Jewish organizations was inadequate to meet the tremendous demands made upon it. Costs were so enormous that they went beyond the capacity of the Polish government alone to deal with the problem. One Polish leader actively involved in the work of *Zegota* estimated that it cost 5,000,000 zlotys every month to maintain 10,000 Jewish orphans.[83]

But budgetary limitations were obviously not the only, or even the most significant, problem facing *Zegota* and the Polish underground in saving Jewish lives. German determination to kill the Jews with the massive apparatus of terror at their disposal was still the dominant factor that Jews themselves recognized limited their ability to survive. As top Jewish leaders of the Jewish underground told Jan Karski, a Polish courier who gave an eyewitness account to western statesmen concerning the plight of Jews in 1942: "We want you to tell the Polish government, the Allied governments, and the great leaders of the Allies that we are helpless in the face of the German criminals. We cannot defend ourselves, and *no one in Poland can defend us* (italics mine). The Polish underground authorities can save some of us, but they cannot save the masses.... We are being systematically murdered. Our entire people will be destroyed .... *This cannot be prevented by any force in Poland, neither the Polish nor the Jewish Underground* (italics mine). Place this responsibility on the shoulders of the Allies." *Zegota* endorsed what Jewish leaders declared to Karski and called for an international effort to help save the remnants of European Jewry in 1943. It never came.[84] Conspicuously absent was even a declaration of support from the Jewish community in Palestine, where many Polish Jews had immigrated before the war.

The primary focus of *Zegota's* work was to save as many Jewish children as possible. Proof of the importance the organization attached to child rescue was revealed by the appointment of Irena Sendler to head *Zegota's* Children's Bureau. Her vast experience in rescuing children from the Warsaw Ghetto and her extensive contacts proved invaluable in *Zegota's* work. *Zegota* acted primarily as a coordinating agency which identified the individuals who needed assistance and funded a variety of establishments where Jewish children were hidden—convents, special care centers like the Home of Father Gabriel Boduen, agencies run by the *Rada*, and private homes. In the Warsaw region, Zegota was responsible for the care of approximately 2,600 children, of whom 500 were in convents, 200 in the Home of Father Boduen, 500 in establishments run by the *Rada*, 1,300 in the homes of Polish families and 100 placed with partisans outside the city.[85]

The needs of the children were not always the same. Some needed shelter; others were already well cared for by Polish families but needed proper documents to avoid arrest and execution. Many Poles who took care of Jewish children were so poor they needed funds to support themselves and the Jewish children they sheltered. Some families did not need money but required access to medical assistance, a major problem in occupied Poland because of the high mortality of Polish and Jewish physicians.

Polish activists involved in aiding Jews, whether connected with *Zegota* or other organizations, constantly had to be wary of the Gestapo who dogged them, forcing operatives to change names and addresses frequently. The Gestapo arrested, tortured and murdered some of them. Irena Sendler had several close calls with the Nazis who suspected her of underground activities. On one occasion the Gestapo conducted a three-hour inspection of her home where she had hidden the addresses of all the Jewish children under *Zegota*'s care. The Gestapo found nothing. But, in October, 1943, Sendler's luck ran out. An associate, under torture, revealed her name to the Gestapo who promptly arrested her and confined her to the notorious Pawiak prison where she was tortured. She expected to be shot. But her life was spared, thanks to a well-placed bribe by *Zegota* to a Gestapo official. After she was released from prison, Sendler had to live like the Jewish children she had rescued—in hiding. When her mother died, she could not attend the funeral. "I was alone and I gave all my energy to the activities of *Zegota*," she said.[86]

While Sendler concentrated on Jewish children in the Warsaw region, Wladyslawa Choms, an equally remarkable woman, headed the Lwow branch of *Zegota*. Using the *nom de guerre*, "Dionizy," she and her co-workers provided food, money and medical care for Jews inside and outside the Lwow Ghetto. She smuggled Jewish children from the ghetto in sewers and garbage wagons. Jewish mothers, realizing they were doomed, gave their children to Choms, called the "Angel of Lwow," who personally cared for 60 children. According to one Jewish survivor, "The stinking sewers were a dangerous rescue route and they claimed many casualties. The route could be used only by night." Sometimes sackfuls of bread were smuggled into the ghetto and the empty sacks were later used to carry Jewish children to the Polish side of the city where the youngsters were dispersed among convents and Polish families.

Two young Jewish women remarked how Choms had brought them out of the Lwow Ghetto on false papers. When one of them contracted typhus, Choms brought a physician who saved her life. "It goes without saying that everything she did for us was at grave risk to her own life," one of the women commented. In addition to shelter, food, money and false papers, Choms uplifted the morale of those she helped. According to one account, "Wladyslawa did much for those she saved, visiting them and, most important of all, encouraging them with the promise that the Nazis' downfall was at hand." In 1943, when the Germans began to pursue her, she fled from Lwow to Warsaw, where she continued her activities in the Polish underground.[87]

In addition to the *Rada* and *Zegota*, there were other Polish organizations, such as the *Spoleczna Organizacja Samoobrony* (SOS or Civic Organization of Self-Defense), composed of several groups, that cooperated with the Polish underground's Directorate of Civil Resistance and aided Jewish children. By mid-1943, it was responsible for placing approximately 700-1,000 Jewish children in private homes and clerical establishments. The *Polski Czerwony Krzyz* (Polish Red Cross) also hid Jews, especially those who had fled from the Warsaw Ghetto.[88]

The Catholic Church played a critical role in aiding unfortunate people, including Jews, during the war. This was especially evident in the assistance extended to Jewish children. It was an extremely difficult task for the clergy at a time when the Nazis virtually destroyed the church in the annexed lands and seriously curtailed its activities in the General Government.

By partitioning Poland into two sections—the annexed lands and the General Government—the Germans wreaked havoc with the organizational structure of the church. In the annexed lands, the church lost most of its bishops and clergy. In 1941,

500 priests from this area alone ended up in concentration camps. Almost 50 percent of the clergy in Wroclaw and Lodz died. Nuns in the annexed lands shared the same fate as priests. The Germans closed convents, seized their property and sent many into forced labor. The clergy in the General Government was not persecuted as much as their confreres in the annexed lands. But even there the Germans killed hundreds of priests. Out of a total of 10,017 secular clergy in Poland in 1939, almost 20 percent died during the war.[89] In addition, almost 1,000 monks and nuns perished.[90]

These clerical losses were enormous, especially in a country where they numbered only a fraction of the French and Italian clergy, and affected the church's ability to continue one of its missions of helping the unfortunate victims of the war. Nevertheless, priests, nuns and monks met the enormous challenges imposed upon them by the Germans and did what they could in conducting charitable and humanitarian work on behalf of Christians and Jews.

The church was not only weakened and divided but also had no national spiritual leader to shepherd it during the German occupation. The Polish Primate, Augustus Cardinal Hlond, had fled into exile. That meant that individual bishops and priests, not imprisoned by the Nazis yet, had to assume individual leadership in their respective dioceses and parishes in meeting the demands made upon them for relief and assistance by Christians and Jews. Their work on behalf of Jews had to be conducted surreptitiously; any kind of public declarations concerning aiding Jews by bishops, priests and nuns would have been suicidal for everyone involved in the process.

The ranking Polish clergyman, Archbishop Adam Sapieha of Krakow, strongly supported the *Rada* and urged the clergy to help Jews, especially those in prisons and Jewish converts to Catholicism.[91] Bishop Karol Niemira and Canon Roman Archutowski set the tone for the clergy in Warsaw by helping Jews. "These men were tireless in finding ways to help Jewish families," Rev. Jan Januszewski said.[92] Various clerical leaders in Warsaw offered to hide Jewish rabbis during the occupation and one chose to avail himself of the offer by hiding in the library of the Ordinary of the Diocese of Warsaw. Under the leadership of Romuald Jalbrzykowski, the Metropolitan of Vilna, the clergy hid Jews in churches and convents.[93]

There is substantial evidence of sporadic and individual assistance to the Jews by parish priests and monks. Emmanuel Ringelblum observed how parish priests in Warsaw urged their parishioners to forget sometimes bitter relations between Christians and Jews and opposed Nazi actions toward the Jewish people. Even some former anti-Semitic priests, notably Rev. Marceli Godlewski, put aside past animosities to help Jewish children and adults. On one occasion, Godlewski hid under his cassock small Jewish children trying to elude Nazi pursuers. Several priests and monks helped Jews by providing false baptismal documents which allowed them to function freely as Aryans.[94] One monk, Sylvester Paluch, was responsible for arranging documents for 500 Jews.[95] Rev. Franciszek Zak in Dolina arranged for the flight of Jews from Poland to Romania and Hungary. In Krakow, Karol Wojtyla, the future Pope John Paul II, cooperated with the Jewish leadership to aid Jews.[96]

Even though Polish priests were not in the best position to help Jews, one prominent member of the *AK* declared, "I never heard of an instance where Polish clergy ever refused help to Jews."[97]

Parish priests were too visible and their rectories inadequate to provide long-term shelter to Jews. Those who did often ended up paying with their lives. Some, like Rev. Jozef Pochoda, had to flee his parish before the Gestapo caught up with him for having christened two Jewish children. Father Michael Sopocko personally sheltered a 5-year-old Jewish child until he was forced to send it to a village. Other priests, like Father Witold Szymczukiewicz, used his influence to place a Jewish boy and his father in the home of a parishioner.[98] Sometimes Jewish children passed from one rectory to another. Rev. Konstanty Cabaj accepted a Jewish child from a mother on her way to her death. He took care of the child until the Gestapo got too inquisitive. Cabaj then sent the child to a priest in another city who cared for it.[99]

Father Maximilian Kolbe, head of the Franciscan monastery at Niepokalanow, and his confreres were responsible for giving food and shelter to approximately 1,500 Jews, many of whom were children, that were refugees from Poznan. Most of the friary in 1940 had been turned over to Jewish and Christian refugees who had been expelled by the Germans from the Poznan region. The Germans arrested Kolbe for the aid he gave Jews. Sent to Auschwitz, Kolbe gave his life for another Pole. Before his death, Kolbe befriended Sigmund Gorson, a 13-year-old Jewish boy, whom he comforted and helped win back to a belief in God after the death of Gorson's family. "He was like an angel to me," Gorson said. "Like a mother hen, he took me in his arms. He used to wipe away my tears. He knew I was a Jewish boy. That made no difference. His heart was bigger than persons—that is, whether they were Jewish, Catholic or whatever. He loved everyone. He dispensed love and nothing but love." He added, "I will love him until the last moments of my life."

In addition to the Franciscans, there were a number of other monastic orders involved in the work of aiding Jews, including children. These included the Congregation of Father Missionaries of St. Vincent a Paolo, the Congregation of the Most Holy Redeemer, the Salesian Society, the Association of Catholic Apostleship, the Congregation of Marist Friars, Capuchins, and Dominicans.[100]

The focal point for much of the activity of laymen and clergy in Warsaw in behalf of Jewish children was the Home of Father Boduen. *Zegota*, which could not operate without the support of the clergy, placed approximately 200 Jewish children in the home, directed by Dr. Maria Prokopowicz-Wierzbowska. Jewish children whose appearance compromised them, especially circumcised boys, were sent to Klarysew and Gora Kalwaria, outside of Warsaw. They hid under clothes in wagons whose drivers routinely carried vodka and kielbasa to pay off snoopy policemen. Despite the fact that it was common knowledge that many Jewish children resided at Boduen, no one informed to the Gestapo.[101]

For many reasons Polish nuns were in the best position to care for Jewish children on a prolonged basis. There were more than three times as many nuns as monks in Poland and a greater number of monks than nuns died at the hands of the Germans. In 1939, there were 84 female congregations with 2,289 houses in Poland.[102] To be sure, nuns lost hundreds of their houses in the annexed lands where organized religious life had ceased to exist but many of them were allowed to operate in the General Government where the German policy aimed at control, not liquidation, of the church. Moreover, many of the convents were scattered in some of the more remote areas of the country, mitigating some of the scrutiny of the Gestapo.

Polish nuns saw their most important work as caring for children, the most helpless and vulnerable victims of the war. They looked after not only Poles but also Jews, Gypsies, Ukrainians, and later in the war, German children. One historian has located 189 convents, almost one-third of which were in the Warsaw region alone, that hid Jewish children during the war.[103] Four orders accounted for almost 25 percent of Polish nuns—the Sisters of Charity (Grey Sisters), Little Servant Sisters of the Immaculate Conception, Franciscans of the Family of Mary and the Order of St. Elizabeth—all actively engaged in hiding Jewish children. Probably as many as two-thirds of the religious communities in Poland were involved in hiding Jewish children and adults.[104]

Although the decision to take Jews into the convent was to a large degree the decision of mother superiors, there were cases where individual nuns rescued children and influenced their superiors to approve of their actions. Admitting Jewish children into a convent or a facility run by nuns was not new to Polish sisters who had operated scores of institutions where a number of Jewish children resided before the war.[105]

During the early stages of the German occupation of Poland, sisters gathered a number of Jewish children but in many cases *Judenrats* demanded that the children be returned to the ghettos. In December, 1939, when the Germans eliminated the bishop of Krakow's sanatorium for children with tuberculosis, the Grey Ursulines took 15 children into their convent. Two of them were Jewish. The chairman of the *Judenrat* of Nowy Targ ordered that the children be brought to the Warsaw Ghetto. One of them, Anita Goldman, age 10, remained in the care of nuns but Rysio Krupka, who was 10 or 12 years old, went back to the Warsaw Ghetto where he died in the deportations of August, 1942.[106]

Once the Nazis began to liquidate the ghettos in 1942 and

1943, Jewish children began to arrive at convents and orphanages in larger numbers. Some Jewish parents and guardians brought the children to the nuns. One Jewish dentist simply brought his son to the door of a convent at Turkowiec where he told the mother superior, "I will live for as long as I am useful to the Germans, but I will surely not survive. I have brought my son. If you can, I would ask you to take him in." When the Germans liquidated the Ostrowiec Ghetto, an old Jewish man ran to a convent window and hurled a baby boy, called Antos, to a nun saying, "Hide him! He's yours now!"[107] A Jewish physician left his wife and son with nuns in Nowogrodek during the anti-Jewish pogroms there in 1941. The nuns hid them until the physician returned in 1943 and took them away because of German searches of the convent.[108]

Most Jewish parents and guardians who wanted their youngsters placed with the sisters usually went through Polish laymen, parish priests, or, as has been seen, operatives working for the *Rada* or *Zegota*, who acted as intermediaries for them. Often priests sought out Jewish children on their own and brought them to the nuns. Rev. Piotr Tomaszewski, chaplain of the Boduen home, "excelled in this activity." One woman, a Polish school teacher by the name of Kitowna, brought several Jewish children to a convent and probably paid with her life.[109]

Most Jewish children arrived at convents as foundlings. Laymen and clergy found them everywhere—on doorsteps, streets, abandoned houses, gates, porches. In three months, 57 Jewish girls and 65 boys arrived at the Home of Father Boduen. The Grey Sisters had to deal with so many foundlings they established a special creche near the hospital in Kielce in 1942. An Albertine nun in Krakow said, "During the anti-Jewish actions the number of children left at the creche increased. They could be recognized as the boys were circumcized or had Semitic features."[110]

As news began to spread about the murder of Poles who sheltered Jews, some Poles, unable to overcome their fear, turned over their charges to nuns. One farmer brought a 3-year-old girl to the Albertines in Siedlce because he was too frightened to keep her any longer. One Lublin nun related, "There were a few Jewish girls hiding from the Germans. One of them, 10- or 11-years-old, whose parents had been shot and whose house had been burnt [*sic*] down, tried to run away and hid first of all with some Polish farmers. But they were afraid to hide a Jewish child and sent her to us."[111] One Jewish boy, thrown out of a train headed for Auschwitz, was rescued by a Polish couple and remained with them until they found a permanent home for him with nuns in Pruszkow.[112]

Sometimes older Jewish children who had escaped from the ghetto found their own way to the nuns or were directed there by Polish people who were afraid to take them. Icek, a young Jewish boy, rang the door bell at the convent of the Samaritan Sisters in Henrykow and pointedly asked a nun, "Will I get something to eat?" When the nun ushered Icek inside the convent and fed him, Icek confided that his sister, Lola, waited for him some distance away. When they arrived at the place where Lola was hiding, Icek called to her, "Lola, come on over here. There's bread and sausage as well and it's warm in the house. White walls and these ladies in funny clothes." But Lola had already died of cold and hunger. Icek stayed with the nuns, along with other children and adults, and survived the war.

Often nuns themselves sought out Jewish children to bring to the convent. One nun found a 5-year-old boy near the Children's Institute of Wolomin. Some Polish boys had chased him away and even threw stones at him. When one of the nuns saw that, she called the boy and gave him food and clothes. "At first he was frightened and timid, but he changed after a few days and the [Polish] boys came to like him very much," Sister Magdalena Kaczmarzyk said. The boy remained at the institute until 1946 when his mother reclaimed him.[113] Even nuns unconnected with a convent but part of the civilian labor force aided Jews. Sister Stanislawa Blandzinski worked in a cannery in Galicia, and every day sent food to a Jewish woman and her children.[114]

One of the most active orders in rescuing Jewish children was the Franciscan Sisters of the Family of Mary. Sister Matylda Getter, mother superior of the Warsaw branch of the order, accepted all Jewish children who fled from the Warsaw Ghetto and placed most of them at the convent in Pludy near Warsaw. Mother Getter, a legend in her own time, was no different from most Polish nuns who were interested in saving the lives of children, not in proselyting them. One nun of the order came regularly to Warsaw to take away Jewish children to the safety of the convent. Two former children who survived the war remarked later that the nuns treated them "like mothers." Altogether this congregation alone saved the lives of at least 500 children and young people and 250 adults. In addition, at least 500 other Jews received help from these nuns.[115]

The Ursulines also helped Jewish children. A prominent Jewish physician, Dr. Sofia Szymanska, was sheltered at a convent-school in Ozarow when a Jewish girl, Jasia, was left at the door. "I'm Jasia. I have no one," she declared. Sister Wanda Garczynska replied, "You are not alone, child, you have me." Jasia, who looked Semitic, had to be hidden when the Nazis visited the convent. On one occasion, Sister Wanda dressed Jasia and another Jewish girl in long white robes and hid them in a wardrobe prior to a German search. German soldiers, suspecting Jewish children in the convent, jabbed their bayonets into the closet but fortunately, the girls later emerged unscathed. The girls thought it was all a game. Despite the fact that Polish children in the school and their parents knew Jasia and another girl were Jewish, no one betrayed them. Dr. Szymanska said, "The children were under the protection of the entire convent and village. Not one traitor existed among them." She added, "The memory of Sister Wanda Garczynska allowed me during the years of rampant cruelty to believe in man."[116]

One of the orders of nuns devoting itself to helping Jewish children was the Little Servant Sisters of the Immaculate Conception. The convent at Turkowiec, located in the Polish countryside, was ideally suited to shelter Jewish children. Mother Superior Stanislawa Polechajllo, a Pole of Tatar background, was, like Mother Getter, committed to saving lives. The nuns hid 33 Jewish children in Turkowiec and 31 other Jewish children at other centers of the order.[117] One Jewish girl, now an adult living in Israel, expressed her gratitude to the nuns saying, "The gift of life belongs to you." Sister Witolda Wielgus's protection of a Jewish boy, Marian Marzynski, at the order's convent at Lazniew enabled him to survive the war and to this day he regards Sister Witolda as his second mother. One of the nuns of the order, upon receiving a prearranged code word from *Zegota*, regularly went to Warsaw to escort Jewish children back to the convent at Turkowiec.[118]

Rare was the convent that did not experience a German search, especially if the Gestapo's suspicion had been aroused that Jews might be in hiding there. Surprisingly, these inspections rarely turned up anything, so adept were the nuns in hiding and camouflaging Jewish boys and girls. Sometimes there was even a comical twist to a potentially tragic event. In one convent, an 11-year-old Jewish girl was under the care of nuns when someone informed the Gestapo that a Jew was in the convent. The Gestapo first inquired of the Polish mayor, a courageous man who told them that the report was false and deliberately got the Germans drunk. While the Germans drank, the mayor sent a messenger to the nuns and warned them of an impending German inspection of the convent. The nuns hid the young girl in the church belfry. The Gestapo never came due to their hangovers. The shrewd mayor got the Germans to sign a document which indicated that they had searched the convent and that the report concerning the nuns had been without merit.[119]

Generally speaking, young Jewish children were not baptized by the nuns without an understanding with either their parents or guardians. As one Jewish father told one of the nuns of the Little Servants of the Immaculate Conception, with whom he entrusted his son, "I give you...a free hand to christen him; if you choose to do so, christen him. If you do not, then don't." Younger children without adults or foster parents sometimes were baptized but not all orders did so, believing that the children would be returned to their families after the war.[120]

The issue, of course, was a sensitive one, especially to religious Jews. When one Jewish leader asked Jan Dobraczynski, head of the Children's Branch of the *Rada*, what would happen to baptized children after the war, he replied that should any Jewish kinsmen claim the child, they could change the child's religion. The Jew accepted the Pole's explanation and thanked him for Polish help to Jewish children.[121] As will be seen later, with only a few exceptions, most of the Jewish children sheltered by Polish nuns survived the war. Some remained in Poland, others were reclaimed by parents, relatives or Zionist organizations who resettled them elsewhere.

Historians document at least 1,500 Jewish children who were

saved by Polish nuns.[122] More than likely, there were many more children saved by the sisters but the lack of records and the difficulty in some cases of establishing how many of the children left with the nuns were Jewish make it difficult to calculate the number with any kind of precision. What is known is that the Jewish children came mostly from assimilated Jewish families, people who knew and trusted Poles and did not subscribe to the negative stereotypes about them that circulated widely among unassimilated Jews. Regarding Polish Catholic nuns, Szymon Datner, a distinguished Jewish historian, concluded, "In my research I have found only one case of help being refused. No other sector was so ready to help those persecuted by the Germans, including the Jews.... this attitude, unanimous and general, deserves recognition and respect."[123]

Some Jewish children survived the war as nomads, moving from place to place in the countryside. Sometimes they stayed for a few days in one place, sometimes longer. They found shelter in barns, chicken coops, under bridges and in haystacks, virtually anywhere that gave them adequate protection. When they changed locations, it usually was at night to avoid detection. They begged for food and picked out what was edible from garbage dumps. The reception they received from peasants was often warm, sometimes it wasn't, especially when the Germans warned Poles that they would be shot for even feeding a Jew. Peasants were well aware of Poles who had been shot or burned alive by the Germans for aiding Jews.

One 6-year-old boy, described as having "the cunning of a man 36," lived in a peasant's abandoned chicken coop until the farmer chased him off. Later, he became one of hundreds of street kids who hawked newspapers, matches, and pornographic books during the day and slept under bridges and empty streetcars at night.[124]

Two Jewish boys survived for a time in a dug-out in a garden of a ruined house in Mokotow, a Warsaw suburb, and received food from kindly Poles before they were eventually placed with a Polish guardian. One day in Mokotow, the boys found a scooter which they put back into working order. Completely oblivious to their dangerous circumstances, the boys drove around the area on their scooter until someone reported to the Germans, "There are Jews riding on the streets and disturbing the peace." When the police arrived the boys fled, passing an old woman selling apples in a stall. When she saw the gendarmes gaining on the boys, she deliberately knocked over her own stall so that the scattered apples impeded the police chase. It worked. The boys managed to get back to their hiding place.[125]

Sometimes Jewish children, like the famous novelist Jerzy Kosinski, hid their Jewish identity as they wandered around doing odd jobs for people. Yuzik, a 12-year-old who looked Polish, kept his identity secret while he sold newspapers on the corner of Krolewska and Krakowskie Streets in downtown Warsaw. There were even some loving liaisons of mutual help as in the case of a 5-year-old orphaned Polish girl and a young Jewish boy who teamed up and begged together on the streets of Warsaw.[126]

We will never know the number of Poles who perished at the hands of the Nazis for aiding Jews. Few records were kept and that which existed in the archives of the Polish underground was destroyed in the massive devastation accompanying the Warsaw Uprising of 1944. So far one Polish research group has estimated that approximately 2,300 Poles lost their lives for aiding Jews.[127] But it rightly makes no claim to accuracy because as everyone knows who has studied the subject, it is doubtful that anything more than a small number of Poles who died in their efforts to help Jews will ever be known. Some estimates reach as high as 50,000. According to one scholar who has recently published a book on the subject, "I succeeded to identify... a few thousand of them and every time I make a trip to Poland this number increases by 30 or 40."[128] Among those Poles killed by the Germans for helping Jews were 200 people in Berecz and Podiwanowka, 43 in Bor Kunowski, 30 in Przewrotne, 25 in Klobuczyn, 25 in Cisie, and on the list goes. According to one Jewish historian and eyewitness to the deaths of Poles for aiding Jews, "In 38 cases of Jews saved by Poles, as established on the basis of one source, the Nazis murdered 97 Poles, including 30 women, 14 children and 1 infant."129

Often Polish children died with their parents. On June 22, 1943, the Germans shot 7 Poles, including 2 infants, in Posadza. In Pustelnik, the Germans learned that Marianna Banaszek had helped a Jewish family. When the Germans arrived at her home, they only found 17-year-old Stanislawa and her older brother.

Enraged at being unable to find the Jews, the Germans shot Banaczek's children at a nearby pond. In Radgoszcz, the German military police shot Zofia Wojcik and her two children, ages 2 and 3, along with the Jew who had lived with the family. There is an account of the SS burning alive 10 Poles, 6 of whom were children between the ages of 3 and 13, for harboring Jews.[130] In Ciepielow Stary, the Germans murdered three families—the Kowalskis, Obuchs and Kosiors–for hiding Jews. Half of the family members were children.[131]

In 1942, a group of Polish Boy Scouts tried to smuggle badly needed anti-typhoid shots to fight the epidemic that killed large numbers of Jews in the Warsaw Ghetto. The Germans killed 7 of the young boys in this operation. One boy, Staszek, whose family name is unknown, was 16-years-old. Caught by the Germans with one of the ampules in his hand, Staszek swallowed it to prevent the Gestapo from learning the purpose of his mission. He died soon afterwards.[132]

Rather than murder all Poles in a village for aiding Jews, the Germans sometimes selected only a certain number of them for execution. This is what happened in Przewrotne on March 13, 1943, when the Germans selected 36 villagers for a public execution. Among those shot to death were 3 children, ranging in ages from 2 months to 19, of the Klecha family, and a teenage boy of the Warzocha family.[133]

One of the most devastating retribution raids conducted by the Nazis occurred on July 12-13, 1943, in Michniow, where the Germans herded people into barns and houses and burned them alive for helping a Jewish partisan unit. Over 200 people died, including almost 70 children. The youngest was only 9 days old.[134]

Chapter Notes

1. Dobroszycki, *Chronicle of the Lodz Ghetto*, p. xxv.
2. See Lukas, *Forgotten Holocaust*, pp. 121-26.
3. Silkes Papers in YIVO.
4. *Ibid.* According to a distinguished Jewish physician, Jews in the Warsaw Ghetto did not seriously look for Polish help until May, 1942, shortly before the deportations began. Szymanska, *Bylam Tylko Lekarzem*, pp. 144-45.
5. Film, Documentaries International, "Zegota: A Time to Remember."
6. Ringelblum, *Kronika Getta Warszawskiego*, p. 425.
7. Nir, *Lost Childhood*, p. 44.
8. Interview with Stanislaw Makuch, September 17, 1984.
9. Memo, Savery to Allen, July 17, 1944, in FO 371/ 39524 C 9465/7711/55, PRO; Stewart Steven, *The Poles* (New York: Macmillan, 1982), pp. 313-14.
10. Eugene Kusielewicz, "Some Thoughts on the Teaching of the Holocaust," *Perspectives*, 14 (March-April, 1984), Insert D.
11. Emmanuel Ringelblum, *Polish-Jewish Relations during the Second World War.* Edited by Joseph Kermish and Shmuel Krakowski (New York: Howard Fertig, 1976), p. 53; Ringelblum, *Notes from the Warsaw Ghetto*, p. 322; Wladyslaw Bartoszewski and Sofia Lewin, *The Samaritans: Heroes of the Holocaust* (New York: Twayne, 1970), p. 58.
12. Rose Zar, *In the Mouth of the Wolf* (Philadelphia: Jewish Publication Society of America, 1983), pp. 23, 192.
13. Geve, *Youth in Chains*, p. 93.
14. In the introduction to Vladka Meed's book, Elie Wiesel makes the astonishing suggestion that Poles were morally flawed, "But how many good-hearted, upright Poles were to be found at the time in Poland. Very few." See Vladka Meed, *On Both Sides of the Wall: Memoirs from the Warsaw Ghetto* (New York: Holocaust Library, 1979), p. 4. There is no evidence for Wiesel's indictment

while there is much to the contrary. Meed herself makes several tendentious statements about the Poles in her book.

15. Harold Schulweis, "The Fear and Suspicion of Goodness," in *Moral Courage during the Holocaust: Select Papers from the Jewish Foundation for Christian Rescuers' 1990 Conference* (New York: Jewish Foundation for Christian Rescuers, Anti-Defamation League, 1990), pp. 1-4.

16. Prekerowa, *Konspiracyjna Rada Pomocy Zydom*, p. 194.

17. For the statistics, see *ibid.*, p. 478; and Bednarczyk, *Obowiazek Silniejszy*, p. 112.

18. Lukas, *Forgotten Holocaust* pp. 126-27.

19. Wladyslaw Bartoszewski, *The Blood Shed Unites Us: Pages from the History of Help to the Jews in Occupied Poland* (Warsaw: Interpress, 1970), p. 222.

20. Eyewitness Accounts (137-90), Series I, No.90, in YIVO.

21. See *Hiding Experience Directory: The First International Gathering of Children Hidden during World War II, May 26-27, 1991*.

22. Bartoszewski and Lewin, *Samaritans*, p. 3; Stanislaw Wronski and Maria Zwolakowa, *Polacy Zydzi, 1939-1945* (Warsaw: Ksiazka i Wiedza, 1971), p. 258; Wladyslaw Zarski-Zajdler, *Martyrologia Ludnosci Zydowskiei i Pomoc Spoleczenstwa Polskiego* (Warsaw: 1968), p. 16. Some estimates of the number of Poles who helped Jews are ridiculously low. One of these lists a total of 160,000-360,000 Poles, Belorussians and Ukrainians who helped Jews. Teresa Prekerowa, "Aid to Jews by Poles," *Encyclopedia of the Holocaust*, I, 9.

23. Wladyslaw Bartoszewski and Zofia Lewin, *Righteous Among Nations: How Poles Helped the Jews, 1939-1945* (London: Earlscourt, 1969), p. 39.

24. Riwash, *Resistance and Revenge*, p. 139.

25. Lukas, *Out of the Inferno,* pp. 156-58.

26. Huberband, *Kiddush Hashem*, pp. 91-101.

27. Geve, *Youth in Chains*, p. 171.

28. Protokol Przesluchania Swiadka, Leokadia Soltys (Symoniuk) April 22, 1987, in OKL/Kpp 2/97, in DS 23/68, AGKBZHP.

29. Peter Hellman, *Avenue of the Righteous* (New York: Atheneum, 1980), pp. 168-267.

30. Ziemian, *Cigarette Sellers*, pp. 37-54.

31. Lukas, *Out of the Inferno*, pp. 179-80. Brzuska, known as

"Grandma" to those she helped, was a legendary Warsaw personality. In addition to feeding and sheltering Jewish children, she hid escapees from a nearby German workshop, stored Jewish underground literature and hid false documents. Her shop was a critical link for the Jewish underground movement. Ziemian, *Cigarette Sellers*, p. 28; Bartoszewski and Lewin, *Righteous Among Nations*, pp. 175-80.

32. *Canadian Jewish News*, July 10, 1986.

33. Meed, *On Both Sides of the Wall*, pp. 192-93. Pero was one of hundreds of officers and men in the *AK* who independently looked after Jews in Warsaw. See the comments of Henryk Wolinski, who headed the Jewish Office of the Bureau of Information and Propaganda of the High Command of the *AK*, in Lukas, *Out of the Inferno*, p. 179. Also see Bednarczyk, *Obowiazek Silniejszy*, pp. 106ff.

34. Douglas E. Huneke, *The Moses of Rovno* (New York: Dodd, Mead, 1985), p. xvi.

35. Lukas, *Out of the Inferno*, pp. 116-23.

36. *Ibid.*, pp. 110-16.

37. Ltr., Rys to Glowna Komisja Badania Zbrodni Hitlerowskich w Polsce, June 1, 1985, in DS 23/68, AGKBZHP.

38. Martin Gilbert, *The Second World War* (London: Stodart, 1989), p. 505.

39. Prekerowa, *Konspiracyjna Rada Pomocy Zydom*, p. 205.

40. Meed, *On Both Sides of the Wall*, p. 113.

41. Dobraczynski, *Tylko w Jednym Zyciu*, pp. 244-45.

42. Adina Blady Szwajger, *I Remember Nothing More: The Warsaw's Children Hospital and the Jewish Resistance*, Trans. by Tasja Darowska and Danusia Stok (London: Collins Harvill, 1990), pp. 137-38.

43. Prekerowa, *Konspiracyjna Rada Pomocy Zydom*, p. 202.

44. Nir, *Lost Childhood*, p. 54.

45. Eisenberg, *Lost Generation*, p. 184.

46. Nir, *Lost Childhood*, pp. 54-55. Dr. Feliks Kanabus, a member of the clandestine Coordinating Committee of Democratic and Socialist Physicians, specialized in plastic surgery to remove the effects of circumcision. Bartoszewski and Lewin, *Righteous Among Nations*, p. 66.

47. Kuchler-Silberman, *One Hundred Children*, p. 121.

48. Zar, *In the Mouth of the Wolf*, p. 9.

49. Prekerowa, *Konspiracyjna Rada Pomocy Zydom*, pp. 201-202.

50. Meed acknowledges that lower-class Jews, who constituted the overwhelming majority of Jews in Poland, did not know Polish well enough to pass for gentiles. Meed, *On Both Sides of the Wall*, p. 182.

51. Interview with Staszek Jackowski, July 30, 1984; Prekerowa, *Konspiracyjna Rada Pomocy Zydom*, pp. 191-92.

52. Bohdan Vitvitsky, "Slavs and Jews: Consistent and Inconsistent Perspectives on the Holocaust," in *A Mosaic of Victims: Non-Jews Persecuted and Murdered by the Nazis*. Edited by Michael Birenbaum (New York: New York University Press, 1990), p. 107.

53. Szwajger, *I Remember Nothing More*, p. 161.

54. Prekerowa, *Konspiracyjna Rada Pomocy Zydom*, p. 208.

55. Games, *Escape into Darkness*, p. 93; Bartoszewski and Lewin, *Righteous Among Nations*, p. xxii.

56. Andrzej and Karolina Jus, *Our Journey in the Valley of Tears* (Toronto: University of Toronto Press, 1991), p. 180.

57. Komisja Polskiego Sztabu Glownego w Londynie, *Polskie Sily Zbrojne*. Vol. III: *Armia Krajowa*, 473; Joseph Kermish, "The Activities of the Council for Aid to Jews (*Zegota*) in Occupied Poland," in *Rescue Attempts during the Holocaust: Proceedings of the Second Yad Vashem International Historical Conference* (Jerusalem: Yad Vashem, 1977), p. 368. There were many executions of informers which were not recorded.

58. Edmund Golecki, "Ludzie i Zwierzeta," in Turski, *Byli Wowczas Dziecmi*, pp. 294-98.

59. Meldunek Organizacyjny, Bor do N.W., August 31, 1943, in Studium Polski Podziemnej, *Armia Krajowa w Dokumentach*, III, 75; Tadeusz Zenczykowski, *General Grot: U Kresu Walki* (London: Polonia Book Fund, 1983), pp. 170-72.

60. Lukas, *Out of the Inferno*, pp. 32-35.

61. Protokol Przesluchania Swiadka, Wladyslaw Milewski, Komisja Badania Zbrodni Hitlerowskich w Bialymstoku, October 27, 1986, in DS 23/68, AGK BZHP.

62. *Toronto Star*, December 3, 1990.

63. Film, Documentaries International, "The Other Side of Faith."

64. Ltr., Aniela Hessek do Glowna Komisja Badania Zbrodni Hitlerowskich w Polsce, November 10, 1987; Ltr., Deutsches Rotes Kreuz to Stanislaw Staniec, October 28, 1971, DS 23/68, AGK BZHP.

65. Deposition, Dr. Leonard Lukaszuk, November 25, 1991.

66. Judith Kestenberg, et. al., "Jewish Christian Relationships As Seen Through the Eyes of Children, Before, During and After the Holocaust" (Sand's Point, N.Y.: Jerome Riker International Study of Organized Persecution of Children, n.d.), p. 14.

67. *Ibid.*, p. 15.

68. Meed, *On Both Sides of the Wall*, p.114.

69. Bogdan Kroll, *Rada Glowna Opiekuncza*, 1939-1945 (Warsaw: Ksiazka i Wiedza, 1985), pp. 125, 164-65; Hrabar, *Fate of Polish Children*, p. 174.

70. Kroll, *Rada Glowna Opiekuncza*, pp. 223-27; Bogdan Kroll, "Rada Glowna Opiekuncza," *Encyclopedia of the Holocaust*, 111, 1217-18.

71. Prekerowa, *Konspiracyjna Rada Pomocy Zydom*, p. 190; Irena Sendler, "People Who Helped Jews," in Bartoszewski and Lewin, *Righteous Among Nations*, pp. 41ff.

72. Dobraczynski, *Tylko w Jednym Zyciu*, pp. 235-38.

73. Prekerowa, *Konspiracyjna Rada Pomocy Zydom*, pp. 211-13; Sendler, "People Who Helped Jews," p. 43.

74. Dobraczynski, *Tylko w Jednym Zyciu*, pp. 241-47; *Slowo Powszechne*, April 19, 1968.

75. Prekerowa, *Konspiracyjna Rada Pomocy Zydom*, p. 191.

76. Szwajger, *I Remember Nothing More*, pp. 122-24.

77. Marek Arczynski and Wieslaw Balcerak, *Kryptonim Zegota: Z Dziejow Pomocy Zydom w Polsce, 1939-1945* (Warsaw: Czytelnik, 1983), pp. 76-80; Sendler, "People Who Helped Jews," pp. 41-42.

78. Arczynski, *Kryptonim Zegota*, pp. 76-80; Bartoszewski, *Blood Shed Unites Us*, pp. 89-106; Raport Specjalny, Kalski do Premiera, May 25, 1944, in A.9III. 24-27; Raport, Zegota, 12/42-10/43, in Sprawy Zydowskie-E, X-1, PI/GSHM. Krakow's *Zegota* cared for about 1,000 Jews.

79. For *Zegota's* activities, see Arczynski, *Kryptonim Zegota* and Prekerowa, *Konspiracyjna Rada Pomocy Zydom*. For some officers involved in Zegota's activities, see Bartoszewski and Lewin, *Samaritans*, pp. 116-18.

80. Madajczyk, *Polityka Rzeszy*, 1, 343; II, 337; Arczynski, *Kryptonim Zegota*, pp. 95, 188; Bartoszewski, *Blood Shed Unites Us*, pp. 100-101; Kermish, "Activities of the Council for Aid to Jews," pp. 374, 394.

81. Arczynski, *Kryptonim Zegota*, pp. 87-88.

82. *Ibid.*, pp. 90, 136; Kermish, "Activities of the Council for Aid to Jews," p. 374.

83. Arczynski, *Kryptonim Zegota*, p. 89.

84. Karski, *Story of a Secret State*, p. 323; Depesza do Mikolajczyka, January 8, 1943, in Sprawy Zydowskie-E III-9 in PI/GSHM; Depesza, Rada Pomocy Zydom do Rzadu, July 22, 1943, in T.78, Polish Underground Study Trust. Hereinafter cited as PUST.

85. Prekerowa, *Konspiracyjna Rada Pomocy Zydom*, pp. 213-17. Prekerowa correctly notes that the actual number of Jewish children rescued from the Warsaw Ghetto was "much greater" than 2,600 because there were, after all, other avenues of rescue open to Jews than *Zegota*.

86. Sendler, "People Who Helped Jews," pp. 56-59.

87. Arieh L. Bauminger, *The Righteous Among the Nations* (Jerusalem: Yad Vashem, 1990), pp. 135-39; Mordecai Paldiel, "Wladyslawa Choms," *Encyclopedia of the Holocaust*, I, 289-90; Kurt R. Grossman, "The Angel of lvov," in Bartoszewski and Lewin, *Righteous Among Nations*, pp. 105-07.

88. Bednarczyk, *Obowiazek Silniejszy*, pp. 45-48, 196-97.

89. Lukas, *Forgotten Holocaust*, pp. 11-12.

90. Jerzy Kloczowski, "The Religious Orders and the Jews in Nazi-Occupied Poland," *Polin*, No.3 (1988), p. 238.

91. Zenon Fijalkowski, *Kosciol Katolicki na Ziemiach Polskich w Latach Okupacji Hitlerowskiej* (Warsaw: Ksiazka i Wiedza, 1983), pp. 199-200; Zygmunt Zielinski, *Zycie Religijne w Polsce pod Okupacja Hitlerowska*, 1939-1945 (Warsaw: Osrodek Dokumentacji i Studiow Spolecznych, 1982), p. 338.

92. Fijalkowski, *Kosciol Katolicki*, p. 202; Interview with Rev. Jan Januszewski, August 1, 1982.

93. Fijalkowski, *Kosciol Katolicki*, p. 202: Zygmunt Zielinski, *Zycie Religijne w Polsce pod Okupacja, 1939-1945: Metropolie Wilenska o Lwowska, Zakony* (Katowice: Wydawnictwo Unia, 1992), p. 51. The activities of the clergy spurred many young Catholic Poles to get involved in helping Jews. For one significant example, see *ibid.*, p. 344.

94. Fijalkowski, *Kosciol Katolicki*, pp. 201-02; Bednarczyk, *Obowiazek Silniejszy*, p. 53.

95. Zygmunt Mazur, "Dominikanie Lwowscy w Podwojnej Niewoli," *Gazeta 144 (Toronto)*, 1991, p. 15.

96. Zielinski, *Zycie Religijne: Zakony*, p. 157; Fijalkowski, *Kosciol Katolicki*, p. 203.

97. Bednarczyk, *Obowiazek Silniejszy*, p. 55.

98. Zielinski, *Zycie Religijne: Zakony*, pp. 51-54, 157.

99. Tadeusz Seweryn, "Wielostronna Pomoc Zydom w Czasie Okupacji Hitlerowskiej," *Przeglad Lekarski*, No. 1 (1965), pp. 167-77.

100. Treece, *A Man For Others*, pp. 104, 152-53. There has been a barrage of savage attacks on Kolbe by a variety of individuals, including a nationally known attorney, who are unqualified to speak about the priest's life and work. The criticism focuses on Kolbe's alleged anti-Semitism, supposedly reflected in his writings. One historian addressed the point and discovered that out of 1,400 publications edited by Kolbe, only 14 of them referred to Jews, and of those, 5 could be construed as negative. This is hardly a basis to calumniate a man, especially one who went to Auschwitz for aiding Jews and non-Jews at his monastery. Zygmunt Zielinski, "Polska w Oczach Zydow Amerykanskich," *Wiez* (June, 1991), pp. 20-21; Bartoszewski and Lewin, *Righteous Among Nations*, p. ixxxiii.

101. Prekerowa, *Konspiracyjna Rada Pomocy Zydom*, pp. 205-08; Slomczynski, *Dom. Ks. Boduena*, pp. 117, 119.

102. Kloczowski, "Religious Orders and the Jews," p. 238.

103. Ewa Kurek-Lesik, "The Conditions of Admittance and the Social Background of Jewish Children Saved by Women's Religious Orders in Poland from 1939-1945," *Polin* (1988), p. 245.

104. *Ibid.*, p. 246; Ewa Kurek-Lesik, "Udzial Zenskich Zgromadzen Zakonnych w Akcji Ratowania Dzieci Zydowskich w Polsce w Latach 1939-1945," *Dzieje Najnowsze*, XVIII (1986), 250.

105. Kurek-Lesik, "Conditions of Admittance and Social Background," pp. 246-48.

106. *Ibid.*, p. 249.

107. *Ibid.*, pp. 250-51.

108. Zielinski, *Zycie Religijne:Zakony*, p. 407.

109. Kurek-Lesik, "Conditions of Admittance and Social Background," pp. 251-52.

110. *Ibid.*, pp. 252-53.

111. *Ibid.*, pp. 254, 259.

112. Zielinski, *Zycie Religijne: Zakony*, pp. 336-37.

113. Kurek-Lesik, "Conditions of Admittance and Social Background," pp. 255-57.

114. Zielinski, *Zycie Religijne: Zakony*, p. 158.

115. Kloczowski, *Religious Orders and the Jews*, p. 241; Prekerowa, *Konspiracyjna Rada Pomocy Zydom*, p. 209.

116. Szymanska, *Bylam Tylko Lekarzem*, pp. 151-76.

117. Ewa Kurek-Lesik, "Wybor Zrodel do Pracy Doktorskiej—Udzial Zenskich Zgromadzen Zakonnych w Akcji Ratowania Dzieci Zydowskich w Polsce w Latach, 1939-1945" (Unpublished paper, Lublin, 1989), pp. 220, 225.

118. Sister Janina W(olossyp), "Zgromadzenie Siostr Sluzebniczek Najswietszej Maryi Panny Niepokalanie Poczetej/Starowiejskie w Diecezji Lubelskiej w Latach 1918-1980" (Unpublished M.A. Thesis, Catholic University of Lublin, 1984), p. 113; Typescript, Sister Jolanta Kolata and Sister Maria Lewicka, "Pomoc Udzielana Zydom w Latach 1939-1945 Przez Zgromadzenie Siostr Sluzebniczek N.M.P.," p. 3; Sendler, "People Who Helped Jews," p. 51.

119. Zielinski, *Zycie Religijne: Zakony*, p. 448.

120. *Ibid.*, p. 158; Kurek-Lesik, "Wybor Zrodel," p. 226; Sister Joanna Bodzak, "Sluzebniczki Najswietszej Maryi Panny Niepokalanie Poczetej/Starowiejskie w Archidiecezji Warszawskiej w Latach 1920-1985" (Unpublished M.A. Thesis, Catholic University of Lublin, 1990), p. 173.

121. Dobraczynski, *Tylko w Jednym Zyciu*, pp. 243-44.

122. Kurek-Lesik, "Conditions of Admittance and Social Background," p. 246. Nuns allowed their convents to be used as a refuge for Jewish underground activists. One of these, Arie Wilner, hid in the Carmelite convent in Warsaw.

123. Kloczowski, "Religious Orders and the Jews," p. 243. It is odd that Yad Vashem has recognized so few Polish clergy—priests and nuns—for aiding Jewish adults and children during the Holocaust. Even so, 40 percent of all Christians decorated by Yad Vashem for aiding Jews are Poles.

124. Kuchler-Silberman, *One Hundred Children*, pp. 166-67.

125. Szwajger, *I Remember Nothing More*, pp. 139-40.

126. Jerzy Kosinski, *The Painted Bird* (New York: Modern Library, 1983); Meed, *On Both Sides of the Wall*, pp. 201-02; Ziemian, *Cigarette Sellers*, pp. 62-63.

127. Zielinski, "Polska w Oczach," p. 17, n. 27.

128. Ltr., Waclaw Zajaczkowski to author, June 5, 1984.

129. Wronski and Zwolakowa, *Polacy Zydzi*, pp. 262, 275-77, 361, 421ff, 445ff; Duraczynski, *Wojna i Okupacja*, p. 413; Sytuacja w Polsce, October, 1943, in Ciechanowski Papers, Hoover Institution on War Revolution and Peace, Stanford, CA; Bartoszewski and Lewin, *Samaritans*, p. 119; Bartoszewski and Lewin, *Righteous Among Nations*, p. lxxxi.

130. Waclaw Zajaczkowski, *Martyrs of Charity* (Washington, D.C.:St. Maximilian Kolbe Foundation, 1987), pp. 205, 210, 213.

131. Eugeniusz Fafara, *Gehenna Ludnosci Zydowskiej* (Warsaw: Ludowa Spoldzielnia Wydawnicza, 1983), pp. 396-400.

132. Zajaczkowski, *Martyrs of Charity*, p. 245.

133. *Ibid.*, pp. 207-08.

134. *Ibid.*, pp. 184-89.

Chapter VII

The War and Child Survivors

1945: Armistice with Germany. The war in Europe was over. Fascism and all it stands for had surrendered.

Someone turned the knob of our radio set to search the ether. It was filled with the peals of victory. There was jubilation everywhere: London's reverberating victory gong, giving the V sign—enthusiastic voices singing the rousing *Marseillaise*—the solemn, monumental tunes of the Soviet anthem, the chimes of the Kremlin—Berliners rising from the ruins to celebrate.

I turned about in my pillow and contemplated. It was peace. What could we make of it? Soon I would be sixteen. Before long I, too, would have my say.

Then I dozed off, dreaming about the future.[1]

THOMAS GEVE'S HOPE for the future was shared by other child survivors of the war. But they brought into that future the physical and psychic scars that the war had bequeathed to them.

Children who survived the camps, the labor gangs, and homes where their protectors were impoverished themselves ended up with diseases associated with diet deficiencies. Some had boils, fistulas, rickets, anemia, enlarged lymph glands and protruding bellies. It was common to find children with large heads and small bodies. Jewish children, whose food rations were less than others, were often more shrunken than others. Dental deficiencies were perhaps the most common physical symptoms found in medical examinations of child survivors.[2]

One social worker who visited a feeding center for children in Warsaw after the war observed a high incidence of scurvy, rickets and tuberculosis of the bones. "Their faces were gray and they seemed to be half asleep," he said. There was a playground at the center but few children were on it. Some children were so weakened they couldn't even walk. One Polish child, found in a German nursery, could not walk or talk. He never smiled. As soon as someone approached his bed, he screamed wildly.[3]

The psychological impact of the war on the children was enormous and many of them grew to adulthood without being able to deal effectively with the traumas they experienced during their younger years. Health care professionals observed immediately after the war that many children had ticks, fainting spells, enuresis and extreme sweating, results more of the psychological than the physical impact of the war. When Allied health care workers began to care for child survivors, it was apparent that large numbers of the children had developed a psychological appetite associated with hunger. Even though now they had ample food, they suffered from chronic hunger. "Even small babies wish to eat, eat, eat and scream furiously when food is not forthcoming," one UNRRA report stated.[4]

Deprived of a sense of security for so long, children developed a distrust of others, shrinking away from the touch or friendly overture of an adult and suspecting the motives, orders and anything that varied from their own thinking. Too often in the past a friendly gesture by an adult meant he or she wanted to have a homosexual liaison with the youngster or to use him as an informer.[5]

Children displayed aggressive behavior, not too difficult to understand when one remembers the cruelties and atrocities most of them had witnessed and experienced. One young boy who had survived Auschwitz had been so traumatized that he seized a gun and threatened anyone who wore a uniform after the war.[6] When a journalist visited a group of children at an

Allied reception center, he noted their aggressive attitude, characterized by a kind of sadistic fantasy. The youngsters stubbornly defended their own modest property—usually a few old playthings—as if their lives depended on it. "Everything dear to them had been wrested from them for too long," he remarked.

A former prisoner of Buchenwald personally observed the aggressive behavior of young teenage inmates during the last months of the war. He noted that 10-year-olds could still cry, "but not those of fourteen, who were impudent, bullying and sometimes dangerous." At Buchenwald, the children did not play childish games, which they labeled "silly" or "disgusting" but engaged in "watching." When they were asked what they were "watching," it became immediately apparent that they enjoyed watching the brutality and cruelty of the SS men who beat, tormented and killed people. "What other children in normal society act out through play, these children witnessed in reality. And if play was absent, guilt over aggression seemed also absent," he said. That is why they frequently hit each other, oblivious to where they punched their victim and what the consequences might be of the blow.[7]

Younger children often identified with the Germans in their games. One boy admitted he and his friends in the ghetto used to scream, "*Juden Heraus!*" (Jews Out) and familiar German expressions like, "*Verfluchter Jude*" (Accursed Jews). Despite scoldings from neighbors, he and his friends screamed like their German persecutors and spoke only in German.[8]

Whether they came from the ghetto, concentration camp or the streets of Warsaw, child survivors had brutal images seared into their psyches that explained much of their aggressive behavior. Henry Michinelk, a 14-year-old Polish boy, painted beautiful frescoes of jolly half-human ducks and geese which would have impressed Walt Disney but he also drew a black and white drawing of five men and women hanging like broken dolls from a gibbet, an astonishing glimpse into his past.[9]

Little wonder children displayed callousness to sickness, tragedy and even death. When a young friend left the room during an interview, a child casually referred to him as "dead." One day an adult inmate, who had tried to befriend some young child prisoners at Buchenwald, got ill in the camp

203

kitchen where he worked. While he struggled to the door to leave the area, not one of the children offered him any assistance. "They just sat there peeling potatoes as if I was no concern of theirs," he said. "Had I died then, they would have carried on as usual." Yet, months later, when bonds of friendship had been forged between him and the children, the youngsters began to experience nightmares and depression. "It seems as though their feeling of guilt increased as they began to form relationships," he added.[10] Commenting on the insensitivity of a group of Jewish children, one observer stated:

> Blood, pain suffered by others, the most terrible stories, made little impression upon them. The younger children are not scared by terror tales, while the older are not frightened by threats. They have lived through and seen far too much misery, which is why they are so insensitive. The reply of a child of twelve who explained in the following terms his indifference to a sick comrade, is typical: "That is nothing. I would be able to see the whole world die and would go on playing." Another child said: "If you had seen as many people dying as I have you wouldn't worry about a sick person." A child of seven used to relate quietly how his father had been murdered.[11]

To some children death was something they expected at a young age. They had no concept of living a long healthy life. "Some longed for death because they were tired of running or accepted the verdict of the 'superior race' that they deserved to die," wrote Judith Kestenberg and Yolanda Gampel.[12]

Compensating for the loss of relatives, children often developed strong emotional bonds among themselves. Deriving a sense of security from belonging to a group, even adolescent boys became deeply attached to younger children at institutions where they lived after the war. "It was not uncommon to see a gawking adolescent boy taking a baby for a walk in a carriage, or to find the adolescents in the nursery playing with the small children." Sometimes these close relationships resulted in homosexual bonds.[13]

Forced to become independent early in their lives, these children without childhoods had to sharpen their skills to survive the Germans and their informers. Little wonder they cheated, deceived, stole and adapted their behavior to the specific situation they encountered. Dishonesty and cunning were crucial to their survival. Now, after the war, social workers told them it was anti-social behavior.

Most of the children had to lie so much to survive they were incapable of relating an honest account of their wartime experiences. Their story varied with each telling. Sometimes the trauma they experienced was so crippling they developed amnesia, which resulted in blocking out their own names or those of their family members, the name of the place they lived and their nationality.[14]

In reading the reports of UNRRA one senses a confident, if somewhat naive, belief that the behavioral patterns of these children could be treated by health experts who would be able to integrate these youngsters into a normal life. To be sure there were some successes but there were also many failures. One UNRRA report opined, "The Jewish children presented even more serious problems. They had been in concentration camps, had lost their parents, and for years had lived by their wits— cheating, stealing, homosexuality and evasion of the law were behavior problems presented by this group."[15]

Most Jewish children under 12 years of age in Poland had died during the Holocaust. Those who survived shared not only the physical and psychological problems of gentile child survivors but also problems that were peculiar to them because they were Jewish. One of the most unique aspects of the Jewish child survivor was that since the Nazis had condemned Jews as evil and beyond any redemption, those who survived "carried with them the image of the world persecuting them." Children lost faith not only in their parents who could not protect them but also in the entire culture they once had shared. One young boy, liberated from a camp when he was 4-years-old, blamed his father for his misfortunes. He told an interviewer the Nazis didn't harm him but his father did.[16]

If a Jewish parent left the child with a Pole without some parting expression of love, the sense of abandonment and betrayal was virtually complete. That is what had happened to Halina who grew attached to her Polish foster mother. Halina had to leave her foster parents after the war because they were poor and some neighbors had ridiculed the woman for caring for a Jewess.

Yet when parents expressed their love and concern for their

children as they left them with Polish protectors, sometimes that was sufficient to sustain the child through the long ordeal of separation. "In a sense the parting words became the child's companions, the living remnants of the parents' love and their desire for the child to survive, which was incorporated into the superego," wrote Judith Kestenberg.[17]

It was common to find Jewish children blaming their tribulations on their parents, not the Nazis. Even the word "Jew" terrified many Jewish children who associated it with death and destruction. "For years they had evaded the word," one Jewish social worker said. "They had become expert at lying about their background."[18] The feeling of loss and distrust was so great that often postwar reunions between Jewish children and their parents were unhappy, "overshadowed by the resentment, generated by persecution, separation from parents and indoctrination with an anti-Jewish mentality." When children and parents were finally reunited, often they had forgotten what their parents looked like. Neither was the same. Some children "thought that these strange adults pretended to be their parents."[19]

Sometimes Jewish children identified with a lost parent through a relationship with a pet. Abram was a 13-year-old Jewish boy who found a home with loving Polish peasants. *Siwek*, a horse, helped Abram deal with the loss of his parents. He said:

> I became attached to a little horse, who filled my free time and gave me a great deal of joy. He was my best friend and my most beloved being. I called him *Siwek* (Gray) and he too liked me and came only to me. The best part of my food, bread, I saved for *Siwek*. He was the speediest in the whole village. He jumped over ditches, over fields and my *Siwek* was always first. I trained him that well.

The Polish peasants who protected Abram could not help him mourn. But by riding and taming Siwek, Abram felt at one with the animal who helped the boy to restore his self-esteem. "The horse was his friend and loved him and in this capacity was a substitute for his mother," a prominent psychiatrist wrote.[20]

Many Jewish children who survived the war living with Polish families or institutions run by the clergy were exposed to the Catholic religious experience. For some, the experience affected their emotional development and caused identity problems. Many children were impressed by the loving relationship between Jesus and His mother, Mary, and the impressive liturgy of the Catholic Mass. The beauty, structure and values of the church made them feel better, safer and gave them hope. Prayers at Mass also helped them to develop a sense of at least minimal control over their future.[21] By comparison, Judaism to some youngsters was a failed religion, one that could not prevent the calamities that had befallen them and their families. The fact that an impressionable child embraced Christianity did not mean that the child's Christian protectors were anti-Semitic. The youngster simply saw the Christian God as a stronger one. As one 9-year-old boy declared, "The Jewish God killed my parents. He burned my home. Jesus Christ saved me."[22]

One girl, who lived with a religious Polish woman, said, "I liked to go with her to church. I felt safe. The Germans will never suspect me to be a Jew, I thought. The whole atmosphere was like a theater. Till today I know nothing more beautiful than a Catholic Mass." She reasoned that if Jews were so hated, "Maybe they are horrible people." She wanted to become like the Christians and end her Jewishness which she saw as the cause of her problems.[23]

One young girl was so impressed by the story of Christ's death at the hands of Jews she wanted to atone for being a Jew. She lived in a convent and was distraught when she left it. Some Jewish children, who had been baptized, remained in the church after the war and experienced guilt for abandoning Judaism.[24] It wasn't easy for some Jewish children who decided to remain Catholic after the war; often their Jewish friends were not supportive of their decision.

Psychologists agree that the curative effects of recovering memories and integrating the past with its losses into the life of the child survivor are important to the restoration of the emotional health of the survivor.[25] No doubt the reason many former child and adult survivors have written accounts of their experiences is to deal with the losses they suffered and to integrate these into their lives. But, from a historical point of view, these accounts are often flawed and do not always make clear distinctions and differentiations between victims and victimizers. In many of these accounts one finds Poles and other Slavs, even those who risked their lives for Jews, often being dismissed as anti-Semites and co-villains in the drama of the Holocaust. Largely because of such accounts, the popular myth persists that Poles are anti-Semites which has as much validity as defining Jews as Polonophobes or Israelis as Zionist imperialists.

Oddly, one finds stronger feelings and more attention to uncomplimentary details about their former protectors—i.e., they talked nasty about Jews, they took money for keeping me—than the Germans who victimized them. Perhaps this phenomenon is due to the fact that the emotional development of former child survivors was so damaged by their endless premature struggle for existence that they had expectancies from Polish Christians which some Poles for reasons that had nothing to do with anti-Semitism were unable to meet. Disappointment of some child survivors, ironically, led to hatred toward the people who had saved them.

From a psychological point of view, it is quite understandable why someone would wish to deny the existence of the Germans who had brought such horror to the life of a Jewish child. But it isn't very good history to ignore the perpetrators of the crimes and to criticize former caretakers, who risked their lives for their Jewish charges, for real or alleged lapses. Polish protectors were not all saints. Most fed, clothed, sheltered and even loved Jewish children without any thought of material rewards. But some were less altruistic, believing that the risks they assumed entitled them to financial compensation.

The war left 350,000 orphaned, abandoned and neglected children in Poland. In addition, there were over 1 million children under the age of 18 who had lost one of their parents during the war and were in need of food and medical care. Only a fraction of the sick and injured Polish children could receive medical care because there were no more than 6,000 physicians in the entire country. For the 90,000 children in Warsaw after the war, there was only one hospital with 50 beds; the Germans had destroyed all the other children's hospitals. In addition to the usual diseases associated with malnutrition, there were large numbers of Polish children who had been wounded or blinded.[26]

Without the support of the United Nations Relief and Rehabilitation Administration (UNRRA), the postwar Polish government would have been unable to provide the needed food, medicine and shelter that the orphaned and needy children required. Unfortunately, the Cold War between the East and West had begun in the immediate postwar years and UNRRA became a pawn in the struggle, caught in the barrage of charges and countercharges hurled by governments on both sides.

Nevertheless, Poland had received $480,000,000 worth of aid from UNRRA during the period 1945-47, making it the largest single beneficiary of the international aid program. The biggest single item the Poles received was food.[27] One of the unique contributions by UNRRA to the Poles was the provision of modern apparatus for the Madame Curie Institute for Cancer Research. This included X-Ray machines, equipment for laboratories and operating rooms, and radium. According to one knowledgeable insider, the UNRRA Mission to Poland "was a success story from the beginning to the end."[28]

One Polish official, expressing Poland's gratitude for the aid, said, "Here was a friend and here were good men. There was a crime and here was assistance; there was devastation and here was construction." Individual Poles responded enthusiastically to the assistance. Since most of the items shipped to Poland carried a "Made in the U.S.A." or "Shipped from the U.S.A." label on them, Poles popularly referred to the aid as "UNRRA-Amerykanski." One American observer in Warsaw at the time said Poles talked of "the wonderful America" that had sent help.[29] But by 1947, Cold War passions scuttled the program which even its defenders could not deny buttressed the postwar communist government in Poland and in other Iron Curtain countries.

Apart from UNRRA, a host of private relief organizations operated in Poland in the immediate postwar years, including the American Relief for Poland, American Red Cross, War Relief Services of the National Catholic Welfare Conference, and the American Joint Distribution Committee. Polish and Jewish children benefited from the aid of all these groups. In addition, the Quaker Relief Mission, the British Save the Children Fund, and the Danes provided food supplements to children. The YMCA cared for 15,000 young boys and an additional 8,000 in day camps. The American Ambassador to Poland, Arthur Bliss Lane, said that the outpouring of American aid to the Poles helped to rebuild "the bridge of understanding and affection between the American and Polish peoples, which had been closed to traffic during the Nazi occupation."[30]

When World War II ended, there were millions of Poles, including hundreds of thousands of children, who found themselves in the Allied occupation zones of Germany and in the Soviet Union. The Polish government estimated there were 1.7 million people east of the Bug River who needed to be repatriated to Poland and 2.3 million Poles, most of whom lived in the American and British occupation zones of Germany. In other words, at least 4 million Poles had been uprooted by the war and lived outside of the country. As a result of the Nazi Germanization program, approximately 200,000 Polish boys and girls had been deported to the Reich.[31]

One of UNRRA's responsibilities was to see that Polish children were repatriated from Germany, a major priority of the Polish government. Poland wanted all children under 18 years of age returned home. Once the Polish nationality of the child had been established, UNRRA automatically repatriated children under 12 years of age.[32] That meant that older children, essentially teenagers, had a voice in determining whether or not they chose to return home. Jewish children of Polish citizenship of any age had the option of going to any country of their choice. As will be seen later in greater detail, most Jewish children who had survived the war in Poland went to Palestine, to western European countries and to the United States.

The criteria for repatriation established by UNRRA and the roadblocks erected by the Germans made it difficult for Poland to recover anything more than 15 to 20 percent of the 200,000 children who had been deported for Germanization.[33] UNRRA's policy was that a child could not be repatriated unless it was established beyond doubt that the youngster was Polish. That, of course, was difficult, if not impossible, to establish in most cases because the authentic records of these children had been destroyed by the Nazis and replaced by bogus papers.

Perhaps the most dramatic discoveries of genuine records

that had not been destroyed by the Nazis were in Lodz and Katowice where the names and photographs of Polish children who had been given German identities were found. The records also revealed information about the child's family and an evaluation concerning whether the child was suitable from the Nazi point of view for Germanization. Despite the large number of records found in Lodz, only 443 children had been accounted for by the end of 1946.[34]

Moreover, Allied officers had to work with German administrators of orphanages and other institutions where many of the Polish children lived during the war. Often these officials proved less than cooperative in identifying the children and seeing that they were returned to Poland. In Hesse, the Germans reported that there were no Polish children; yet Allied occupation authorities identified 72. In some districts of Bavaria, the Germans claimed there were no Polish children; Allied officials identified 660. The worst example of German duplicity occurred in Baden-Wurtemberg where officials reported the existence of 276 children while the Allies uncovered 3,000.

To be sure, some German administrators were helpful with the consequence that the success UNRRA had in recovering Polish children came largely from German institutions, not from German families where the Nazis had placed a large number of Germanized Polish boys and girls.[35]

It was more difficult to locate Polish children living with German families. Many German households tended to be uncooperative in reporting foreign children to Allied authorities. The process of finding a child in a family was complicated by the fact that children sometimes had several foster families during the course of the war. In some cases, German families genuinely assumed when they received or adopted a child, especially a young one, that it was German. When the *Lebensborn* offered children for adoption, it frequently used the ruse that they were German orphans. Since it was easier to denationalize young Polish children than older ones, the young boy or girl came to the German family purged of their Polish past and spoke German like a native.

When Allied investigators either suspected or identified a foreign child in an institution, there was no certainty there would be a successful resolution. Sometimes the Germanization process had been so advanced that children remembered little or nothing about their past. Even in the postwar period in many instances foreign children continued to be subjected to Germanization policies in children's homes by being denied the right to speak their native language. Sometimes peer pressure helped to continue the Nazi legacy. When children were overheard by others lapsing into their own language, they had to bear the brunt of jokes and teasing. The result is they tried to cover up their knowledge of languages other than German.[36]

When Allied welfare workers conducted interviews with children, German administrators, teachers and nuns were usually present which was sufficient to intimidate the child into affirming its alleged German nationality. One Allied official, who had interviewed 11 children suspected of being Polish at St. Joseph's Kinderheim in Kaufleuren, remarked that it was obvious the German nuns had prepared the children for the interview during which the children appeared to be afraid and looked nervously at the nuns. All of the children declared they were German, not Polish. When the Allies transferred the children to an UNRRA facility in Prien, the investigator met smiling children who greeted him in Polish and asked him to transfer their sisters and brothers to the new facility.[37]

Sometimes during an interview conducted in German, an unexpected question elicited a spontaneous reply of *Tak* (Yes) in Polish. Eleven-year-old Eva Kim stubbornly affirmed she was German but immediately after boarding a train for Poland, she began to speak fluent Polish and completely identified with the other Polish children. At the Aglosterhausen Children's Center, there was a group of Polish girls originally selected for Germanization during the war. At first the girls denied their Polish background, which they considered inferior to German. But within a few months, they began to learn Polish and wanted to sing songs in their native language. "They were some of the best advocates we had for repatriation as they influenced some of the other children to go back to Poland," one UNRRA official reported. "By the time that they had made the decision to return to Poland, they were identified with the Polish group and had thus severed their relationships with their German friends."[38]

Allied investigators found a variety of obstacles erected by the Polish children themselves in establishing their nationality. Life had been harsh for the children and they distrusted everyone. "They tended to accept a known situation, even if it were bad, rather than to test a new [one]," one history of UNRRA related. In many cases, the children did not know or could not remember the facts of their background. Since many of them were young when the Germans seized them, they remembered very little. Other boys and girls were slow; some may have been victims of medical experimentation. Since children often lied to survive the war, it is possible they could not give a truthful coherent account of who they were and where they came from. All this made it very difficult to establish the nationality of children in postwar occupied Germany.[39]

There were also special problems arising from a lack of historical understanding by Allied authorities concerning certain groups of people who were obvious candidates for repatriation. American officials betrayed their lack of historical knowledge of *Volksdeutsch* children by affirming they were German, even though their parents had come from Poland.[40]

The most tragic cases involved children, stolen from their parents when they were young, who had been so completely Germanized that they forgot their Polish parents and wanted to remain with their German foster parents, the only ones they ever knew. This is what happened to Eugenia Ewertowska, seized by the Germans from her mother, Bronislawa. When a child welfare officer completed his investigation of the matter, he told the Polish mother that Eugenia was now Irene Ewert and lived with German parents who took good care of her. "Irene does not remember well her heritage; she forgot how to use the Polish language and can not adequately explain how she was taken away from her parents," he said. "All she remembers is that she was taken away by the police. It would be shocking to her and especially to her German foster parents if she had to leave their home."[41] There were many cases like Irene's where Allied investigators opted in favor of allowing a Polish child to remain with its new parents rather than compound their emotional problems by returning them to Poland.

Astonishingly, postwar German courts also had an important role in allowing adoptions of Polish children by German families. The Germans kidnapped 7-year-old Marian Gajewy in Poznan, took him to Germany as Martin Gawner, and gave him to the Karl Dengler family who lived in Esslingen. A Polish investigator traced the child to the Denglers in 1946 and began the laborious process of repatriation. When the Denglers discovered they might lose Marian, they went to a German court to adopt the child legally. Despite the fact that postwar adoptions of children were prohibited by the Allies in Germany, unless they cleared them, Dengler won his case and registered the adoption in 1948.[42]

An equally striking commentary on the postwar German judicial system came in the case of Alojzy Twardecki, renamed Alfred Hartmann by the *Lebensborn*. Stolen from his bed at night, Twardecki ended up with a German family, who hid him for weeks while a Polish investigation team was in the area after the war. Twardecki's foster mother, when finally confronted by an investigator about her child's being Polish and that his real mother wanted him returned to her, insisted the boy was a German orphan. Twardecki's foster parents were deeply attached to him and they, too, lost little time in adopting him by using false information. Twardecki's story had a happier ending than the Gajewy case. After Alfred's foster mother died, he quarrelled with his father's new wife and decided one day to return to Poland where his mother still waited for him. Fifteen-year-old Twardecki said later:

> I had become a fanatical Nazi. I wept with rage when the men condemned at the Nuremberg trial were hanged. It took years before I stopped hating the Poles, as I had been taught, and then the French, who occupied our city of Koblenz. Actually it was a coincidence, for purely family reasons, that I became Polish again. My German mother was dead, and my Polish mother wanted me back. So one day I cleared off.[43]

Most Polish refugees in the West decided to return to Poland after the war. To be sure, many of them were children who for a number of reasons found themselves in one of the Allied occupation zones. But there were also some unattached children who joined adult Poles in refusing to return to Poland. Many of these refugees had come from eastern Poland and had bitter memories of the treatment they had received from the Soviets. They had no intention to return to a postwar Poland

governed now by a Provisional Government that was domi-
nated by Communists. One observer at the time pointed out
that these Poles "would commit suicide rather than return to
Poland."[44] Even Lt. Gen. Sir Frederick Morgan, a top UNRRA
official, told the chief of the UNRRA Mission to Poland, "Were
I myself a Polish DP, I am just about damned if I'd go."[45]

The Polish government launched a propaganda campaign to
encourage adults and children in displaced persons camps to
return home. They printed and distributed pamphlets to induce them to do so; one of the publications was entitled "Our
Country Is Calling" and another "What Are You Waiting For?"
There were specific appeals to Polish children in Germany from
their peers which appeared in the publication *Repatriant*.[46]

The United States and Great Britain tried to facilitate the
repatriation of Polish children and adults who wanted to return
to Poland. The flood of displaced persons in the western occupation zones was so huge that it clogged communications and
strained available food supplies. So anxious were American
authorities to get rid of as many Poles as possible, they seriously suggested an operation reminiscent of what the Nazis
had won notoriety for—namely, foot-marching as many Poles
as possible out of the western zones before the end of 1945.
American eagerness to expedite the repatriation of Poles eastward gave rise to charges that the Allies forced refugees against
their will to return to Poland.[47]

Although there was no conclusive evidence to prove that the
Allies practiced the involuntary repatriation of Poles, Polish
American leaders, led by Charles Rozmarek, president of the
Polish American Congress, went to Germany, visited refugee
camps, and concluded, "UNRRA has embarked on a course to
make life so miserable for Displaced Persons that they will
accept repatriation as the lesser of two evils."[48] The Allies had
stooped to using food as a political weapon; they cut back on
rations of the refugees in the displaced persons camps and
increased those who had decided to return home.[49]

The American military establishment had no reservations
about pressuring the refugees with warnings to them that they
would face worse economic conditions in occupied Germany
than if they returned to Poland. However, the claim was con-
tradicted by Poles who had returned to the West after having

been repatriated to Poland. Once Polish refugees in the West learned that Poland was one of the worst places in postwar Europe from the standpoint of the availability of food, repatriation dropped overnight.[50]

Apparently UNRRA officials believed that the less attractive housing conditions were the more likely the Poles would go home. Rozmarek complained that as soon as the DPs made a more decent life for themselves by planting a garden or starting a school for their children, they were shifted to another refugee camp, "where bare walls and ruined barracks are the only things left by the previous occupants."[51] Under these circumstances, deep-seated resentments by Polish refugees toward UNRRA officials were inevitable.

Polish camp leaders were convinced that a well-organized cultural life was the last thing UNRRA officials wanted to see developed because it encouraged the refugees to remain in Germany. Rozmarek reported that in one camp he had visited, the Poles had established schools, a theater, choir, library, pharmacy and even a camp newspaper. "Before moving the inmates to another camp," Rozmarek said, "UNRRA confiscated textbooks, school supplies, sporting and recreational equipment, music sheets and sewing machines, presented to the camp by a relief organization." The departing Poles could take only their clothing and bedding with them. Rozmarek's claim was supported by a directive from UNRRA's Stuttgart office which read, "Effective October 1st, 1946, all educational, recreational and other cultural activities are to be discontinued in all camps caring for one hundred or more Polish Displaced Persons."[52]

In the campaign to induce Poles to leave the refugee camps, UNRRA officials directed that Polish refugees should not be employed. One office memorandum declared, "Do not employ Poles—repatriate them, as they must go home.... no such thing as a unrepatriable Pole.... Hire outsiders, even Germans, to replace essential Poles, but fire Poles and get them home."[53]

Of particular concern to the Polish American Congress was the large number of Polish youths who fled from Poland after the war but were not accorded DP status. Apparently many of them had belonged to the Polish underground during the war. Rozmarek charged that when American and British military police caught the young men they were handed over to the

Soviets. "They disappear never to be heard of again," he claimed.[54]

Although UNRRA denied the claims of Rozmarek and other Polish American leaders, the denials were not entirely convincing. Even less emotionally involved observers recognized that the Allies strongly pressured the Poles to return home. "People in the camps are denied any semblance of the Four Freedoms," William Henry Chamberlin wrote.[55]

While the Warsaw regime tried to get as many Poles in the West to rebuild the war-ravaged homeland, Polish liaison officers who worked closely with Allied administrators in Germany tried to sabotage repatriation efforts and even kidnapped some Polish children scheduled to return to Poland. These liaison officers were passionately loyal to the Polish government, which had fled into exile to London after the fall of France in 1940, and was the legal government of Poland until the summer of 1945, when the United States, Great Britain, and the Soviet Union extended diplomatic recognition to the new Communist-dominated regime. For Poles in the West, the western policy of appeasement toward the Soviets was more than they could bear.

A few over-zealous Poles, loyal to the Polish government in London, which continued to function even without the recognition of the Big Three, abducted a number of Polish children, some of whom had parents in Poland, to prevent their repatriation to Poland by transporting them to Italy, Spain and England. Although UNRRA officials estimated there may have been as many as 1,000 children removed from refugee camps, the Polish government had specific information on only 210.[56]

For those children returning to Poland, it was exciting to board the repatriation train. The first group of unaccompanied children repatriated from the American zone in Germany left Funk Kaserne on June 2, 1946, more than one year after VE Day. Accompanied by Polish Red Cross personnel, which included physicians and nurses, 111 Polish children left Germany amidst a chorus of singing and cheering. As they approached the Czech-Polish frontier, the excitement level ran high but it was also tinged with some anxiety about the new life that awaited the children in Poland. When the train finally arrived at Katowice, one of the child welfare escorts noted the heightened tension and drama that awaited the first Polish child repatriants in Poland:

> It was a dramatic moment as the train pulled into the station. Children were again waving flags from the windows and singing Polish songs. A band was playing at the station, and little girls handed flowers in through the windows. Boy Scouts stood by, and the Polish Red Cross was ready to pass cocoa onto the train as it stopped. The station was thronged with people and we were all excited—adults no less than children. Many were laughing and crying at the same time.[57]

One of the most unfortunate groups of young boys, ranging in age from 10 to 18, were the G.I. mascots who had attached themselves to Allied armies in the West. A majority of the youngsters were German but there were some Polish youths in the group who hoped to get to the United States.

Intelligent, bold and aggressive, they were spoiled by the servicemen who took them to theaters, shows, and gave them food, candy, cigarettes and liquor. "Their ideas of America were gleaned from the glorious stories of home told by homesick and boastful GIs as well as impressions from their way of life which indicated that America was a land flowing with milk and honey and with a PX open to them on every corner," one UNRRA report stated. When their GI friends left them, sometimes quickly and abruptly, these children became despondent. They had nothing but contempt for the DPs and children's centers and always ran away when Allied officials tried to confine them. The mascots were the envy of other children who gawked in admiration at these little GIs who sometimes appeared dressed in military uniforms, complete with side arms. The incorrigible mascots found by Allied officials were placed in a special center run by the YMCA which sought to prepare the young boys to readjust to postwar life.[58]

One Jewish expert has estimated that out of approximately 1 million Jewish children under 14-years-of-age before World War II, about 5,000 survived the war in Poland. Since this estimate is based upon lists prepared by ad hoc Jewish committees after the war, it is, at best, a rough estimate.[59] These survivors were joined by thousands of others whom the Soviets repatriated after the defeat of the Nazis. Most Jewish adults and children chose not to remain in Poland after the war. There were several reasons for this. Between 1945 and 1947, Poland was under a Communist regime that rapidly established a Moscow-style totalitarianism over the country. Moreover, few Jews wanted to remain in a land which the Germans had selected to become the major killing center of European Jewry. Also, Poland was a devastated country, one of the worst in Europe and it would take many years to recover in contrast to the promise that western Europe, the United States and Palestine had to offer. Finally, Poland, like other eastern European countries, experienced a number of anti-Semitic outbreaks which further spurred Jewish emigration from the country.

Representatives of Jewish organizations traveled throughout Poland trying to identify and retrieve Jewish children, most of whom had been hidden by Polish families and religious institutions. Most Poles willingly gave up the children to whom they had become attached and expected no financial rewards for their sacrifices. Some families who had received children through *Zegota* had hoped to adopt them. But this was against *Zegota's* policy not to denationalize Jewish youngsters. Polish foster parents were aware that they would have to return the children after the war either to parents, relatives or representatives of Jewish organizations.[60] But there were Poles who had acquired Jewish children in a number of ways other than through *Zegota* or the *Rada* and quietly kept them after the war much like German families kept Polish children. That is why it is most probable that more than 5,000 Jewish children survived the war in Poland. Some Poles, motivated by mercenary considerations, returned Jewish children they had sheltered and expected financial payment.[61]

Jewish representatives were often single-minded in their objective of scouring the Polish countryside and recovering children without adequate consideration for the close relationships that had often developed between Polish foster parents and the children. One Jewish social worker who was responsible for the recovery of 20 Jewish children from Poland, observed a touching loving bond between a young Jewish girl, Marysia, and a Polish nurse, and had serious reservations about taking the child away from the family. But her second thoughts didn't last very long. "If I want to continue with my work, I must not be burdened with such sentiments," she said. "I grabbed Marysia... and went to Lodz."[62]

The methods employed by some Jewish officials in recovering Jewish children in Poland were neither moral nor legal. One Jewish historian admitted, "In the belief that the end justified the means, some children were taken from their families under pretenses or through outright lies; some were torn from families to whom they were deeply attached." In doing so, it soothed the consciences of some zealots to paint Poles with the broad brush of anti-Semitism.[63]

These actions seemed largely, though not exclusively, the result of the work of the Coordination Committee, a consortium of four Zionist groups who met in Warsaw early in 1945 and passionately devoted itself to the recovery of Jewish youth.[64] This was an interesting reversal of Jewish policy because when Jan Dobraczynski had approached the American Joint Distribution Committee, a Jewish organization, for aid to help with the upkeep of Jewish children in Polish centers, a Jewish representative of the group told him, "These aren't our children, but yours." A few months later, the Joint reversed itself and began to help. By the summer of 1946, the Joint contributed to the support of 5 Catholic orphanages and helped various children's summer camps.[65]

Zionists were so dedicated to getting as many Jews as possible to Palestine they participated in a number of unauthorized and illegal movements of children and adults.[66] *Bricha*, which means "flight" in Hebrew, was a Jewish underground organization that actively smuggled Jews out of Poland and other countries to displaced persons camps in Austria and Germany from where the refugees were escorted to Mediterranean ports for the voyage to Palestine.[67] Lt. Gen. Sir Frederick Morgan of UNRRA believed the entire operation was a Zionist scheme to force the British to open immigration to Palestine. Morgan was close to the mark because even David Ben Gurion admitted, "If we succeed in concentrating a quarter million Jews in the American zone, it will increase the American pressure [on the British]." The pressure would not be financial, Ben Gurion explained, "but because they see no future for these peoples outside *Eretz Yisrael*." By 1947, there were 122,313 Jews, including thousands of children, from Poland who received UNRRA assistance in western Germany.[68]

After recovering Jewish children from Polish homes and institutions, Jewish leaders usually sent them to Allied reception centers in Austria and Germany. Most of them were members of *kibbutzen*, groups of children numbering 70-80 under the supervision of young adults called *madrichim*. The majority of orphans and a high percentage of children who had parents were members of a *kibbutz*. Many parents gave up their children to a *kibbutz*, believing that they would join their sons and daughters later in Palestine. "For many children the promise of a secure life in Palestine plus the belief that their parents would soon follow them gave them the fortitude to remain with their *kibbutz* group," one UNRRA report stated. The intense political feeling among the children was revealed by one 7-year-old who looked intently at and confidently told a stranger, "I'm going to Palestine; of course, I'm Zionist."[69]

Each *kibbutz*, dedicated to pioneer work in Palestine, had its own religious and political beliefs. Orphaned children found a home, a sense of security and purpose, and affection in a *kibbutz*, which filled a void for them. About 90 percent of the children in a *kibbutz* were in the 10-17 age bracket. There was a great deal of competition between the groups and a certain amount of proselytizing in order to recruit children into various *kibbutzen*.[70]

The solidarity the youngsters felt in a *kibbutz* is illustrated by what happened one day after four Allied officials had taken four of their leaders into custody for attempting to move the children without Allied permission. The children started a hunger strike. Even youngsters as young as 7- and 8-years-old joined teenagers in refusing to eat. But later that day, when representatives of the Jewish Agency prevailed upon them, the boys and girls called an end to the strike.[71] There were several incidents like these, revealing the unwillingness or inability of the *madrichim* to accept supervision and control by Allied authorities in Austria and Germany.[72]

Postwar anti-Semitic outbreaks in Poland, most of which were the work of criminal elements associated with the nationalistic right wing of the Polish underground, were an important factor that convinced many Jews to leave Poland after the war.

The scope and effect of the attacks were often exaggerated in the western press. Stanislaw Mikolajczyk, the respected leader of the Polish Peasant Party who served as deputy premier in the coalition government in postwar Poland and its only states- man of international stature, pointed out that while he was in the cities of Radom and Krakow, the western press reported pogroms in these cities when, in fact, there were political demonstrations against the Communists.[73]

Some of the anti-Jewish feeling in postwar Poland was due in large part to the presence of many Jews who were members of the Communist Party and the hated security police in which Jews had a virtual monopoly. Since most Poles regarded the regime as an alien-imposed system, the obvious prominence of Jews within the government, along with those who had re- turned to Poland from the Soviet Union after the war, created a very tense situation. Gerald Keith, the American Chargé in Warsaw, described it this way, "It is a paradox that after a period of six years when Jews were more mercilessly killed off than any other race, *this country finds itself under a very marked Jewish governing and industrial influence* (italics mine)." Though Keith found it difficult to estimate what percentage of the resentment toward the government stemmed from the part played by Jews, he flatly stated, "It is surely of considerable consequence."[74]

Polish officials were well aware that anti-Jewish currents in postwar Poland represented an expression of hostitlity toward the Polish and Soviet regimes. Foreign Minister Wincenty Rzy- mowski admitted that the outbreaks were "aimed primarily against the present regime in Poland and only in the second place against the Jews."[75]

The most notorious assault on Jews in postwar Poland oc- curred in Kielce on July 4, 1946. Prior to the outbreak, vicious rumors had circulated about the Jews in the area, including the libel of ritual murder of gentile children which was so charac- teristic of Russian-inspired pogroms. On July 1, the day after a controversial political referendum which pitted Communists against anti-Communists, an 8-year-old boy disappeared from his home, only to return in a few days with a story of his alleged confinement in a Jewish home where he claimed he had seen the bodies of Christian children. His father took him to the police on July 4, when the boy related his incredible story. Not long afterward, an ugly crowd assembled in front of a house occupied by several Jewish families and attacked them. As a result, 41 Jews and 4 Poles died.

Although the Communists blamed the Polish Peasant Party and the still active anti-Communist underground for the tragedy, the anti-Communists blamed the regime for orchestrating the grim event to divert attention from a fraudulent referendum, the prelude to a Communist dictatorship. The evidence strongly implicated the regime, especially the security police, militia, and army in the Kielce tragedy. Both sides agreed on one thing—Kielce was not a spontaneous outpouring of anti-Semitic feeling by a mass of Poles.[76]

Understandably, panic gripped the surviving Jewish community in Poland. Jews had emigrated at the rate of 70 per week before the Kielce incident. After July 4, 1946, the number skyrocketed to 700 per day.[77] Tragically for Poland, the incident played into the hands of opportunists inside and outside Poland who used it to their political advantage.

To be sure, not all Jews left Poland. Although the Polish government did not create obstacles to Jewish emigration, it organized a network of cultural and local Jewish groups in 235 towns and villages in postwar Poland. Major Jewish centers could be found in Lodz, Warsaw, Krakow, Czestochowa, Katowice, Wroclaw and Szczecin. Polish Jewry developed its own cultural institutions and until 1947 was free to remain in contact with Jews abroad. After that, Jewish political and other activities increasingly came under Communist control.[78] Jewish relief and welfare organizations tended to give more assistance to their kinsmen who decided to emigrate than to those Jews who preferred to remain in the country they considered their home.[79]

Chapter Notes

1. Geve, *Youth in Chains*, p. 245.

2. History of Child Welfare, pp. 81ff, in PAG 4/4.2: Box 81, UN-RRA/UNA.

3. Joseph Wechsberg, "Hell's Orphans," *Saturday Evening Post* (October 23, 1948), p. 119; Hrabar, *Hitlerowski Rabunek*, p. 89.

4. History of Child Welfare, pp. 81-82.

5. *Ibid.*; Eugene Heimler, "Children of Auschwitz," in *Prison: A Symposium*, ed. by George Mikes (London: Routledge and Kegan Paul, 1963), p. 10.

6. Wanda Poltawska, "Z Badan nad 'Dziecmi Oswiecimskim'," *Przeglad Lekarski* (1965), p. 22; Hrabar, *Fate of Polish Children*, p. 180.

7. Heimler, "Children of Auschwitz," p. 12.

8. Judith S. Kestenberg, "Coping with Losses and Survival," in *The Problem of Loss and Mourning: New Psychoanalytic Perspectives*, ed. by Peter Shabad and D.R. Dietrich (New York: International Universities Press, 1987), p. 16.

9. Quotations from Returning Europe's Kidnapped Children, in History of Child Welfare, p.2.

10. Hrabar, *Fate of Polish Children*, p. 180; Heimler, "Children of Auschwitz," pp. 12-13.

11. T. Lavi, "A Psychological Study of Jewish Children in Rumania during the Catastrophe," *Yad Vashem Bulletin* (December, 1962), p. 48.

12. Judith S. Kestenberg and Yolanda Gampel, "Growing Up in the Holocaust Culture," *Israel Journal of Psychiatry and Related Sciences*, XX (1983), p. 142.

13. Report, Greene, May 5, 1947 (Exhibit 31), in History of Child Welfare (DP #US 22); History of Child Welfare, pp. 81, 84.

14. History of Child Welfare, pp. 81-84.

15. *Ibid.*, p. 81.

16. Judith S. Kestenberg and Milton Kestenberg, "Psychoanalyses of Children of Survivors from the Nazi Persecution: The Continuing Struggle of Survivor Parents," *Victimology: An International Journal*, V (1980), 368-71.

17. Kestenberg, "Coping with Losses and Survival," pp. 11-13.

18. Kuchler-Silberman, *One Hundred Children*, pp. 122-23.

19. Kestenberg and Gampel, "Growing Up in the Holocaust Culture," pp. 129-42.

20. Kestenberg, "Coping with Losses and Survival," pp. 14-15.

21. Flora Hogman, "The Experience of Catholicism for Jewish Children during World War II," *The Psychoanalytic Review*, LXXV (Winter, 1988), pp. 520-21.

22. My interpretation of the youngster's remark differs from Mahler who seems fixated on Polish anti-Semitism. Ella Mahler, "About Jewish Children Who Survived World War II on the Aryan Side," *Yad Vashem Bulletin* (December, 1962), p. 50.

23. Hogman, "The Experience of Catholicism," p. 516.

24. *Ibid.*, pp. 514-15.

25. Judith Kestenberg, "Child Survivors of the Holocaust—40 Years later: Reflections and Commentary," presented as a Discussion at the American Psychiatric Association in 1983, p. 410. A study of scores of former child inmates of the Lodz camp for children revealed they suffered from a higher percentage of neuroses and psychoses compared to the Polish population as a whole after the war. Andrzej Zasepa, "Wyniki Badan Medycznych i Psychosocjologicznych Bylych Wiezniow Obozu Koncentracyjnego dla Dzieci w Lodzi," *Wojna i Okupacja a Medycyna: Materialy* (Krakow: Akademia Medyczna im. Mikolaja Kopernika w Krakowie, 1986) pp. 80-85.

26. Permanent Social Welfare (Appendix 22), in PAG-4/3.0.17.1.3:3 (Centres in Poland), UNRRA/UNA; Macardle, *Children of Europe*, pp. 79-80.

27. Thad Paul Alton, *Polish Postwar Economy* (Westport, Conn.: Greenwood, 1974), pp. 268-69.

28. George Woodbridge, *UNRRA: The History of the United Nations Relief and Rehabilitation Administration* (3 vols.; New York: Columbia University Press, 1950), II, 227; Oral History Account, Robert G.A. Jackson in Herbert H. Lehman Papers and Suite, School of International Affairs, Columbia University, N.Y., N.Y.

29. Address by Kazimierz Rusinek, June 27, 1947, in *ibid.*; Thomas

G. Paterson, *Soviet-American Confrontation: Postwar Reconstruction and the Origins of the Cold War* (Baltimore: Johns Hopkins University Press, 1973), p. 85; Irving Brant, *The New Poland* (New York: Universe, 1946), p. 18.

30. Summary of Foreign Voluntary Agencies—Information to Date 8/28/46, in Polish Mission, 75,039, UNRRA/UNA; Arthur Bliss Lane, *I Saw Poland Betrayed: An American Ambassador Reports to the American People* (Indianapolis: Bobbs Merrill, 1948), p. 216. For more detailed information on UNRRA aid to Poland, see Richard C. Lukas, *Bitter Legacy: Polish-American Relations in the Wake of World War II* (Lexington, Ky.: University Press of Kentucky, 1982), Chapter VI.

31. Memo, Stein to Menshikov, August 27, 1945, in Menshikov Files (RF 9), PAG-4/3.0.17.0: Box 1, UNRRA/UNA; Hrabar, *Fate of Polish Children*, p. 147. According to one Polish historian, over 2 million Poles returned home from the West during the years 1944-49. Wladyslaw Gora, *Polska Rzeczpospolita Ludowa*, 1944-1974 (Warsaw: Ksiazka i Wiedza, 1974), p. 192.

32. History of Child Welfare, pp. 93-104.

33. Hrabar, *Fate of Polish Children*, p. 147. One official estimate put the figure at 250,000 children. *Gazeta Ludowa*, October 16, 1947.

34. History of Child Welfare, p. 44.

35. Hrabar, *Fate of Polish Children*, pp. 147-48. One UNRRA report bluntly stated, "Very few children have been found in German families." Report, location of United Nations Children in the U.S. Zone, Germany, n.d., in PAG-4/1.3.1.2.10, Box 1, UNRRA/UNA.

36. History of Child Welfare, pp. 47-48.

37. *Ibid.*, pp. 49-50.

38. *Ibid.*, p. 47; Report by Greene, May 5, 1947 (Exhibit 31) in History of Child Welfare (DP #US 22).

39. History of Child Welfare, pp. 47-48.

40. Wnuk, *Dzieci Polskie Oskarzaja*, p. 247.

41. *Ibid.*, p. 248.

42. Henry and Hillel, *Children of the SS*, pp. 221-22.

43. *Ibid.*, pp. 222-26.

44. Ltr., Stanton to Byrnes, August 24, 1945, in RG 59, Box 6381, Department of State, National Archives. Hereinafter cited as DS/NA.

45. Ltr., Morgan to Drury, March 19, 1946, in RF 69, Gen. Correspon-

dence; Missions: Germany, 1946, PAG-4/3.0.17.0: Box 9, UN-RRA/UNA.

46. Msg., UNRRA Mission to Poland to UNRRA Central HQS., November 4, 1946; Msg., UNRRA Central HQS. to UNRRA Mission to Poland, November 16, 1946, in *ibid.*

47. Lukas, *Bitter Legacy*, pp. 108-09.

48. Polish American Congress, *A Factual Report on the Plight of Displaced Persons in Germany* (Chicago: Polish American Congress, 1947), p. 1.

49. *Ibid.*, p. 2; Statement by McNarney, September 2, 1946, in Box 75,028, UNRRA/UNA.

50. Statement by McNarney, September 26, 1946; Transcript of lecture by Warren, June 28, 1946, in George Warren Papers, Box 1, Harry S. Truman Library. Hereinafter cited as HST/L.

51. Polish American Congress, *A Factual Report*, p. 2.

52. *Ibid.*, pp. 2-3.

53. *Ibid.*, pp. 4-5.

54. *Ibid.*, p.5.

55. Polish American Congress, *Story of the Polish American Congress in Press Clippings, 1944-48* (Chicago: Alliance Printers and Publishers, 1948), p. 94.

56. Msg., UNRRA Mission to Poland to E.R.0., Welfare and Repatriation Division, September 23, 1946 (with enclosures); Minutes of Meeting held in E.R.O, October 11, 1946; Msg., UNRRA Mission to Poland to UNRRA Mission to Austria, November 19, 1946, in PAG-4/2.0.62-Box 32, UNRRA/UNA.

57. Report, Repatriation to Poland of Unaccompanied Children from Children's Centers at Wartenberg, Deggendorf, and Kloster Indersdorf, June 21, 1946, in PAG-4/4.2: Box 81, UNRRA/NA.

58. History of Child Welfare, pp. 57-59.

59. Alizah Zinberg and Barbara Martin, *An Inventory to the Rescue Children, Inc. Collection, 1946-1985* (New York: Yeshiva University Archives, 1986), p.6.

60. Prekerowa, *Konspiracyjna Rada Pomocy Zydom*, pp. 204-05.

61. The evidence does not support claims that Poles "rushed to get rid of their charges" after the war or that they demanded ransom for Jewish children. These unsubstantiated charges are made by Kuchler-Silberman, *One Hundred Children*, p. 125, and Solomon Goldman, "The Jewish Child during the Holocaust," *Jewish Education*, XLVI (Spring, 1978), 49. Goldman's source was the *Jewish*

Morning Journal, October 13, 1945, which was usually very critical of the Poles.

62. Mahler, "About Jewish Children," p. 52.

63. *Ibid.*, p. 51.

64. *Ibid.*

65. Dobraczynski, *Tylko w Jednym Zyciu*, pp. 245-46; Summary of Foreign Voluntary Agencies—Information to Date, 8/28/46.

66. One of these movements, involving 200 Jewish children, is discussed in Report to Doughty [1947] (Exhibit 25) in History of Child Welfare (D.P. #US 22).

67. Riwash, *Resistance and Revenge*, pp. 84-85.

68. Mark Wyman, *DP: Europe's Displaced Persons, 1945-1951* (Philadelphia: The Balch Institute Press, n.d.), pp. 145ff, 149.

69. Report to Doughty; History of Child Welfare, p. 91. The reception of Jewish children in Palestine was not always a warm one. See Katarzyna Meloch, "Trzy Proby," *Wiez* (Czerwiec, 1991), p. 56.

70. Report to Doughty; History of Child Welfare, pp. 74-75.

71. Report to Doughty.

72. Report on Jewish Infiltree Children (Exhibit 23), in History of Child Welfare (DP U.S. #22).

73. Memo of conversation, November 9, 1945, in Matthews-Hickerson Files, Box 17, DS/NA. Irving Brant, a prominent American Jewish journalist who visited Poland in 1945, blamed the *Narodowe Sily Zbrojne* (NSZ), a small right-wing group, for the attacks on the Jews. Ltr., Brant to Truman, January 14, 1946, in Truman Papers, PSF, Box 186, HST/L.

74. Memo, Keith to Lane, July 11, 1946, in Lane Papers, Box 25, folder 270, Yale University Library.

75. "The Jews in Poland Since the Liberation," May 16, 1946, in OSS/DS Reports, MF Roll 9; memo, Jonas to Anglo-American Committee of Inquiry, December 31, 1945, in OSS/DS Reports, MF Roll 3.

76. For a discussion of the Kielce incident, see Lukas, *Bitter Legacy*, p. 58.

77. *Ibid.*, p. 59.

78. *Ibid.*, p. 57.

79. Statement of Plans for the Care of Polish Children in Allied and Neutral Countries (Prepared for the Jewish Committee of the Warsaw Government), October 4, 1945, in PAG-4/2.0.6.2: Box 32, UNRRA/UNA.

Chapter VIII

Epilogue

"NEVER HAS CHILDHOOD been so assailed and tormented since the beginning of man," one historian of the children of the Second World War wrote.[1] The end of World War II brought physical and psychic problems for most of the child survivors of the war, especially those who had experienced the horrors of concentration camp life. Postwar child psychologists were astonished by the magnitude of the problem of helping child survivors cope with the distress the war had caused them. They saw a large percentage of the younger generation in Europe cut off from a normal, hopeful life. Yet their findings also offered some basis for encouragement, provided the child victims received help as soon after the war as possible.[2]

One of the thorny problems associated with Holocaust research involves the question of statistics. The fact is statistics concerning the war can not be engraved in stone because as new information comes to light, as it has recently, they can and will change. Recently, historian Franciszek Piper of the Auschwitz State Museum has revised the number of victims at that camp. Instead of 4 million victims, Piper is able to document the death of 1.1 million people, 90 percent of whom were Jewish. Now most historians agree that the number of murdered men, women and children at Auschwitz did not exceed 1.5 million.[3]

Based upon the revised estimates of casualties at Auschwitz, it is likely that statistics concerning Jewish and non-Jewish losses during the war will have to be reconsidered. Estimates of victims at other major camps continue to reflect considerable imprecision: 150,000 to 340,000 in Chelmno; 550,000 to 600,000 in Belzec; 200,000 to 600,000 in Sobibor, and 750,000 to 1 million in Treblinka.[4]

As far as child losses are concerned, historians have even greater difficulties in reaching reasonable estimates because the Nazis usually killed young children in concentration camps without counting or registering them. Surviving German documents, which are incomplete, usually use the word "persons," failing to distinguish between adult and child victims in the camps. Even the master of murder at Auschwitz, Rudolf Hoess, could not give any precise data concerning the number of children who died there.[5]

There were some children in virtually every group of people who arrived at Nazi concentration camps. There were usually 1,000 empty prams every day after children had been gassed at Auschwitz. During one 47-day period in late 1944 and early 1945, the Germans shipped from Auschwitz to Germany almost 100,000 sets of children's clothing.[6]

Among the 400,000 Polish prisoners who survived the war in Nazi camps, 17,750 of them were children. Twenty-five years later, only 9,500 were still living.[7]

Allied soldiers had liberated 1,000 children from Buchenwald, 500 from Bergen-Belsen, 500 from Ravensbruck, 1,400 from Dachau, 500 from Auschwitz and 1,000 from Theresienstadt.[8]

According to current estimates, 1 to 1.5 million Jewish children in Europe perished during World War II. According to Jacques Bloch, out of a total of 1.6 million Jewish children under 16 years of age in Europe before the outbreak of hostilities, 175,000 survived the war. Or, put another way, approximately 11 percent of Jewish children alive in Europe in 1939 survived to the conclusion of the war in 1945.[9]

Losses of Jewish and gentile children up to 16-years-of-age in Poland total 1,800,000. Of that number, Polish historians estimate that 1,200,000 were Polish and 600,000 were Jewish children of Polish origin. If one adds children in the 16-18 age bracket, the losses increase to 2,025,000.[10]

Epilogue

The deliberate systematic slaughter of so many children for so long will remain one of the most horrendous crimes of the Nazis against humanity.

Chapter Notes

1. Macardle, *Children of Europe*, p. 13

2. *Ibid.*

3. *Columbus Dispatch*, April 5, 1992. Piper calculates that 1 million Jews died at Auschwitz. He estimates that non-Jewish deaths at Auschwitz included 70,000-75,000 Poles, 21,000 Gypsies, 15,00 Soviet prisoners-of-war and 5,000 gentiles from other countries. In *The Auschwitz Crematoria: The Machinery of Mass Slaughter,* Jean-Claude Pressac suggests that 800,000 people died at Auschwitz. Of these, 700,000 were Jewish. If these figures are accurate, then Treblinka would surpass Auschwitz as the major slaughterhouse of the Jews. *New York Times* (International), October 28, 1993.

4. Konnilyn G. Feig, *Hitler's Death Camps: The Sanity of Madness* (New York: Holmes and Meier, 1981), pp. 266, 277, 285, 296; Raul Hilberg, *The Destruction of the European Jews* (3 vols.; New York: Holmes and Meier, 1985), III, 1201ff. Until the most recent spate of revisions concerning Jewish wartime losses, the most accurate tally of Jews who perished in the Holocaust came from Raul Hilberg. He estimated that 5.1 million Jews died—3 million in concentration camps, 1.3 million in open-air shootings and over 800,000 as a result of privation and ghettoization. See Hilberg, *ibid.*, p. 1219.

5. Kraus and Kulka, *Death Factory*, p. 114; Pilichowski, *Zbrodnie Hitlerowskie*, p. 29.

6. Kraus and Kulka, *Death Factory*, p. 116; Pilichowski, *Zbrodnie Hitlerowskie*, p. 25.

7. Kempisty, *Spraw Norymbergi Ciag Dalszy*, p. 195.

8. Pilichowski, *Zbrodnie Hitlerowskie*, p. 34; "Research News," *Newsletter of the Jerome Riker International Study of Organized Persecution of Children*, VI (Fall, 1989), 8; Milton, "Non-Jewish Children in the Camps," p. 56.

9. Dwork, *Children With a Star*, pp. xxxiii, 274.

10. Roman Hrabar, "Dziecko w Hitlerowskim Systemie Zaglady," in Glowna Komisja Badania Zbrodni Hitlerowskich w Polsce, *Zbrodnie Hitlerowskie na Dzieciach i Mlodziezy Polskiej, 1939-1945* (War-

saw: Wydawnictwo Prawnicze, 1969), p. 15; Pilichowski, *Zbrodnie Hitlerowskie*, p. 43. By including approximately 200,000 Polish children whom the Germans deported to the Reich for Germanization purposes and only a small fraction of whom later returned to Poland, total losses of Polish children, Jewish and gentile, are 2,225,000 or about 35 percent of the total losses suffered by Poland during World War II.

Bibliography

Archival Materials

United States

Hoover Institution on War, Revolution and Peace, Stanford, CA: Ciechanowski Papers

Herbert H. Lehman Papers and Suite, School of International Affairs, Columbia University, New York, New York: R.G.A. Jackson Papers

National Archives, Washington, D.C.: Records of Office of Strategic Services and United States Department of State

Franklin D. Roosevelt Library, Hyde Park, New York: Biddle Report

Sterling Library, Yale University, New Haven, CT: Arthur Bliss Lane Papers

Harry S. Truman Library, Independence, MO: George L. Warren Papers

United Nations Archives, New York, New York: Records of the United Nations Relief and Rehabilitation Administration

YIVO Institute for Jewish Research, New York, New York: Collection of Eyewitness Reports and Genia Silkes Papers

Great Britain

Polish Institute and General Sikorski Historical Museum, London, England: Archiwa—Ministerstwa Spraw Wewnetrznych, Prezesa Rady Ministrow, Prezydenta R.P., Rady Narodowej, Spraw Zydowskich

Polish Underground Study Trust, London, England: Akta dotyczace Spraw Zydowskich

Public Record Office, Kew, Richmond, England: Records of Foreign Office and War Office

Poland

Archiwum Glownej Komisji Badania Zbrodni Hitlerowskich w Polsce,Warsaw, Poland (now Glowna Komisja Badania Zbrodni Przeciwko Narodowi Polskiemu): Records pertaining to children

Archiwum Zgromadzenie Siostr Sluzebniczek, N.M.P., Warsaw, Poland

Interviews and Correspondence

Zbigniew Drecki, November 5 and 6, 1992; Staszek Jackowski, July 30, 1984; Rev. Jan Januszewski, August 1, 1982; Stefan Korbonski, June 7, 1982; Pelagia Lukaszewska, September 22, 1992; Dr. Leonard Lukaszuk, November 25, 1991; Stanislaw Makuch, September 17, 1984; Count Edward Raczynski, July 21, 1986; Waclaw Zajaczkowski, June 5, 1984

Documentary Film

Documentaries International. "The Other Side of Faith." 1990; "Zegota: A Time to Remember." 1992

Theses and Other Papers

Bodzak, Sister Joanna. "Sluzebniczki Najswietszej Maryi Panny Niepokalanie Poczetej/Starowiejskie/w Archidiecezji Warszawskiej w latach 1920-1985." M.A. Thesis. Catholic University of Lublin, 1990.

Kestenberg, Judith S.; Hogman, Flora; Kestenberg, Milton; Fogelman, Eva. "Jewish Christian Relationships as Seen Through the Eyes of Children, Before, During and After the Holocaust." Paper. Jerome Riker International Study of Organized Persecution of Children, n.d.

Kolata, Sister Jolanta and Lewicka, Sister Maria. "Pomoc Udzielana Zydom w latach 1939-1945 przez Zgromadzenie Siostr Sluzebniczek N.M.P." Lodz, 1983.

Kurek-Lesik, Ewa. "Wybor Zrodel do Pracy Doktorskiej—Udzial

Zenskich Zgromadzen Zakonnych w Akcji Ratowania Dzieci Zydowskich w Polsce w latach 1939-1945." Lublin, 1989.

W(olossyp), Sister Janina. "Zgromadzenie Siostr Sluzebniczek Najswietszej Maryi Panny Niepokalanie Poczetej/Starowiejskie/w Diecezji Lubelskiej w latach 1918-1980." M.A. Thesis. Catholic University of Lublin, 1984.

Documents and Official Histories

Arad, Yitzhak; Krakowski, Shmuel; Spector, Shmuel, eds. *The Einsatzgruppen Reports: Selections from the Dispatches of the Nazi Death Squads' Campaign Against the Jews, July 1941-January 1943*. New York: Holocaust library, 1989.

Berenstein, T.; Eisenbach, A.; Rutkowski, A., eds. *Eksterminacja Zydow na Ziemiach Polskich w Okresie Okupacji Hitlerowskiej: Zbior Dokumentow*. Warsaw: Zydowski Instytut Historyczny, 1957.

Central Commission for Investigation of German Crimes in Poland.*German Crimes in Poland*. 2 vols. New York: Howard Fertig, 1982.

Gutman, Israel, ed. *Encyclopedia of the Holocaust*. 4 vols. New York: Macmillan, 1990.

International Auschwitz Committee. *Nazi Medicine: Doctors, Victims, and Medicine in Auschwitz*. New York: Howard Fertig, 1986.

International Labour Office. *The Health of Children in Occupied Europe*. Montreal: International labour Office, 1943.

Komisja Historyczna Polskiego Sztabu Glownego w Londynie. *Polskie Sily Zbrojne w Drugiej Wojnie Swiatowej*. Vol. III: *Armia Krajowa*. London: Instytut Historyczny im. Gen. Sikorskiego, 1950.

Polish American Congress. *Story of the Polish American Congress in Press Clippings, 1944-1948*. Chicago: Alliance Printers and Publishers, 1948.

Polish Ministry of Information. *The Black Book of Poland*. New York: G.P. Putnam's Sons, 1942.

Republic of Poland. *German Occupation of Poland: Extract of Note Addressed to the Allied and Neutral Powers*. New York: Greystone Press, 1942.

Sawicki, Jerzy. *Przed Polskim Prokuratorem: Dokumenty i Komentarze*. Warsaw: Iskry, 1958.

Studium Polski Podziemnej. *Armia Krajowa w Dokumentach, 1939-1945*.4 vols. London: Studium Polski Podziemnej, 1970-77.

Trial of Major War Criminals before the International Military Tribunal. 42 vols. Nuremberg, 1947-49.

Trials of War Criminals before the Nuernberg Military Tribunals under Control Council Law No. 10, Nuernberg, October 1946-April 1949. 15 vols. Washington, D.C.: Government Printing Office, 1949-53.

U.S. Department of State. *Foreign Relations of the United States: Diplomatic Papers, 1939. Vol. I, General. Vol.II, General, the British Commonwealth and Europe.* Washington, D.C.: Government Printing Office, 1956.

U.S. Office of United States Chief of Counsel for Prosecution of Axis Criminality. *Nazi Conspiracy and Aggression.* 10 vols. Washington, D.C.: Government Printing Office, 1946.

Woodbridge, George. *UNRRA: The History of the United Nations Relief and Rehabilitation Administration.* 3 vols. New York: Columbia University Press, 1950.

Memoirs, Autobiographies, Recollections

Adelson, Alan, and Lapides, Robert, comps. and eds. *Lodz Ghetto: Inside a Community Under Siege.* New York: Viking, 1989.

Arczynski, Marek, and Balcerak, Wieslaw. *Kryptonim Zegota.* Warsaw: Czytelnik, 1983.

Barski, Jozef. *Przezycia i Wspomnienia z lat Okupacji.* Wroclaw: Wydawnictwo Polskiej Akademii Nauk, 1986.

Bednarczyk, Tadeusz. *Obowiazek Silniejszy od Smierci: Wspomnienia z lat 1939-1944 o Polskiej Pomocy dla Zydow w Warszawie.* Warsaw: Spoleczne Wydawnictwo Grunwald, 1986.

Berg, Mary. *Warsaw Ghetto: A Diary.* New York: L.B. Fischer, 1945.

Bieberstein, Aleksander. *Zaglada Zydow w Krakowie.* N.C.: Wydawnictwo Literackie, 1985.

Birenbaum, Halina. *Hope Is the last to Die: A Personal Documentation of Nazi Terror.* Translated by David Welsh. New York: Twayne, 1971.

Bor-Komorowski, T. *The Secret Army.* New York: Macmillan, 1951.

Brant, Irving. *The New Poland.* New York: Universe, 1946.

Dobraczynski, Jan. *Tylko w Jednym Zyciu: Wspomnienia.* Warsaw: Instytut Wydawniczy Pax, 1977.

Dobroszycki, Lucjan, ed. *The Chronicle of the Lodz Ghetto,1941-44.* New Haven: Yale University Press, 1984.

Bibliography

Drecki, Zbigniew. *Freedom and Justice Spring from the Ashes of Auschwitz.* Exeter: BPCC Wheatons, n.d.

Eisenberg, Azriel, ed. *The lost Generation: Children in the Holocaust.* New York: Pilgrim Press, 1982.

Frome, Frieda. *Some Dare to Dream: Frieda Frome's Escape from Lithuania.* Ames, Iowa: Iowa State University Press, 1988.

Games, Sonia. *Escape into Darkness: The True Story of a Young Woman's Extraordinary Survival during World War II.* New York: Shapolsky, 1991.

Gelman, Charles. *Do Not Go Gentle: A Memoir of Jewish Resistance in Poland, 1941-45.* Hamden, Ct.: Archon, 1989.

Gershon, Karen, ed. *We Came as Children: A Collective Autobiography.* London: Victor Gollancz, 1966.

Geve, Thomas. *Youth in Chains.* Jerusalem: Rubin Mass, 1958.

Gruber, Samuel. *I Chose Life.* New York: Shengold, 1978.

Hart, Kitty. *I Am Alive: Auschwitz and Birkenau.* New York: Abelard-Schuman, 1961.

Heimler, Eugene. *Night of the Mist.* New York: Vanguard, n.d.

Hilberg, Raul, et.al. *The Warsaw Diary of Adam Czerniakow: Prelude to Doom.* New York: Stein and Day, 1979.

Hirschmann, Ira A. *The Embers Still Burn: An Eyewitness View of the Postwar Ferment in Europe and the Middle East and Our Disastrous Get-Soft-With-Germany Policy.* New York: Simon and Schuster, 1949.

Hoess, Rudolf. *Commandant of Auschwitz: The Autobiography of Rudolf Hoess.* Translated by Constantine Fitzgibbon. London:Pan, 1961.

Huberband, Rabbi Shimon. *Kiddush Hashem: Jewish Religious and Cultural life in Poland during the Holocaust.* Hoboken, N.J.: KTAV Publishing House and Yeshiva University Press, 1987.

Iranek-Osmecki, George, trans. *The Unseen and Silent: Adventures from the Underground Movement Narrated by Paratroops of the Polish Home Army.* London: Sheed and Ward, 1954.

Jus, Andrzej and Karolina. *Our Journey in the Valley of Tears.* Toronto: University of Toronto Press, 1991.

Kaplan, Chaim A. *Scroll of Agony: The Warsaw Diary of Chaim A. Kaplan.* Translated and edited by Abraham I. Katsh. New York: Collier, 1973.

Karski, Jan. *Story of a Secret State.* Boston: Houghton Mifflin, 1944.

Klein, Gerda W. *All But My Life.* New York: Hill and Wang, 1957.

Korbonski, Stefan. *Fighting Warsaw: The Story of the Polish Underground State, 1939-45.* Translated by F.B. Czarnomski. N.C.: Minerva Press, 1968.

Korczak, Janusz. *The Warsaw Ghetto Memoirs of Janusz Korczak.* Translated by E.P. Kulawiec. Washington, D.C.: University Press of America, 1978.

Kraus, Ota, and Kulka, Erich. *The Death Factory: Document on Auschwitz.* Oxford: Pergamon, 1966.

Kruk, Zofia. *The Taste of Fear: A Polish Childhood in Germany, 1939-46.* London: Hutchinson, 1973.

Kuchler-Silberman, Lena. *One Hundred Children.* New York: Doubleday, 1961.

Landau, Ludwik. *Kronika Lat Wojny i Okupacji.* 3 vols. Warsaw: Panstwowe Wydawnictwo Naukowe, 1962.

Lane, Arthur Bliss. *I Saw Poland Betrayed: An American Ambassador Reports to the American People.* Indianapolis: Bobbs Merrill, 1948.

Lengiel, Olga. *Five Chimneys—Story of Auschwitz.* Chicago: Ziff Davis, 1947.

Lewin, Abraham. *A Cup of Tears: A Diary of the Warsaw Ghetto.* Edited by Antony Polonsky. London: Basil Blackwell, 1988.

Lukas, Richard C., ed. *Out of the Inferno: Poles Remember the Holocaust.* Lexington: University Press of Kentucky, 1989.

Meed, Vladka. *On Both Sides of the Wall: Memoirs from the Warsaw Ghetto.* Translated by Steven Meed. New York: Holocaust Library, 1979.

Muller, Filip. *Auschwitz Inferno: The Testimony of a Sonderkommando.* Translated by Susanne Flatauer. London: Routledge and Kegan Paul, 1979.

Mussmano, Michael A. *The Eichmann Kommandos.* New York: Macrae Smith, 1961.

Newman, Judith Sternberg. *In the Hell of Auschwitz: The Wartime Memories of Judith Sternberg Newman.* New York: Exposition Press, 1963.

Nir, Yehuda. *The Lost Childhood.* San Diego: Harcourt, Brace, Jovanovich, 1989.

Nyiszli, Miklos. *Auschwitz: An Eyewitness Account of Mengele's Infamous Death Camp.* New York: Seaver, 1986.

Bibliography

Poltawska, Wanda. *And I am Afraid of My Dreams*. Translated by Mary Craig. New York: Hippocrene, 1989.

Pres, Terrence des. *The Survivor: An Anatomy of Life in the Death Camps*. New York: Oxford University Press, 1976.

Ringelblum, Emmanuel. *Kronika Getta Warszawskiego*. Edited by Artur Eisenbach. Warsaw: Czytelnik, 1983.

Ringelblum, Emmanuel. *Notes from the Warsaw Ghetto: The Journal of Emmanuel Ringelblum*. Edited and translated by Jacob Sloan. New York: McGraw-Hill, 1958.

Ringelblum, Emmanuel. *Polish-Jewish Relations during the Second World War*. Edited by Joseph Kermish and Shmuel Krakowski. New York: Howard Fertig, 1976.

Riwash, Joseph. *Resistance and Revenge, 1939-1949*. Quebec: 1981.

Rudashevski, Yitshok. *The Diary of the Vilna Ghetto*. Israel: Fighter's House and Hakibbutz Hameuchad, 1973.

Schoenfeld, Joachim. *Holocaust Memories: Jews in the Lwow Ghetto, the Janowski Concentration Camp and as Deportees in Siberia*. Hoboken, N.J.: KTAV, n.d.

Singer, Elisabeth. *Children of the Apocalypse*. London: Hodder and Stoughton, 1967.

Stroop, Juergen. *The Stroop Report: The Jewish Quarter of Warsaw Is No More!* Translated by Sybil Milton. New York: Pantheon, 1979.

Szwajger, Adina Blady. *I Remember Nothing More: The Warsaw Children's Hospital and the Jewish Resistance*. Translated by Tasja Darowska and Danusia Stok. Collins: Harvill, 1990.

Szymanska, Zofia. *Bylam Tylko Lekarzem*. Warsaw: Instytut Wydawniczy Pax, 1979.

Tec, Nechama. *Dry Tears: The Story of a lost Childhood*. New York: Oxford University Press, 1984.

Tory, Avraham. *Surviving the Holocaust: The Kovno Ghetto Diary*. Cambridge, Mass.: Harvard University Press, 1990.

Trunk, Isaiah. *Jewish Responses to Nazi Persecution: Collective and Individual Behavior in Extremis*. New York: Stein and Day, 1979.

Turski, Marian, ed. *Byli Wowczas Dziecmi*. Warsaw: Ksiazka i Wiedza, 1975.

Wells, Leon Weliczker. *The Janowska Road*. New York: Macmillan, 1963.

Wiernik, Yankel. *A Year in Treblinka*. New York: American Representation of the General Jewish Workers' Union of Poland, n.d.

Wiesenthal, Simon. *The Murderers Among Us: The Simon Wiesenthal Memoirs.* New York: McGraw Hill, 1967.

Zar, Rose. *In the Mouth of the Wolf.* Philadelphia: Jewish Publication Society of America, 1983.

Ziemian, Joseph. *The Cigarette Sellers of Three Crosses Square.* Translated by Janina David. London: Vallentine, Mitchell, 1970.

Zuker-Bujanowska, Liliana. *Liliana's Journal: Warsaw, 1939-1945.* New York: Dial, 1980.

Secondary Works

Ainsztein, Reuben. *Jewish Resistance in Nazi-Occupied Eastern Europe.* New York: Barnes and Noble, 1974.

Alton, Thad Paul. *Polish Postwar Economy.* Westport, Connecticut: Greenwood, 1974.

Bartnikowski, Bogdan. *Dziecinstwo w Pasiakach.* Warsaw: Nasza Ksiegarnia, 1989.

Bartoszewski, Wladyslaw. *The Blood Shed Unites Us: Pages from the History of Help to the Jews in Occupied Poland.* Warsaw: Interpress Publishers, 1970.

————. *Warsaw Death Ring, 1939-1945.* Warsaw: Interpress Publishers, 1968.

Bartoszewski, Wladyslaw and Lewin, Sofia, eds. *Righteous Among Nations: How Poles Helped the Jews, 1939-1945.* London: Earlscourt Publications, 1969.

————. *The Samaritans: Heroes of the Holocaust.* New York: Twayne Publishers, 1970.

Bauminger, Arieh L. *The Righteous Among the Nations.* Jerusalem: Yad Vashem, 1990.

Berenbaum, Michael, ed. *A Mosaic of Victims: Non Jews Persecuted and Murdered by the Nazis.* New York: New York University Press, 1990.

Berenstein, Tatiana, and Rutkowski, Adam. *Assistance to the Jews in Poland, 1939-1945.* Warsaw: Polonia Publishing House, 1963.

Borkiewicz, Adam. *Powstanie Warszawskie.* Warsaw: 1957.

Borowski, Tadeusz. *This Way for the Gas, Ladies and Gentlemen.* Trans. Barbara Vedder. New York: Penguin, 1976.

Browning, Christopher R. *Fateful Months: Essays on the Emergence of the Final Solution.* New York: Holmes and Meier, 1985.

Burstin, Barbara Stern. *After the Holocaust: The Migration of Polish*

Jews and Christians to Pittsburgh. Pittsburgh: University of Pittsburgh Press, 1989.

Council for the Protection of Monuments to Struggle and Martyrdom, *The World Remembers Those Children*. Warsaw: Ruch Publishers, 1971.

Cyganski, Miroslaw. *Z Dziejow Okupacji Hitlerowskiej w Lodzi*. Lodz: Wydawnictwo Lodzkie, 1967.

Datner, Szymon. *Las Sprawiedliwych*. Warsaw: Ksiazka i Wiedza, 1968.

Deschner, Gunther. *Warsaw Uprising*. New York: Ballantine, 1972.

Dunin-Wasowicz, *Resistance in the Nazi Concentration Camps, 1933-1945*. Warsaw: PWN-Polish Scientific Publishers, 1982.

Dobroszycki, Lucjan *Centralny Katalog Polskiej Prasy Konspiracyjnej, 1939-1945*. Warsaw: Wydawnictwo Ministerstwa Obrony Narodowej, 1962.

Duraczynski, Eugeniusz. *Wojna i Okupacja: Wrzesien 1939-Kwiecien 1943*. Warsaw: Wiedza Powszechna, 1974.

Dwork, Deborah. *Children With a Star: Jewish Youth in Nazi Europe*. New Haven: Yale University Press, 1991.

Elkins, Michael. *Forged in Fury*. New York: Ballantine, 1971.

Epstein, Helen. *Children of the Holocaust*. New York: G.P. Putnam's Sons, 1979.

Fafara, Eugeniusz. *Gehenna Ludnosci Zydowskiej*. Warsaw: Ludowa Spoldzielnia Wydawnicza, 1983.

Feig, Konnilyn G. *Hitler's Death Camps: The Sanity of Madness*. New York: Holmes and Meier Publishers, 1981.

Fijalkowski, Zenon. Kosciol Katolicki na Ziemiach Polskich w latach Okupacji Hitlerowskiej. Warsaw: Ksiazka i Wiedza, 1983.

Friedman, Philip. *Their Brothers' Keepers*. New York: Holocaust Library, 1978.

Garlinski, Jozef. *Polska w Drugiej Wojnie Swiatowej*. London: Odnowa, 1982.

Gellately, Robert. *The Gestapo and German Society: Enforcing Racial Policy, 1933-1945*. Oxford: Clarendon Press, 1990.

Gilbert, Martin. *The Second World War*. London: Stodart, 1989.

Glowna Komisja Badania Zbrodni Hitlerowskich w Polsce. *Zbrodnie Hitlerowskie na Dzieciach i Mlodziezy Polskiej, 1939-1945*. Warsaw: Wydawnictwo Prawnicze, 1969.

Gora, Wladyslaw. *Polska Rzeczpospolita Ludowa, 1944-1974*. Warsaw: Ksiazka i Wiedza, 1974.

Gross, Jan T. *Polish Society under German Occcupation: The General Gouvernement, 1939-1944*. Princeton, N.J.: Princeton University Press, 1979.

Gumkowski, Janusz, and Leszczynski, Kazimierz. *Poland under Nazi Occupation*. Warsaw: Polonia Publishing House, 1961.

Gutman, Yisrael. *Fighters Among the Ruins: The Story of Jewish Heroism during World War II*. Washington, D.C.: B'nai B'rith, 1988.

————. *The Jews of Warsaw, 1939-1943: Ghetto, Underground, Revolt*. Bloomington, Indiana: Indiana University Press, 1982.

Gutman, Yisrael, and Krakowski, Shmuel. *Unegual Victims: Poles and Jews during World War Two*. New York: Holocaust Library, 1986.

Gutman, Yisrael, and Zuroff, Efraim, eds. *Rescue Attempts during the Holocaust: Proceedings of the Second Yad Vashem International Conference, Jerusalem, April 8-11, 1974*. Jerusalem: Yad Vashem, 1977.

Hanson, Joanna K.M. *The Civilian Population and the Warsaw Uprising of 1944*. Cambridge: Cambridge University Press, 1982.

Harris, Whitney R. *Tyranny on Trial: The Evidence at Nuremberg*. Dallas, Texas: Southern Methodist University Press, 1954.

Hellman, Peter. *Avenue of the Righteous*. New York: Atheneum, 1980.

Henry, Clarissa, and Hillel, Marc. *Children of the SS*. Translated by Eric Mosbacher. London: Hutchinson, 1975.

Hilberg, Raul. *The Destruction of the European Jews*. 3 vols. New York: Holmes and Meier, 1985.

Hrabar, R.Z. *Hitlerowski Rabunek Dzieci Polskich, 1939-1945*. Katowice: 1960.

Hrabar, Roman; Tokarz, Zofia, and Wilczur, Jacek E. *The Fate of Polish Children during the Last War*. Warsaw: Interpress, 1981.

Huneke, Douglas E. *The Moses of Rovno*. New York: Dodd and Mead, 1985.

Infield, Glenn B. *Secrets of the SS*. New York: Stein and Day, 1982.

Iranek-Osmecki, Kazimierz. *He Who Saves One Life*. New York: Crown Publishers, 1971.

Jewish Foundation for Christian Rescuers/ADL. *Moral Courage during the Holocaust: Select Papers from the Jewish Foundation for Christian Rescuers' 1990 Conference*. 1990.

Kamenetsky, Ihor. *Secret Nazi Plans for Eastern Europe: A Study of Lebensraum Policies*. New York: Bookman, 1961.

Kempisty, Czeslaw. *Spraw Norymbergi Ciag Dalszy*. Warsaw: Panstwowe Wydawnictwo Naukowe, 1975.

Kenrick, Donald, and Puxon, Grattan. *The Destiny of Europe's Gypsies*. New York: Basic, 1972.

Koehl, Robert L. *RKFDV: German Resettlement and Population Policy, 1939-1945*. Cambridge: Harvard University Press, 1957.

Kogon, Eugen. *The Theory and Practice of Hell*. New York: Farrar, Straus and Cudahy, 1950.

Krakowski, Shmuel. *The War of the Doomed: Jewish Armed Resistance in Poland, 1942-1944*. New York: Holmes and Meier, 1984.

Krannhals, Hanns von. *Der Warschauer Aufstand, 1944*. Frankfurt am Main: Bernard and Graefe Verlag fur Wehrwesen, 1962.

Kroll, Bogdan. *Rada Glowna Opiekuncza, 1939-1945*. Warsaw: Ksiazka i Wiedza, 1985.

Lagnado, Lucette Matalon, and Dekel, Sheila Cohen. *Children of the Flames: Dr. Josef Mengele and the Untold Story of the Twins of Auschwitz*. New York: William Morrow, 1991.

Lappin, Ben. *The Redeemed Children: The Story of the Rescue of War Orphans by the Jewish Community of Canada*. Toronto: University of Toronto Press, 1963.

Le Chene, Evelyn. *Mauthausen: The History of a Death Camp*. London: Methuen, 1971.

Levin, Dov. *Fighting Back: Lithuanian Jewry's Armed Resistance to the Nazis, 1941-1945*. New York: Holmes and Meier, 1985.

Lewandowska, Stanislawa. *Polska Konspiracyjna Prasa Informacyjno-Polityczna, 1939-1945*. Warsaw: Czytelnik, 1982.

Lifton, Betty Jean. *The King of Children: A Biography of Janusz Korczak*. New York: Farrar, Straus, Giroux, 1988.

Lifton, Robert Jay. *The Nazi Doctors: Medical Killing and the Psychology of Genocide*. New York: Basic, 1986.

Lukas, Richard C. *The Forgotten Holocaust: The Poles under German Occupation, 1939-1944*. Lexington, Kentucky: University Press of Kentucky, 1986; New York: Hippocrene Books, 1990.

Macardle, Dorothy. *Children of Europe: A Study of the Children of Liberated Countries; Their War-Time Experiences, Their Reactions, and Their Needs, with a Note on Germany*. Boston: Beacon Press, 1951.

Madajczyk, Czeslaw. *Die Okkupationspolitik Nazideutschlands in Polen, 1939-1945*. Berlin: Akademie-Verlag, 1987.

————. *Polityka III Rzeszy w Okupowanej Polsce*. 2 vols. Warsaw: Panstwowe Wydawnictwo Naukowe, 1970.

Maier, Charles S. *The Unmasterable Past: History, Holocaust and German National Identity*. Cambridge: Harvard University Press, 1988.

Marczak-Oborski, Stanislaw. *Teatr Czasu Wojny: Polskie Zycie Teatralne w latach II Wojny Swiatowej, 1939-1945*. Warsaw: Panstwowy Instytut Wydawniczy, 1967.

Marszalek, Jozef. *Majdanek*. Warsaw: Interpress, 1986.

Mazur, T., and Tomaszewski, J. *Poland's Losses in World War II*. Warsaw: 1961.

Meltzer, Milton. *Rescue: The Story of How Gentiles Saved Jews in the Holocaust*. New York: Harper and Row, 1988.

Michel, Henri. *The Shadow War: European Resistance, 1939-1945*. New York: Harper and Row, 1972.

Mikes, George, ed. *Prison: A Symposium*. London: Routledge and Kegan Paul, 1963.

Muller-Hill, Benno. *Murderous Science: Elimination by Scientific Selection of Jews, Gypsies, and Others in Germany, 1933-1945*. Oxford: Oxford University Press, 1988.

Neuman, Gerard G. *Origins of Human Aggression: Dynamics and Etiology*. New York: Human Sciences Press, 1987.

Paterson, Thomas G. *Soviet-American Confrontation: Postwar Reconstruction and the Origins of the Cold War*. Baltimore: Johns Hopkins University Press, 1973.

Pawelczynska, Anna. *Values and Violence in Auschwitz: A Sociological Analysis*. Translated by Catherine S. Leach. Berkeley, California: University of California Press, 1979.

Pilichowski, Czeslaw, ed. *Dzieci i Mlodziez w latach Drugiej Wojny Swiatowej*. Warsaw: Panstwowe Wydawnictwo Naukowe, 1982.

————. *Zbrodnie Hitlerowskie na Dzieciach i Mlodziezy Polskiej*. Warsaw: Rada Ochrony Pomnikow Walki i Meczenstwa, 1972.

Polish American Congress. *A Factual Report on the Plight of Displaced Persons in Germany*. Chicago: Polish American Congress, 1947.

Polonsky, Antony, ed. *'My Brother's Keeper?': Recent Polish Debates on the Holocaust*. London: Routledge, 1990.

Posner, Gerald L., and Ware, John. *Mengele: The Complete Story*. New York: McGraw Hill, 1986.

Pospieszalski, Karol. *Polska pod Niemieckim Prawem*. Poznan: Wydawnictwo Instytutu Zachodniego, 1946.

Bibliography

Prekerowa, *Teresa. Konspiracyjna Rada Pomocy Zydom w Warszawie, 1942-1945.* Warsaw: Panstwowy Instytut Wydawniczy, 1982.

Proch, Franciszek. *Poland's Way of the Cross, 1939-1945.* New York: Polish Association of Former Political Prisoners of Nazi and Soviet Concentration Camps, 1987.

Rittner, Carol, and Myers, Sondra, eds. *The Courage to Care: Rescuers of Jews during the Holocaust.* New York: New York University Press, 1986.

Roiphe, Anne. *A Season for Healing: Reflections on the Holocaust.* New York: Simon and Schuster, 1988.

Schwarberg, Gunther. *Dzieciobojca Eksperymenty Lekarza SS w Neuengamme.* Warsaw: Czytelnik 1987.

Shabad, Peter, and Dietrich, D.R., eds. *The Problem of Loss and Mourning: New Psychoanalytic Perspectives.* New York: International Universities Press, 1987.

Slomczynski, Adam. *Dom. Ks. Boduena, 1939-1945.* Warsaw: Panstwowy Instytut Wydawniczy, 1975.

Smolski, Wladyslaw. *Losy Dziecka: Opowiesc Wojenna.* Warsaw: Instytut Wydawniczy Pax, 1961.

Sosnowski, Kiryl. *The Tragedy of Children under Nazi Rule.* New York: Howard Fertig, 1983.

Steven, Stewart. *The Poles.* New York: Macmillan, 1982.

Tec, Nechama. *When light Pierced the Darkness: Christian Rescue of Jews in Nazi-Occupied Poland.* New York: Oxford University Press, 1986.

Treece, Patricia. *A Man for Others: Maximilian Kolbe Saint of Auschwitz in the Words of Those Who Knew Him.* San Francisco: Harper and Row, 1982.

Trunk, Isaiah. *Judenrat: The Jewish Councils in Eastern Europe under Nazi Occupation.* New York: Macmillan, 1972.

Wojna i Okupacja a Medycyna: Materialy. Krakow: Akademia Medyczna im. Mikolaja Kopernika w Krakowie, 1986.

Wnuk, Jozef. *Dzieci Polskie Oskarzaja.* Lublin: Wydawnictwo Lubelskie, 1975.

Wroniszewski, Jozef K. *Ochota: 1944.* Warsaw: Wydawnictwo Ministerstwa Obrony Narodowej, 1970.

Wronski, Stanislaw, and Zwolakowa, Maria. *Polacy Zydzi, 1939-1945.* Warsaw: Ksiazka i Wiedza, 1971.

Wyman, Mark. *DP: Europe's Displaced Persons, 1945-1951.* Philadelphia: Balch Institute Press, n.d.

Wytwycky, Bohdan. *The Other Holocaust: Many Circles of Hell.* Washington, D.C.: Novak Report, 1980.

Yahil, Leni. *The Holocaust: The Fate of European Jewry, 1932-1945.* New York: Oxford University Press, 1990.

Zajaczkowski, Waclaw. *Martyrs of Charity.* Washington, D.C.: St. Maximilian Kolbe Foundation, 1987.

Zarski-Zajdler, Wladyslaw. *Martyrologia Ludnosci Zydowskiej i Pomoc Spoleczenstwa Polskiego.* Warsaw: 1968.

Zenczykowski, Tadeusz. *General Grot: U Kresu Walki.* London: Polonia Book Fund, 1983.

Zielinski, Zygmunt. *Zycie Religijne w Polsce pod Okupacja Hitlerowska, 1939-1945.* Warsaw: Osrodek Dokumentacji i Studiow Spolecznych, 1982.

——. *Zycie Religijne w Polsce pod Okupacja 1939-1945: Metropolie Wilenska o Lwowska, Zakony.* Katowice: Wydawnictwo Unia, 1992.

Zinberg, Alizah, and Martin, Barbara. *An Inventory to the Rescue Children Inc. Collection, 1946-1985.* New York: Yeshiva University Archives, 1986.

Articles and Periodicals

Baron, Alexander. "The Anniversary." *The Jewish Quarterly* (Spring, 1954): 7-10.

Biuletyn Glownej Komisji Badania Zbrodni Hitlerowskich w Polsce. 1946-58.

Bronsen, David. "Child of the Holocaust." *Midstream* (April, 1981): 50-56.

Cahn, Theresa I. *"The Diary of an Adolescent Girl in the Ghetto: A Study of Age-Specific Reactions to the Holocaust." The Psychoanalytic Review* (Winter, 1988): 587-617.

Cousins, Norman. "The Ravensbruck Lapins." *Dimensions: A Journal of Holocaust Studies* 6 (1991): 22-24.

Drozdowski, Marian M. "Refleksje o Stosunkach Polsko-Zydowskich w Czasie Drugiej Wojny Swiatowej." *Kwartalnik Historyczny* 97 (1990): 177-84.

Ehrlich, B.H. "Jewish Children in the Days of the Nazi Catastrophe." *Jewish Forum* 33 (June, 1950): 102.

Fejkiel, Wladyslaw. "The Health Service in Auschwitz Concentration Camp No. 1 (Main Camp)." *Przeglad Lekarski* (1962): 13-20.

Fogelman, Eva. "Psychological Origins of Rescue." *Dimensions* 3 (1982): 9-12.

Glinska, Alicja. "Kierunek Przeksztalcen Moralnych wsrod Wiezniow Oswiecimia." *Przeglad Lekarski* (1969): 53-57.

———. "Z Badan nad Moralnoscia Wiezniow Oswiecimia." *Przeglad Lekarski* (1967): 37-45.

Goldman, Solomon. "The Jewish Child during the Holocaust." *Jewish Education* 46 (Spring, 1978) 40-51.

Hogman, Flora. "Displaced Jewish Children during World War II: How They Coped." *Journal of Humanistic Psychology* 23 (Winter, 1983): 51-66.

———. "The Experience of Catholicism for Jewish Children during World War II." *The Psychoanalytic Review* 75 (Winter, 1988): 511-32.

———. "Role Memories in Lives of World War II Orphans." *Journal of the American Academy of Child Psychiatry* 24 (1985): 390-96.

Kestenberg, Judith. "History's Role in Psychoanalyses of Survivors and Their Children." *The American Journal of Social Psychiatry* 3 (1983): 26.

Kestenberg, Judith, and Gampel, Yolanda. "Growing Up in the Holocaust Culture." *Israel Journal of Psychiatry and Related Sciences* 20 (1983): 129-44.

Kestenberg, Judith, and Kestenberg, Milton. "Psychoanalyses of Children of Survivors from the Nazi Persecution: The Continuing Struggle of Survivor Parents." *Victimology: An International Journal* 5 (1980): 368-73.

Kloczowski, Jerzy. "The Religious Orders and the Jews in Nazi-Occupied Poland." *Polin* (1988): 238-43.

Klodzinski, Stanislaw. "Z Zagadnien Ludobojstwa: Sterylizacja i Kastracja Promieniami Roetgena w Obozie Oswiecimskim Dr. Horst Schumann." *Przeglad Lekarski* (1964): 105-111.

Kosciuszkowa, Janina. "Losy Dzieci w Obozie Koncentracyjnym Oswiecimiu." *Przeglad Lekarski* (1961): 60-61.

Kurek-Lesik, Ewa. "The Conditions of Admittance and the Social Background of Jewish Children Saved by Women's Religious Orders in Poland from 1939-1945." *Polin* (1988):244-75.

———. "Udzial Zenskich Zgromadzen Zakonnych w Akcji Ratowania Dzieci Zydowskich w Polsce w Latach 1939-1945." *Dzieje Najnowsze* 18 (1986): 249-77.

Kusielewicz, Eugene. "Some Thoughts on the Teaching of the Holocaust." *Perspectives* 14 (March-April, 1984), Insert D.

Lavi, T. "A Psychological Study of Jewish Children in Rumania during the Catastrophe." *Yad Vashem Bulletin* (December, 1962): 45-49.

Levin, Meyer. "They Saved the Children." *Saturday Evening Post* (January 20, 1945): 41-44.

Mahler, Ella. "About Jewish Children Who Survived World War II on the Aryan Side." *Yad Vashem Bulletin* (December, 1962): 49-56.

———. "The Fate of Jewish Children during the Holocaust." *Yad Vashem Bulletin* (August, 1964): 48-54.

Mazur, Zygmunt. "Dominikanie Lwowscy w Podwojnej Niewoli." *Gazeta 144 (Toronto)* (1991): 14-15, 28.

Meloch, Katarzyna. "Trzy Proby." *Wiez* (June, 1991): 42-57.

Milton, Sybil. "Non-Jewish Children in the Camps." *Simon Wiesenthal Center Annual* 5 (1988): 49-60.

Muszkat, M. "Research on the Problem of Youth during the Holocaust." *Yad Vashem Bulletin* (December, 1962): 79-83.

Newsletter. Jerome Riker International Study of Organized Persecution of Children. (Fall, 1989).

Oschlies, Wolf. "The Thesaurus of Hell: Twenty-Six Years of the Periodical *Przeglad Lekarski-Oswiecim*." *Simon Wiesenthal Center Annual* 5 (1988): 255-68.

Papanek, Ernst, and Linn, Edward. "The Boy Who Survived Auschwitz." *Saturday Evening Post* (April 11, 1964): 34-41.

Peck, Abraham J. "The Agony of the Lodz Ghetto, 1941-44." *Simon Wiesenthal Center Annual* 4 (1987): 341-56.

Piekut-Warszawska, Elzbieta. "Dzieci w Obozie Oswiecimskim: (Wspomnienia Pielegniarki)." *Przeglad Lekarski* (1967): 204-205.

Polish Fortnightly Review. 1942.

Poltawska, Wanda. "Z Badan nad 'Dziecmi Oswiecimskimi.'" *Przeglad Lekarski* (1965): 21-25.

Prekerowa, Teresa. "*Podziemie Zydowskie a Podziemie Polskie*." *Odra* (Kwiecien, 1991): 30-35.

Rosenblum, Zofja. "Jewish Children in Ghettos, Camps and Woods, 1939-1945." *American OSE Review* 4 (Spring, 1947): 25-33.

Ruziczka, A. "Refugee Children from the Ghetto Struggle for Their Lives." *Yad Vashem Bulletin* (October, 1963); 59-63.

Sawicka, S. "Zbrodnaia Niemiecka nad Dzieckim Polskim." *Przeglad Zachodni* (1947): 730-36.

Seweryn, Tadeusz. "Wielostronna Pomoc Zydom w Czasie Okupacji Hitlerowskiej." *Przeglad Lekarski* (1965): 162-83.

Sterkowicz, Stanislaw. "Przyczynek do Zagadnienia Moralnosci Wiezniow Obozow Hitlerowskich." *Przeglad Lekarski* (1969): 47-52.

Wechsberg, Joseph. "Hell's Orphans." *Saturday Evening Post* (October 23, 1948): 26-27, 118-19, 150.

Zielinski, Zygmunt. "Polska w Oczach Zydow Amerykanskich." *Wiez* (June, 1991): 9-29.

Other

Ka-Tzetnik 135633. *Atrocity.* New York: Lyle Stuart, 1963.

Kestenberg, Judith. "Child Survivors of the Holocaust—40 Years Later: Reflections and Commentary." Discussion, American Psychiatric Association. Los Angeles, 1983.

Kosinski, Jerzy. *The Painted Bird.* New York: Modern Library, 1983.

Newspapers

Canadian Jewish News

Columbus Dispatch

Gazeta Ludowa

Gazeta (Toronto)

New York Times

Slowo Powszechne

Toronto Star

Zywia i Bronia

Index

THE MOST COMPREHENSIVE ACCOUNT
OF JEWISH RELATIONS WITH POLAND
EVER PUBLISHED

JEWS IN POLAND
A Documentary History

Iwo Cyprian Pogonowski

Introduction by Professor Richard Pipes
of Harvard University

This eye-opening and monumental work describes the rise of Jews as
a nation and how the Polish-Jewish community played a key role in this
development. The book details the progress from the autonomous
Congressus Judaicus to the Knesset in Israel. Pogonowski describes
how the Congressus Judaicus was the only Jewish Parliament between
the Sanhedrin of Biblical times and the Knesset of the modern State of
Israel and thus, how the Jewish legal, governmental, and educational
systems, as well as philosophical and religious beliefs, evolved in
Poland between the 16th and 18th centuries.

Jews in Poland includes a new English translation of the Charter of
Jewish Liberties and an illustrated description of the cultural, social,
and political issues of the 500 years of Jewish autonomy in Poland.
Pogonowski shows that during the entire history of the Diaspora, the
Jewish nation existed only in Poland—with their own culture, social
classes, and legal and economic systems—the Jews referred to the
country as the "New Holy Land."

The book includes a detailed chronicle of the Holocaust, with ample
annotations explaining the war-time situation.

384 pages 172 b/w photos 114 historical maps
0-7818-0116-8 $22.50 hc

HISTORY & POLITICS
FROM HIPPOCRENE BOOKS

THE FORGOTTEN HOLOCAUST
The Poles Under German Occupation, 1939-1944
Richard C. Lukas
This landmark study shows that Nazi treatment of Polish Gentiles was scarcely less barbaric than that of their Jewish compatriots. "An absorbing, meticulously documented study." —**National Review**
"Lively and engaging ... will appeal to scholars and laymen alike." —**Polish Heritage**
300 pages, 5 x 7
0-87052-632-4   *$9.95pb*

POLAND
A Historical Atlas
Iwo Cyprian Pogonowski
Poland has been a vital force in shaping Europe as we know it today. This atlas illustrates the central role Poland has occupied in the history of Europe. With over 170 maps, the book covers such diverse topics as political history, language evolution, cultural achievement, and social history.
320 pages, 8 1/2 x 11, 175 maps
0-7818-0117-6   *$16.95pb*

POLISH GENEOLOGY AND HERALDRY
Janina Hoskins
115 pages, 5 1/2 x 8 1/2, 14 b/w illus., photos, maps
0-87052-940-4 $10.00pb

THE LAST DECADE OF IMPERIAL RUSSIA
V.V. Shulgin
0-87052-928-5 $11.95pb

HISTORY & POLITICS
FROM HIPPOCRENE BOOKS

THE MURDERERS OF KATYN
Vladimir Abarinov

On October 15, 1992, the *New York Times* and newspapers around the world announced definitive proof that on March 5, 1940, Stalin personally approved the genocide of 15,000 Polish prisoners—the Katyn massacre.

The historic disclosure provided the missing documentary link for the courageous Russian journalist Vladimir Abarinov, who reached the same shocking conclusion in the *Labyrinth of Katyn*, published in Russia two years ago. Hippocrene presents the English translation of this unprecedented history—the only book by a Russian on Stalin's crime—under the title of *The Murderers of Katyn.*

In uncovering truth behind the Katyn massacre, Abarinov stripped away 50 years of lies generated by the Soviet propaganda machine. Stalin's cover-up included the unsuccessful attempt to have the Nuremberg tribunal convict the Nazis of the crime. Even Gorbachev, in his public admission in 1990, never revealed Stalin's complicity.

Abarinov relies exclusively on Russian sources, including interviews with over 100 witnesses, some of them retired NKVD executioners. Taking advantage of glasnost, a policy still in formation during much of his research, Abarinov cites many documents never before published in any language.

5 1/2 x 8, 250 pages
0-7818-0032-3   *$19.95 hc*

HIPPOCRENE
JUDAICA BOOKS

POLAND'S JEWISH HERITAGE *by Joram Kagan*
This new guide is a must-have for Jewish travelers to Poland, a country which had the second largest Jewish community in the world prior to World War II. The guide includes historical background, as well as chronological tables showing the history of Polish Jewry. A hundred maps and photos complement the guide's detailed lists of synagogues, cemeteries and other places of Jewish heritage.
0-87052-991-9 $16.95

GLASSMAKERS: An Odyssey of the Jews *by Samuel Kurinsky*
The only work of its kind on the topic of glassmaking, it is fascinating reading for those interested in early Judaica lore.
"Eight years of research, begun in Venice and followed back into the archaeological digs of the Near East, show that glassmaking was an ancient art of the Jews which they carried with them as they moved from one area to another. Eleven chapters packed with facts and stories are a wonderful introduction to the history of ancient civilizations and their connections to the present."
—*Association of Jewish Libraries Newsletter*
32 photos
0-87052-901-3 $29.50

ENGLISH-HEBREW/HEBREW-ENGLISH DICTIONARY
by David Gross
7,000 transliterated, Romanized entries followed by helpful hints on pronunciation make up this compact dictionary.
"Ideal for those planning to visit Israel or beginning conversational Hebrew...useful phrases and maximum encouragement to start talking Hebrew."—*The Jewish Week*
"Beautifully arranged in a clear, concise type..."
—*Association of Jewish Libraries Newsletter*
0-87052-625-1 $7.95

JUDAICA HIGHLIGHTS
FROM HIPPOCRENE

GOLEM by G. Meyrink
This version of the traditional Hebrew tale of a clay figure endowed
with life was first published in 1915 and remains a classic today.
0-946626-12-X $11.95 pb

CHOOSING JUDAISM by L. Kukoff
This book is for those who have already come to Judaism through
conversion as well as for those considering it. In his introduction,
Rabbi Daniel Syme says of author Lydia Kukoff: "She makes a
difference in the way people see themselves and their future as Jews...it
is must reading for Jewish spouses, in-laws, rabbis, educators,
congregational leaders—indeed for any thinking, caring Jew."
"Interesting and touching, splendid advice"—*Jewish News*
0-87052-070-9 $7.95 pb

THE CHRISTIAN PROBLEM:
A Jewish View by Stuart E. Rosenberg
This book is most timely as it raises questions that must be addressed
in a meaningful Christian-Jewish dialogue.
"...This is not an assault or an attack against anti-Semitism. It is a scholar's heartfelt plea
for Jews and Christians to talk to each other with candor, and it is presented against the
background of the Holocaust and the still-extant anti-Semitism found in the Christian
community.—*The Jewish Week*
0-87052-50903 $15.95 hc $8.95 pb

HOW TO BE JEWISH *by David Gross*
"This straightforward explanation provides a primer on Judaism for the layman who seeks to increase his knowledge of Jewish heritage, holidays, beliefs, and even language."—*The Jewish Week*
0-87052-069-5 $7.95 pb

JUDAISM *by David Gross*
From chapters on "Ancient Origins" and "Belief in God" to those focusing on Judaism and the family, this book is a concise yet complete grounding in the Jewish religion. Includes a chronological history of Judaism.
0-87052-068-7 $14.95 hc
0-7818-0237-7 $11.95 pb

ADDITIONAL TITLES OF JEWISH INTEREST

JEWS IN OLD CHINA *by Sidney Shapiro*
0-87052-553-0 $8.95 pb

WARS OF THE JEWS *by Rosenthal and Mozesom*
0-87052-786-X $16.95 hc

WANDERING JEW *by E. Sue*
0-94662-6332 $22.50 pb

YIDDISH-ENGLISH/ENGLISH-YIDDISH DICTIONARY
by D. Gross
0-87052-969-2 $7.95 pb

All prices subject to change.

Order directly from HIPPOCRENE BOOKS by sending a check or mail order for the price of the book, plus $4.00 shipping and handling for the first book, and $.50 for each additional book to: HIPPOCRENE BOOKS, 171 MADISON AVE., NEW YORK, NY 10016

NEW FROM HIPPOCRENE
*A POWERFUL WORK ADDRESSING THE MOST COMPELLING
ISSUES OF CONTEMPORARY JUDAISM*

WHY REMAIN JEWISH?
David C. Gross

One of America's premier Jewish authors tackles the number one issue facing the American Jewish community—the large number of young Jewish people, teens and young adults, who are abandoning Judaism and the Jewish community. The high rate of intermarriage—now exceeding 50% of all marriages involving American Jews—along with the significant number of Jews who convert to another religion, missionary sect or cult, has caused a widespread feeling of dismay and sorrow throughout the Jewish community as a result of these losses.

Why Remain Jewish presents a wide range of arguments, facts and figures, and historical and contemporary insights designed to reverse the current trend. The book shows young people that Judaism is a religion and a way of life that brings fulfillment and serenity to its practitioners, and adds a meaningful dimension to their lives; and that being Jewish is a glorious, lifeflong commitment to intellectual growth and ethical insight.

244 pages
0-7818-0216-4 $9.95 pb

All prices subject to change.

Order directly from HIPPOCRENE BOOKS by sending a check or mail order for the price of the book, plus $4.00 shipping and handling for the first book, and $.50 for each additional book to: HIPPOCRENE BOOKS, 171 MADISON AVE., NEW YORK, NY 10016

POLISH LITERARY CLASSICS
FROM HIPPOCRENE

QUO VADIS? *by Henryk Sienkiewicz* (NEW in paperback). Also available in hardcover.

0427	ISBN 0-89870-475-8	**$14.95 pb**
0005	ISBN 0-7818-0010-1	**$22.50 cloth**

THE TEUTONIC KNIGHTS *by Henryk Sienkiewicz. Translated by Alicia Tyszkiewicz, and newly edited and revised by Miroslaw Lipinski* (NEW), 740 pages.

0558	ISBN 0-7818-0121-4	**$24.95 cloth**

THE DOLL *by Boleslaw Prus*, 700 pages. With a stunning cover by Czachorski, here is one of the most striking portraits of a woman in fiction.

0097	ISBN 0-7818-0158-3	**$16.95 pb**

PHARAOH *by Boleslaw Prus. Translated by Christopher Kasparek*, 691 pages. First published in 1896, *Pharaoh* is considered one of the great novels of Polish literature, and a timeless and universal story of the struggle for power.

0008	ISBN 0-87052-152-7	**$25.00 cloth**

THE DARK DOMAIN *by Stefan Grabinski. Newly translated by Miroslaw Lipinski*, 192 pages. Explorations of the extreme in human behavior combining the macabre and bizarre to send a chill down the reader's spine.

----	ISBN 0-7818-0211-3	**$10.95 pb**

TALES FROM THE SARAGOSSA MANUSCRIPT, OR TEN DAYS IN THE LIFE OF ALPHONSE VAN WORDEN *by Jan Potocki*, 192 pages. The celebrated classic of fantastic literature in the tradition of *Arabian Nights*.

0717	ISBN 0-87052-936-6	**$8.95 pb**

THE GLASS MOUNTAIN:Twenty-Six Ancient Polish Folktales and Fables, *told by W.S. Kuniczak.* Illustrated by Pat Bargielski, 160 pages and 8 illustrations. It is an heirloom book to pass on to children and grandchildren.

0183	ISBN 0-7818-0087-0	**$14.95 cloth**

OLD POLISH LEGENDS, *retold by F.C. Anstruther Wood and illustrated with engravings by J. Sekalski*, 66 pages and 11 woodcut engravings. Now in its second printing, this fine collection of eleven fairy tales has an introduction by Zygmunt Nowakowski.

0098	ISBN 0-7818-0180-X	**$10.00 cloth**

PAN TADEUSZ *by Adam Mickiewicz.* Translated by Kenneth R. MacKenzie, 553 pages with Polish and English text side by side. Poland's greatest epic poem in what is its finest English translation.

0237	ISBN 0-7818-033-1	**$19.95 pb**

HIPPOCRENE FOREIGN LANGUAGE DICTIONARIES
Modern • Up-to-Date • Easy-to-Use • Practical

POLISH-ENGLISH/ENGLISH-POLISH
PRACTICAL DICTIONARY (Completely Revised)
by Iwo Cyprian Pogonowski
Contains over 31,000 entries for students and travelers. Includes a phonetic guide to pronunciation in both languages, a handy glossary of the country's menu terms, a bilingual instruction on how-to-use the dictionary, and a bilingual list of abbreviations.
0450   ISBN 0-7818-0085-4 $11.95 pb

Romanian-English/English-Romanian Dictionary
0488   ISBN 0-87052-986-2 $19.95 pb

Russian-English/English-Russian Standard Dictionary
0440   ISBN 0-7818-0083-8 $16.95 pb

Russian-English/English-Russian Concise Dictionary
0262   ISBN 0-7818-0132-X $11.95 pb

Slovak-English/English-Slovak Dictionary
1052   ISBN 0-87052-115-2 $9.95 pb

Ukrainian-English/English Ukrainian Practical Dictionary
1055   ISBN 0-87052-116-0 $8.95 pb

English-Yiddish/Yiddish-English Conversational Dictionary (Romanized)
1019   ISBN 0-87052-969-2 $7.95 pb

To order these dictionaries or any other Hippocrene titles, send a check or money order for the total price of the book/s plus $4.00 shipping/ handling for the first title and $.50 for any additional title to: Hippocrene Books, Order Dept., 171 Madison Avenue, New York, NY 10016.

*Please note, all prices subject to change.